WITH A UNITY OF PURPOSE

With a Unity of Purpose

How the First World War Changed Newfoundland

MICHAEL R. WESTCOTT

McGill-Queen's University Press
Montreal & Kingston • London • Chicago

ISBN 978-0-2280-2258-9 (paper)
ISBN 978-0-2280-2259-6 (ePDF)
ISBN 978-0-2280-2260-2 (ePUB)

Legal deposit third quarter 2024
Bibliothèque nationale du Québec

Printed in Canada on acid-free paper that is 100% ancient forest free (100% post-consumer recycled), processed chlorine free

This book has been published with the help of a grant from the Federation for the Humanities and Social Sciences, through the Awards to Scholarly Publications Program, using funds provided by the Social Sciences and Humanities Research Council of Canada.

Funded by the Government of Canada | Financé par le gouvernement du Canada | Canada | Canada Council for the Arts | Conseil des arts du Canada

We acknowledge the support of the Canada Council for the Arts.

Nous remercions le Conseil des arts du Canada de son soutien.

McGill-Queen's University Press in Montreal is on land which long served as a site of meeting and exchange amongst Indigenous Peoples, including the Haudenosaunee and Anishinabeg nations. In Kingston it is situated on the territory of the Haudenosaunee and Anishinaabek. We acknowledge and thank the diverse Indigenous Peoples whose footsteps have marked these territories on which peoples of the world now gather.

Library and Archives Canada Cataloguing in Publication

Title: With a unity of purpose: how the First World War changed Newfoundland / Michael R. Westcott.

Names: Westcott, Michael R., author.

Description: Includes bibliographical references and index.

Identifiers: Canadiana (print) 20240353609 | Canadiana (ebook) 20240353668 | ISBN 9780228022589 (paper) | ISBN 9780228022602 (ePUB) | ISBN 9780228022596 (ePDF)

Subjects: LCSH: World War, 1914-1918—Newfoundland and Labrador. | LCSH: World War, 1914-1918—Social aspects—Newfoundland and Labrador. | LCSH: World War, 1914-1918—Economic aspects—Newfoundland and Labrador.

Classification: LCC D547.N55 W47 2024 | DDC 940.3/718—dc23

This book was typeset by Marquis Interscript in 10.5/13 Sabon.
Copyediting by Kathryn Simpson.

This book is dedicated to my parents:
Janitia and Paul Westcott. My mother instilled in me a love of reading and a thirst for knowledge. My father inspired my passion for military history. This book would not exist without their unwavering love and support.

Contents

Chronology of Major Events

4 August 1914	Britain declared war on Germany.
12 August 1914	Governor Walter Davidson announced the formation of the Newfoundland Regiment.
31 August 1914	Margaret Davidson announced the formation of the Women's Patriotic Association.
September 1914	The house of assembly and legislative council passed the War Measures Act, Volunteer Force Act, and Foodstuffs Act.
4 October 1914	The first five hundred soldiers of the Newfoundland Regiment departed on the *Florizel* for training in England.
9 January 1915	The Newfoundland Regiment withdrew from Gallipoli with the rest of the Allied forces. Forty-four men from the regiment died during the Gallipoli Campaign.
13 January 1915	HMS *Viknor* sunk off the coast of Ireland. 24 Newfoundland Royal Naval Reservists were killed. These were Newfoundland's first casualties of the war.
20 September 1915	The Newfoundland Regiment landed in Suvla Bay as part of the Gallipoli campaign.
30 October 1915	The department of justice sent twenty-five German POWs to detention camps in Canada.
November 1915	The first contingent of Voluntary Aid Detachments depart for England.
4 November 1915	The Prohibition Plebiscite passed.

1 January 1916	Prime Minister Morris announced a maximum price of $10 for a tonne of coal.
10 January 1916	The Newfoundland government seized all coal stocks in the dominion after coal dealers refused to follow government-imposed maximum pricing.
1 July 1916	The Battle of Beaumont Hamel, the Newfoundland Regiment was decimated and suffered 710 casualties.
1 January 1917	The Prohibition Act came into force, banning the consumption, manufacture, and possession of beverages above 2 per cent alcohol by volume.
4 April 1917	Governor Walter Davidson formed the Newfoundland Forestry Corps to supply the British army with the labour it needed to provide lumber for the war effort. By the end of the war, nearly 500 men enlisted with the corps.
19 May 1917	The First Contingent of the Newfoundland Forestry Corps departs for Scotland.
16 July 1917	Prime Minister Morris formed a national government and leaves for London. W.F. Lloyd becomes acting prime minister.
20 August 1917	The Newfoundland government passed the Business Profits Tax Act.
15 September 1917	Walter Davidson's term as governor ended, and Governor Charles Alexander Harris was appointed.
31 December 1917	Edward Morris officially resigned as prime minister.
5 January 1918	W.F. Lloyd was formally sworn in as prime minister.
26 April 1918	The Military Service Act passed, ushering in conscription in Newfoundland.
27 April–6 May 1918	The Newfoundland constabulary occupied the *Plaindealer* to prevent the publication of any articles opposing conscription.
28 April 1918	Anti-conscription riot in Wesleyville.

30 April 1918	Due to a lack of new recruits, the Newfoundland regiment was removed from frontline duty and appointed to garrison duty at Haig's headquarters.
13 May 1918	The Newfoundland government passed the Income Tax Act.
30 May–5 June 1918	The Newfoundland constabulary occupied the offices of the *Daily Star* to prevent the publication of any articles that opposed conscription.
1 July 1918	The Food Control Board imposed a regulation that required the purchase and use of one pound of flour substitutes for every four pounds of wheat flour.
11 November 1918	The armistice was signed and the war ended.

YOU'LL BE SURE TO FIND IT IN "The MAIL and ADVOCATE."

THE MAIL AND ADVOCATE.

Official Organ of The Fishermen's Protective Union of Newfoundland.

Vol. III. No. 224. ST. JOHN'S, NEWFOUNDLAND, THURSDAY, OCTOBER 5, 1916. Price: 1 Cent.

Interest in War Shifts to Russian-Roumanian-Macedonia Fronts

Heavy Fighting is in Progress on all of These Fronts—Rain Still Hampers Operations on West Front—Enemy Forces still Hold Back Russians Who are Trying to Push Through to Lemberg

RUSSIAN DEAD NUMBER THOUSANDS

Roumanians Record Fresh Gains Against Teutons in Dobrudja—Also in Region of Odorkin—Central Powers Admit Retirement Before Serbs on Western End Macedonia Front—British Maintain Their Positions Along the Struma River and Have Taken Town of Jenikoi—Serb Territory Recaptured by Allies Now Aggregates 250 Square Kilometres

Cabinet Making Becoming an Art

MEN AND MORE MEN NEEDED

Britain Needs Men For Work in Munition Factories and For the Army—Men Now Engaged in Private Work Will be Diverted to Government Work or Released For Army

MAKES APPEAL FOR MORE MEN

Genl. Sir Wm. Robertson, Chief of Imperial Staff, Says That While Allies Are Winning Slowly but Surely the Need Grows For More Men For Army and Munition Factories

MEN MORE MEN

"Pardon me, May I carry your grip?"
"You'd look better carrying a gun!"

British Navy Quickly Stops Germany's Attempt to Close English Channel

Special Cable to the New York World says Germany Last Week Sent all her Available Submarines to the English Channel—This New Menace Was Quickly Met by the British Navy—Move is Regarded in Naval Circles as Symptom of Germany's Intention to Resume Submarine Campaign on a Serious Scale

Grand Duke Nicholas to Command Armies in the Drive on Constantinople

Roumanian Success

All Over Again

Dutch Salted Herring For States

Conscription for Ireland May Throw the Country Into Hands Sinn Feiners

OFFICIAL CASUALTY LIST FIRST NEWFOUNDLAND REGIMENT

J. R. BENNETT, Colonial Secretary

ANOTHER ATTEMPT TO UNSEAT ASQUITH

JEWS PROTEST TO BRITAIN

Want Von Tirpitz As Chancellor

At Panama

Paper Supply Reduced in Germany

Operations In Macedonia

WILL CONTINUE RAID LONDON THINKS DERBY

A SMART SUIT

is what you are looking for, and you will get one here.

Our made-to-order suits are guaranteed perfect, in style, and finish, and are made of first class material.

All the newest weaves and patterns in the finest fabrics, that will look stunning, when made to fit you.

The cut, and fit, will without doubt, be better than any you have had before.

We know our business, and strive to satisfy everyone. That's why we have so many permanent customers.

Why not be one yourself?

W. H. JACKMAN,
39 WATER STREET WEST. 2 Doors East Railway Station.
Phone 795. P. O. Box 186.

Mail and Advocate, 5 October 1916, 157. Courtesy of the Centre for Newfoundland Studies, Memorial University of Newfoundland.

MEN MORE MEN
"Pardon me, May I carry your grip?"
"You'd look better carrying a gun!"

THE PEOPLE'S PAPER— DON'T SAY PAPER, SAY "EVENING TELEGRAM." —READ BY EVERY

Our Regiment
is short of men and the need of reinforcements is great.
Your Brothers are urgently calling for help.
What's YOUR reply to their appeal
?
This Space Given to the Regiment by Steer Bros.

SCHOOL SHOES
Start the Children to School this Spring with Good Durable and Comfortable School Shoes!
Most Parents already know that we make a specialty of School Shoes.
We've studied the problem carefully and we believe that we have mastered it at every point.
If you have Children who need School Shoes, bring them here and see how well we meet every requirement.
BOYS' SHOES.
Box Calf, Gun Metal Calf. Solid soles and heels. Lace or Blucher. Perfect fitting and durable, but not clumsy. Tan Leathers, if you prefer.
$2.10 3.00 3.50 to 3.90
According to size.
GIRLS' SHOES.
Patent Colt, Vici and Gun Metal Calf. Medium or Low Heels. Button or Lace.
Trim looking Shoes, but formed to fit the growing foot perfectly.
$2.00 $2.50 $3.00 $4.70
According to size.
PARKER & MONROE, Limited
THE SHOE MEN.

Respectfully Dedicated to
Newfoundland's Heroic Mothers
Who so Unselfishly and Bravely Are Giving Their Boys to Help Their Pals--Over There!

"O! broken woman I, my treasured only son;
Still would I not have ought that he himself has done!
Pitying I see them look sometime as I pass by,
But I have borne A MAN,—tears do not clog my eye.
For I might pitied be, mine perhaps might be the slur
Had I A MAN not raised, but just a yellow cur;

And I a title bear—what ask you then?
I'm of that Motherhood, those who are MOTHERS OF MEN,
Which mothers send their boys—MEN—forward to the fight
To help all mothers' boys who battle for the right."

THIS SPACE GIVEN TO THE REGIMENT BY THE REID NFLD. CO.

CALIFORNIA RAISIN BREAD,
Made with Sun-Maid Raisins.
A delicious, nutritious loaf, filled with luscious, tender, meaty Sun-Maid Raisins from the celebrated San Joaquin Valley of California.
A "QUALITY LOAF" IN EVERY DETAIL.
EVERY LOAF LABELED.
At all Grocers, 15 cents each.
Made at
McGUIRE'S BAKERY.

CALIFORNIA RAISIN PIE,
Made with Sun-Maid Raisins.
Our Raisin Pie will prove a treat for the whole family. The flaky crust is browned to perfection, and is filled with large, juicy, full-flavored Sun-Maid Raisins.
IT IS GOOD, AND GOOD FOR YOU.
At all Grocers, 10 cents each.
Made at
McGUIRE'S BAKERY.

Now's the Day!
Now's the Hour!
YOUR CHUMS
have thrown up their lucrative positions and brilliant prospects to do their bit—
Are you doing the square thing by them in hanging back?
Does Your Employer Know Why You Haven't Offered.
THIS SPACE GIVEN TO THE REGIMENT BY A FRIEND.

Insure with the
QUEEN,
the Company having the largest number of Policy Holders in Newfoundland.
Every satisfaction given in settling losses.
Office: 167 Water Street.
Adrain Bldg. P. O. Box 782
Telephone 658.
QUEEN INS. CO.,
GEO. H. HALLEY,
Agent.

DON'T BE A QUITTER!
ENLIST NOW!
This space given to the Regiment by T. A. McNab & Co.

J. J. ST. JOHN
Don't forget the best
TEA
to be got in Newfoundland is at our Store, retailing at
60c.
per lb.
Sun Ammonia,
10c. package.
English Breakfast COFFEE,
1 lb. tins.
Eddy's Matches.
J. J. ST. JOHN.
Duckworth Street and LeMarchant Road.

FOR SHOEMAKERS!
Kerr's
LINEN FINISH THREAD,
Black, Tan Yellow.
Sizes: 40, 50, 60, 2 oz. Reels.
R. Templeton
333 Water Street.

Woodworking Factory and Construction Work.
Our Factory is modern and up-to-date. We make
DOORS, WINDOWS, STAIRS, OFFICE and STORE FIXTURES, FURNITURE,
and all kinds of Cabinet Work, Mantels, Balusters, and all kinds of Trim. We also build houses and do all kinds of construction work.
All work done in a first-class workmanlike manner, of good materials, and reasonable prices.
PLANS AND SPECIFICATION FREE OF CHARGE TO CUSTOMERS.
Newfoundland Shipbuilding Co'y, Ltd.
HARBOR GRACE.

If Newfoundland Were Belgium.
WHAT THEN
?
IT'S
UP TO YOU
YOUNG FELLOW!
This space given to the Regiment by Geo. Neal.

5c. The Crescent Picture Palace 5c.
PRESENTS TO-DAY
The first of the great "Seven Deadly Sins" Series, entitled
"PRIDE."
With Shirley Mason, Holbrook Blynn and George LeGuere. A great 5 part Photo-Play.
PROF. McCARTHY will sing "Thora" at both afternoon and evening shows.
5c.—LATEST MUSIC, DRUMS AND EFFECTS—5c.

ORANGES, CABBAGE, etc.
Oranges, Cabbage, Apples, Onions.
BURT & LAWRENCE,
14 NEW GOWER STREET.

NO MATTER HOW THE FIRE IS CAUSED
If you're not insured, you're a loser. Take time to see about your policies. We give you the best companies and reasonable rates.
PERCIE JOHNSON
Insurance Agent.

Come in Out of the Wet.
You can't afford to lose much time now. Spring is coming on, so get your pipes, traps and drains in good order and don't delay your house-cleaning.
SEND FOR ME
If you want expert Plumbing or Heating done at Low Rates. Orders left at Parsons' Phone 688, will be taken care of.
Remember, am right on the job and personally perform or supervise my own work.
A. PITTMAN,
PLUMBER, STEAM & HOT WATER FITTER.

The Evening Telegram is The People's Paper

Evening Telegram, 23 April 1918, 164. Courtesy of the Centre for Newfoundland Studies, Memorial University of Newfoundland.

Now's the Day!
Now's the Hour!

YOUR CHUMS

have thrown up their lucrative positions and brilliant prospects to do their bit—

Are you doing the square thing by them in hanging back?

Does Your Employer Know Why You Haven't Offered.

THIS SPACE GIVEN TO THE REGIMENT BY A FRIEND.

.s,tu,th

THE EVENING TELEGRAM, ST. JOHN'S, NEWFOUNDLAND, MAY 3, 1918—5

The Immortal Guards.

Grenadiers, Coldstreams and Irish Held Back the German Onrush.

Fought for Two Days and Nights —Allied Reserves Now Equal Those of the Enemy.

WARNING!

Persons Engaging Young Men For Any Work or Occupation this Season

which young men are, under the Selective Conscription Act, eligible for immediate or early Military Service

Will Do So At Their Own Risk.

It is evident that Class A will have to be called up immediately, and Class B may have to be called up much earlier than some people may think.

Patriotic Newfoundlanders

are not engaging young men who have not anybody particularly dependent upon them and who are eligible for Military Service. Neither are they giving their support or financial backing to parties who might, for their own interests, engage such young men.

Some People Have Been Unwise Enough to Say

that the Selective Conscription Bill will not be enforced by the Government for some time.

Don't Let Anybody Run Away With This Idea!

WE KNOW

that there are too strong reasons why this Bill must be enforced immediately by the Government. And as regards the enforcement of a Conscription Act, every intelligent man, woman and child throughout the Dominion is behind the same, even knowing only some of the necessities.

The Returned Soldiers' and Rejected Volunteers' Assoc.

The Wellington THE UNIVERSAL PIPE

W D C TRADE MARK

PUT your good tobacco into a good pipe —a Wellington Pipe. The well catches the moisture. All you draw through the stem is clean, sweet, dry smoke. Every Wellington bears the W.D.C. triangle trade-mark—mark of pipe quality—sign of good French briar, well seasoned. All shapes and sizes, 75 cents and up. Pick yours.

WM. DEMUTH & CO. New York

Evening Advocate, 3 May 1918, 165. Courtesy of the Centre for Newfoundland Studies, Memorial University of Newfoundland.

WARNING!

Persons Engaging Young Men For Any Work or Occupation this Season

which young men are, under the Selective Conscription Act, eligible for immediate or early Military Service

Will Do So At Their Own Risk.

It is evident that Class A will have to be called up immediately, and Class B may have to be called up much earlier than some people may think.

Patriotic Newfoundlanders

are not engaging young men who have not anybody particularly dependent upon them and who are eligible for Military Service. Neither are they giving their support or financial backing to parties who might, for their own interests, engage such young men.

Some People Have Been Unwise Enough to Say

that the Selective Conscription Bill will not be enforced by the Government for some time.

Don't Let Anybody Run Away With This Idea!

WE KNOW

that there are too strong reasons why this Bill must be enforced immediately by the Government. And as regards the enforcement of a Conscription Act, every intelligent man, woman and child throughout the Dominion is behind the same, even knowing only some of the necessities.

The Returned Soldiers' and Rejected Volunteers' Assoc.

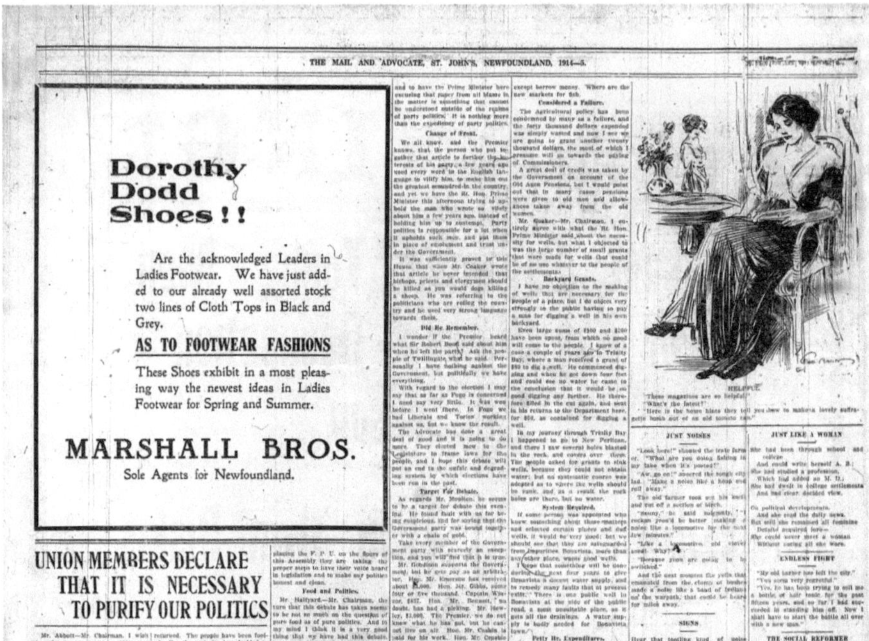

THE MAIL AND ADVOCATE, ST. JOHN'S, NEWFOUNDLAND, 1914—5.

UNION MEMBERS DECLARE THAT IT IS NECESSARY TO PURIFY OUR POLITICS

Willie's Little Game.— By Hoban.

Mail and Advocate, 8 May 1914, 212. Courtesy of the Centre for Newfoundland Studies, Memorial University of Newfoundland. The caption reads, “These magazines are so helpful,” “What's the latest?,” and “Here is the home hints they tell you how to make a lovely suffragette bomb out of an old tomato can.”

HELPFUL

"These magazines are so helpful."

"What's the latest?"

"Here is the home hints they tell you how to make a lovely suffragette bomb out of an old tomato can."

TWELVE PAGES TO-DAY

THE "PEOPLE'S PAPER" IS A LIVE DAILY IN A BUSY CENTRE—STUDY ITS NEWSY ADVERTISING.

TWELVE PAGES TO-DAY

THE EVENING TELEGRAM

VOLUME XL. | PRICE ONE CENT. | ST. JOHN'S, NEWFOUNDLAND, THURSDAY, MAY 2, 1918. | $3.00 PER YEAR. | NUMBER 98.

Are Your Folks Ashamed of You for Not Enlisting?

This space given to Regiment by BOWRING BROTHERS, Limited.

Auction Sales!

FOR SALE BY PUBLIC AUCTION. On Saturday Next, 4th inst. at 11 o'clock, At the Central Auction Mart

M. A. BASTOW, Auctioneer.

FOR SALE!

GEO. G. R. PARSONS, King's Road.

Knock Down Motor Engines.

SEEDS.

PETER O'MARA, The Druggist, 46-48 WATER ST. W.

Canada's Most Famous TOBACCO

IMPERIAL MIXTURE

CASH'S Tobacco Store, Water Street.

Say, Young Fellow!

You Are Just As Good As Those Who Went Before So Come Along.

WHY NOT TODAY?

This space given to the Regiment by Standard Mfg. Co.

Spring Time Offerings at Property Headquarters.

42 Residences ... $350.00 to $13,000.00
7 Farms ... $80.00 to $3,000.00
14 Surburban Properties ... $80.00 to $1,200.00
5 Bungalow Lots ... $2.50 to $15.00 per foot
54 Building Lots ... $2.00 to $30.00 per foot

Look over our offerings before you buy of anyone. Suitable terms.

FRED J. ROIL & Co., Auctioneers, Real Estate & Investment Brokers. Smallwood Building, Duckworth Street.

Watch Our Curtis Offering.

J. J. LACEY & CO., Ltd., Investment Specialists, City Chambers.

Just Arrived!

800 SAX CORNMEAL

HARVEY & CO., Ltd., WHOLESALE.

Forty Years in the Public Service—The Evening Telegram

NEYLE'S HARDWARE (Opp. Bowring Bros.)

ARMY & NAVY Razor, Hone & Strop, Just what is needed for the kit bag, $2.50.

RAZOR STROPS. Good quality, 75c., 80c., $1.00, $1.35 each.

RAZOR HONES. 25c., 40c., 60c., 80c. each.

ENGLISH RAZORS. $1.25 and $1.50 each.

SAFETY RAZOR. Wood Giant Junior, with 4 extra blades, only 60c. complete.

S. Wrenches,

A good quality adjustable Wrench, 6, 8 and 10 inches, for nut and pipe. These are about the most serviceable for use in motor boats.

Ship Auger Bits,

Motor Boat Auger Bits,

FEATHERS in Small Sacks.

ASBESTOS SAD IRONS. Nickel Plated, $3.00 a set.

HARNESS!

We manufacture Carriage and Cart Harness and keep separate parts in stock.

Neyle's Hardware. W. SOPER, Manager.

Why Import Loose Leaf Supplies?

DICKS & CO., Ltd. Manufacturing Stationers.

Insure with the Acada Fire Insurance Company,

and you are assured of prompt and liberal settlement.

BAIRD & Co. 181 WATER STREET, AGENTS.

To Arrive from P.E.I.

M. A. BASTOW, Beck's Cove.

For Sale or to Let!

"Morningside,"

Geo. W. B. Ayre.

W. P. A.

The Workrooms at Headquarters, Sutherland Place, will be open for workers during the summer months on Mondays, Tuesdays, Thursdays and Fridays.

A. N. GOSLING, Hon. Sec'y.

Lodge Tasker Notice.

S. A. CHURCHILL, Secretary.

Come in Out of the Wet.

A. PITTMAN, PLUMBER, STEAM & HOT WATER FITTER.

COAL

Now Landing, 1000 Tons SYDNEY COAL.

H. J. Stabb & Co.

Schooner For Sale!

NOEL PACKET CO., LTD., Noel, Nova Scotia.

NOTICE!

J. T. MEANEY, Convener.

NEW ARRIVALS!

M. A. BASTOW, Beck's Cove.

CLEARING AT COST —

FOR SALE—By M. A. Bastow,

FOR SALE — 3 Horses;

TO LET—For the season or

WANTED TO PURCHASE

PICKED UP — Rejection

FOUND—In C. C. C. Hall,

HELP WANTED

Help Wanted!

WANTED—A Plain Cook
WANTED—A General Servant
WANTED—A Strong Boy
WANTED—A Good General Servant
WANTED—A Reliable Woman
WANTED — Immediately,
WANTED—A Housemaid;
WANTED—A Boy; apply
WANTED—A Young Lady
WANTED—Two Tidy Girls
WANTED — A Cook and
WANTED—A Paper Ruler
WANTED—At Once, Coat
WANTED — A Farmer;
WANTED — A Strong
WANTED—At the Crosbie
WANTED—A Girl for light
WANTED — A Capable
WANTED — A Housemaid,
WANTED — An Assistant
WANTED—A Young Lady
WANTED—A Boy for Cash
WANTED — A Good Plain
WANTED — A Male and
WANTED — A Capable
WANTED—A Young Lady
WANTED — A Cook and

Evening Telegram, 2 May 1918, 158. Courtesy of the Centre for Newfoundland Studies, Memorial University of Newfoundland.

WITH A UNITY OF PURPOSE

Introduction

On the evening of 4 August 1914, a cable arrived at Government House in St John's. It informed Governor Walter Davidson that Britain and its colonies were at war with Germany. With no active soldiers, weapons, or equipment, the Dominion of Newfoundland at that time was hardly prepared to participate in the Great War. The only military presence in Newfoundland was the Newfoundland Royal Naval Reserve (NRNR), which trained sailors for the Royal Navy. Nonetheless, on 8 August, Governor Davidson wired London and committed to sending a force of five hundred Newfoundlanders to support the British war effort. On 12 August, the governor held a public meeting at the Church Lads' Brigade Armoury. He told the cheering crowds that he had committed to sending five hundred soldiers, but he hoped the dominion could send five thousand.

The First World War had a widespread impact on Newfoundland society. By 1918, 11,988 soldiers had enlisted to serve with the Newfoundland Regiment, Newfoundland Naval Reserve, Newfoundland Forestry Corps, and the Canadian Expeditionary Force. Citizens who remained on the home front faced skyrocketing food prices, calls both for voluntary and for compulsory military service, the threat of U-Boat warfare, the loss of their loved ones, and panic over so-called "enemy aliens." To cope with conditions on the home front, the citizens of Newfoundland negotiated what amounted to a new social contract with the government. In this contract, male citizens owed a debt of military service to the state; in return Newfoundlanders expected more help from government to cope with conditions on the home front. This book will examine several areas of life in Newfoundland that became the battleground over new government policies that may be described as socially interventionist. These include policies related to prohibition, food rationing/price control, taxation, recruiting, conscription, the rights of "enemy aliens," and the role of women in Newfoundland society.

THE FIRST WORLD WAR AND THE LIBERAL ORDER

In his seminal article "The Liberal Order Framework: A Prospectus for a Reconnaissance of Canadian History," Ian McKay invited Canadian historians to examine what he called the "Canadian Liberal Revolution," the gradual hegemonic dominance of liberal ideals across the British colonies and Dominion of Canada between 1840 and 1940. He describes the liberal order as a process by which liberalism was implemented in Canadian institutions and inculcated in the dominion's subjects as a totalizing philosophy.[1]

McKay's definition of liberalism comes from Fernande Roy's *Progress, harmonies, liberty: Les liberalism des milieu affairs francophones à Montréal au tournant du siècle*. Roy defines liberalism as a political philosophy that places the utmost importance on the concept of the individual, who is responsible only to themselves and whose freedoms should only be limited by the state when they infringe on the liberty of others. There are three defining characteristics of McKay's liberalism: liberty, equality, and property. The focus on liberty manifested in the importance of the freedom of speech, conscience, labour, and press. The principle of liberty was also used to justify the near-universal acceptance of free-market economics. The tenet of equality was the cornerstone of the Canadian belief that all individuals were equal under the law. Finally, under the liberal order, every individual had the right to own property.[2]

McKay's work has been highly influential on Canadian historiography and inspired a host of historians to examine the development of the liberal order. In 2009, Jean-François Constant and Michel Ducharme edited a volume containing debates about McKay's conception of a Canadian liberal order. Although they concur with McKay that the liberal order made certain compromises in response to the crises of the world wars and the Great Depression, they criticize his assertion that the liberal order framework becomes irrelevant after 1945; in their view, the liberal order was alive and well following the Second World War.[3]

This book examines how the liberal order changed in Newfoundland during the First World War. Like Constant and Ducharme, my research has indicated that the liberal state in Newfoundland underwent profound changes between 1914 and 1919 as its focus shifted from individualistic to communitarian values. The key to understanding these changes is the importance and contradictions of the liberal concept of the "individual." As Constant and Ducharme point out, the liberal "individual" never included all human beings, and also shifted continuously: "It is equally undeniable that, despite its pretensions to universality, liberalism has not always granted the status of the individual to all human beings ... In fact, between the middle of the nineteenth century and the middle of the twentieth, the very definition of an individual was based on a collective consideration of class, race, and gender." To fully comprehend the workings of the liberal state during the war, two things must be understood. The first is, given shifting conceptions of the liberal concept of the individual, one must examine how the war changed Newfoundlanders' conceptions of gender, ethnicity, and class; this is because, as Constant and Ducharme point out, the concept of the liberal "individual" did not extend to everyone in 1914. The second is how the state and citizens understood their rights and responsibilities with respect to each other. This book will argue that, in Newfoundland, during these years, the liberal state underwent a profound change as the war fundamentally altered classical liberalism, transforming it into a burgeoning *social* liberalism. Citizens and the state renegotiated their rights and their responsibilities to each other. Moreover, consensus about *who* should be afforded the status of a liberal individual also changed.[4]

To appreciate the power of war to transform societies, one must understand the requirements of a total war effort. This concept suggests that certain conflicts require societies to commit themselves entirely to the war effort. To wage a total war, the state must harness civilian populations, science, technology, culture, and politics. Elements of society that do not support the war effort must be reforged. In this book, I use the idea of total war to dissect the societal changes that occurred in Newfoundland as the citizens and the state mobilized the dominion for war. Since this preparation involved the mass mobilization money and civilians, the process also turned a spotlight on individuals and social groups and on the categories that identified them: most especially gender, ethnicity, and class. Indeed, one of the outcomes of the war in Newfoundland, and critical ways in which the liberal state changed, was to alter existing ideas about gender, ethnicity, and class to reorient them in support of the war effort.[5]

This book argues that during the First World War, Newfoundland's war effort caused a profound renegotiation of the liberal order as the government and the people sought to cope with the war effort and the conditions on the home front. These renegotiations resulted in a new social covenant between citizens and the state whereby wartime conceptions of gender, ethnicity and class reshaped traditional liberal ideas about the "individual." Furthermore, negotiating this social covenant also required rethinking traditional liberal concepts of liberty. In return for citizens' military and civil service to the state, the people expected greater government protection from adverse conditions on the home front.

Each chapter will focus on a particular proposed social intervention during the war, including the campaign for prohibition, food rationing and price control, the treatment of "enemy aliens," the debate over taxation as a means of paying for military commitments, recruitment of military personnel, the imposition of conscription in 1918, and women's war work. Each topic is a case study into the myriad of ways that the war altered conceptions of race, class, and gender, drastically transforming the liberal order in wartime Newfoundland.

The first significant change stemmed from the war's impact on the local temperance movement. Bolstered by a new discourse of war-related patriotism and sacrifice, temperance advocates convinced people that the state had a duty to prioritize collective needs over those of the individual by prohibiting the consumption of alcohol. As the war impacted Newfoundland's economy, the progressive movement demanded that the government regulate coal and food prices. The government's defence of free-market principles prompted a class-inflected indictment of war profiteering by the St John's business elite as progressives associated patriotism with state intervention and the free market with narrow, class self-interest.

The campaign for a more progressive state intensified when liberal politicians argued that the producing class was bearing the cost of the war effort. They called for fairer forms of taxation that put the burden of the war effort on the shoulders of those who best afford it: Newfoundland's business community. The resulting debate over a business profits tax, an income tax, and a victory loan bond drive were among the most contentious issues of the war.

While working people stood to benefit from the development of a more progressive wartime state, a stronger collective identity based on patriotism intruded on individual rights along ethnic lines. Concerns about the possible subversive presence of enemy aliens within Newfoundland led to the development of ethnic categories of who might be considered "German" or "Austro-Hungarian," regardless of whether one was German or Austro-Hungarian or not. Due to their voluntary public support of the war effort, Syrian immigrants from the Ottoman Empire escaped the restrictions on individual liberties placed on Germans and Austro-Hungarians.

Voluntarism was at the heart of an engendered dimension of emphasizing social obligations over individual rights. To meet the enlistment demands of the Newfoundland Regiment, recruiters across Newfoundland claimed that sacrifice and military service were the highest expressions of masculinity and British identity. This drastically altered perceptions of masculinity, and many decried the unenlisted as selfish, un-British, or unmanly.

When sufficient numbers of men failed to embrace wartime conceptions of masculinity, citizens believed it was the state's duty to compel them through conscription, a policy that came into effect in May 1918, following much public debate. In total, over 1,500 Newfoundlanders were conscripted into military service and sent overseas. For all the divisiveness of the conscription debate, none of these men ever saw combat. They were still in training when the war ended in November.

The wartime emphasis on the rights of the community heavily impacted women in Newfoundland. The role of gender in determining the liberal individual was shifted to an emphasis on patriotism, sacrifice, and service. Every citizen was expected to put the country's needs before their own. As a result, the women of Newfoundland expressed ardent patriotism, sacrifice, and service. In 1914, Margaret Davidson formed the Women's Patriotic Association to "arrange for the providing of necessary articles for the sick and wounded, and also for those who are going to the front to uphold the honour of Newfoundland in defence of Empire."[6] Over the course of the war, women of Newfoundland made huge financial contributions to the war effort, totalling over $250,000 in the first two years alone.[7]

Not all women were content to serve on the homefront. Many trained nurses signed up for frontline service. Dozens of other women enlisted to service with the Voluntary Aid Detachment (VAD). These

VADs received training in England and filled many different roles, such as ambulance drivers, medical assistants, cooks, and clerks. Throughout the war, women exceeded the community's demands for support and met the wartime criteria for the liberal individual. As a result, they demanded and eventually won the prime privilege of the liberal individual: the right to vote.

I will discuss two primary forms of social change throughout these chapters. The first is legislative changes. These are policies, laws, and procedures enacted by the Newfoundland government to rearrange society for the war effort. The impetus for legislative change came from the competing views of various groups of citizens and politicians on how the Newfoundland government could best serve its citizens. The second form of change is public discourse; that is, the issues that were discussed and debated by citizens and how they talked and wrote about them – in newspaper articles, letters to the editor, public speeches, and correspondence between citizens and government officials. I utilize newspaper articles as the primary source for public opinion. By consulting a wide range of newspapers from both urban and rural Newfoundland and from a variety of political backgrounds, I have been able to form an understanding of how various groups of Newfoundlanders felt about a particular issue. While citizens and politicians could not always achieve the legislative change they wanted, public discussion surrounding them was significant. Understanding these conversations and how they changed during the war is critical to understanding how conceptions of gender, ethnicity, class, and the relationship between citizens and the state were reforged to fit the war effort.

This book draws on the study of the construction and reconstruction of gender, especially relevant works by Joy Parr, Susan Grayzel, and Nicoletta Gullace. In *The Gender of Breadwinners: Women, Men, and Change in Two Industrial Towns, 1880–1950*, Parr shows that the local economic conditions in Paris and Hanover, Ontario, had profound impacts on conceptions of gender. Parr's work also highlights that historians can obtain a deeper understanding of the past by examining the interplay between gender, ethnicity, and class. Grayzel, in *Making Peace: The Reconstruction of Gender in Interwar Britain*, argues that, following the war, British society redrew the ideology of "separate spheres" for men and women, providing new spaces for women in public life in hopes of preventing another war. Similarly, Gullace's *The Blood of Our Sons: Men, Women, and the Renegotiation of Citizenship during the Great War* argues that, during the war, women undermined the idea that citizenship was linked to gender. She argues that the prime criteria for citizenship during the war shifted from masculinity, majority, and property to service, patriotism, and British blood.

My methodology follows the work of Parr, Kent, and Gullace by examining the malleability of conceptions of gender, ethnicity, and class. Particularly, I build on the work of Kent and Gullace by extending their work on gender and dissecting how conceptions of gender, ethnicity, and class were reforged to fit the war effort and what impacts this had on the liberal order in the Dominion of Newfoundland.

NEWFOUNDLAND: A BACKGROUND

In 1914, Newfoundland had minimal established military forces. Since the eighteenth century, the colony was host to several iterations of the Newfoundland Regiment, including the Royal Newfoundland Regiment of Foot (1795–1802), the Royal Newfoundland Fencible Infantry (1803–16), and the Royal Newfoundland Companies (1824–62). The coming and going of these infantry regiments left little behind upon which to build a local military force. By 1870, the last British troops had left St John's, leaving the defence of Newfoundland to the Royal Navy.[8]

In 1899, the Newfoundland and British governments formed the Newfoundland Royal Naval Reserve. The purpose of this reserve was to supply the Royal Navy with trained sailors and provide rural Newfoundlanders with seasonal employment. By the time the war broke out, it had over five hundred recruits. Despite the ample number of trained sailors, the only ship the NRNR possessed was the HMS *Calypso*, which was launched in 1883 and given to the NRNR in 1902. By 1914, the *Calypso* could no longer sail under its own power, was permanently moored in St John's, and was used solely as a training vessel. It provided minimal defence for the island.[9]

When it came to a standing army, Newfoundland had no formal military establishment. The closest thing the dominion had to a military force was the various denominational cadet corps, such as the Church of England's Church Lads Brigades, the Catholic Cadet Corps; the Methodist Guards; and the Presbyterian Highlanders. These corps taught young men and boys the basics of drill, physical fitness, marksmanship, and military discipline. Despite their military training, these cadet corps never intended to take any role in combat operations. They would, however, eventually make up most of the initial volunteers for the Newfoundland Regiment.

The dominion's first significant casualties in the First World War came from the Newfoundland Royal Naval Reserve. On 13 January 1915, twenty-four Newfoundlanders stationed on the HMS *Viknor*, as part of the Royal Navy's 10th Cruiser Squadron, were killed when the *Viknor* sank off the coast of Ireland. It is unknown why the *Viknor* was lost, but it likely hit one of the many German mines set off the coast of Ireland. Twenty-two more Newfoundland reservists died on 3 February when the *Clan McNaughton,* a merchant-marine vessel, went down in a massive storm off the coast of Ireland. Tragedy struck a third time on 11 March when eleven reservists were killed on the HMS *Bayano* when a German U-Boat torpedoed it in the Northern Channel.

After preliminary training in St John's and further training in Scotland, the Newfoundland Regiment saw combat for the first time during its four months on the beaches of Gallipoli. The regiment's time there was characterized by mud, cold, and wet. At the end of that four months and the failed attempt at holding Suvla beach, the Newfoundland Regiment helped to protect Australian and New Zealand soldiers as they evacuated. As a result of its actions at Gallipoli, twenty-eight soldiers died, and another eighty were wounded. While the regiment's actions at Gallipoli received widespread press coverage, they were soon overshadowed by the tremendous loss of life on the Western front.[10]

On 1 July 1916, the Newfoundland Regiment and the Essex Regiment were ordered to take part in the first day of the Somme offensive. Its goal was to charge a five-hundred-metre section of no-mans-land and seize part of the German trench at Beaumont Hamel. After a prolonged artillery barrage on the German trenches, the Newfoundlanders left their positions and faced a hail of machine gunfire. The attack was a complete failure and resulted in the death and injury of over seven hundred Newfoundlanders. As it became known in Newfoundland, the battle of Beaumont Hamel sent shockwaves through the home front and would become the defining element of the dominion's participation in the war.

While the Newfoundland Regiment's first engagements had been failures, it had many successes throughout the war. It earned high praise for its accomplishments at the battles of Gueudecourt (October 1916),

Monchy-le-Preux (April 1917), and Cambrai (November 1917), among others. The Newfoundland regiment was issued the prefix Royal for its valour in the field in December 1917.

By the war's end, over 6,000 soldiers enlisted with the Royal Newfoundland Regiment, 2,000 with the Newfoundland Royal Naval Reserve, 500 with the Newfoundland Forestry Corps, and over 3,000 enlisted with the Canadian Expeditionary Force. While the total casualty rate is unknown, over 1,500 Newfoundlanders lost their lives during the war. The patriotism, sacrifice, and service of Newfoundland's soldiers and civilians became a powerful force behind politics, economics, and everyday life.[11]

In 1914, the economy in Newfoundland was much as it had been for hundreds of years: the cod fishery was the primary industry and provided the livelihood for most Newfoundlanders. Fishers across the island caught, split, salted, and dried codfish for export to markets in Spain, the Caribbean, Greece, Italy, and Portugal. The success of Newfoundland's fisheries depended not only on the quantity of fish and the quality of the cure but on the unpredictability of global markets international conflicts, trade barriers, local politics, and competitors like Norway and France profoundly impacted Newfoundland's economic success for better and often for worse.[12]

In addition to the fishery, many people relied on other sources of income to make ends meet. Logging became an important source of income for many Newfoundlanders in the years preceding the war. Significant developments in Newfoundland's pulp and paper industry occurred between 1909 and 1911 when Alfred Harmsworth, a British newspaper financier, and Albert E. Reed, a British paper manufacturer, established pulp and paper mills at Grand Falls and Bishop Falls. By 1914, logging represented over 14 per cent of the dominion's exports and offered a winter income for many fishers.[13]

Sealing was another important source of income, supporting the people of Newfoundland during the spring before the cod fishery began. Since the eighteenth century, fishers have harvested seals for their pelts and fat. Seal fat was a valuable commodity and was the primary reason for the seal harvest. It was rendered to produce oil for lighting, lubrication, and manufacturing products like margarine and paint. Fishers also harvested seal pelts, which were used to make clothing. Seal meat was not a significant part of Newfoundlanders' diets, though, in some areas, people considered seal flippers a delicacy.[14]

Mining was another form of employment across Newfoundland, with mining operations beginning in the mid-nineteenth century. By the early 1900s, mines operated in Tilt Cove, Terra Nova, Bett's Cove, Little Bay, Pilley's Island, and Bell Island. These mines exploited copper, pyrite, iron ore deposits, and small amounts of gold. Mining provided lucrative income for residents of northeastern Newfoundland and Bell Island. To supplement these more traditional forms of employment, people across the island also earned additional money by picking berries, raising livestock, growing vegetables, and fishing for salmon.

Though the dominion had abundant food resources in the form of cod and salmon, the island was always reliant on food imports. The relatively late retreat of glaciers and the island's cold, wet northern maritime climate meant Newfoundland had very little fertile soil and a short growing season. Approximately one-third of the island had no agricultural capacity, and only tiny pockets of land had enough fertile ground for growing crops. Though residents often augmented their diets by raising sheep and cows and growing vegetables, the island could never sustain enough livestock and crops to support the population. As a result, the residents of Newfoundland relied on imports of salt pork, beef, flour, tea, molasses, sugar, butter, oatmeal, peas, hops, malt, beer, wine, brandy, and tobacco. The inability to provide sufficient food for its settler population was a defining element of Newfoundland throughout its history and would become a source of great anxiety during the war.[15]

Three political parties dominated politics in 1914: the Liberal Party, the People's Party, and the Fisherman's Protective Union. The oldest of these parties was the Liberal Party, formed in 1887 by former Premier William Whiteway. The primary goal of Whiteway's Liberal party was to complete the railway that he had worked towards during his time as leader of the Conservative Party and develop Newfoundland's natural resources. Whiteway won elections in 1889 and 1895. In 1897, however, Whiteway's Liberal Party lost to James Spearman Winter, the leader of the Tory Party. After this loss, Whiteway retired from politics, and Robert Bond took control of the Liberal Party in 1899.

Bond's popularity in Newfoundland stemmed from his vocal opposition to the 1897 Reid Contract, which had caused outrage across the island. In exchange for constructing a railway across Newfoundland, the Reid Newfoundland Company received unprecedented compensation from the Newfoundland government, including a right to run the railway for fifty years, after which the company would take possession of the railway. It also received the right to millions of acres in land grants; the dry dock in St John's; the operation of eight coastal steamers, and the development of Newfoundland's first hydroelectric company. As a result, in the 1900 election, Bond won against Spearman, winning thirty-two out of thirty-six seats in the house. Bond's time as premier of Newfoundland Colony and later prime minister of the Dominion of Newfoundland was characterized by three major issues: the settling of the French shore issue in 1904, the development of a pulp and paper mill in Grand Falls, and a reciprocity deal with the United States that Britain eventually vetoed. His work on these issues made Bond and the Liberal Party seem like strong defenders of Newfoundland who pushed back against France and Britain. This persona won him two more elections, and he served as prime minister until 1914.[16]

Another major party was Edward Morris's People's Party. Morris first entered politics in 1885 when he ran in a general election as an independent. He campaigned door to door, promoting himself as a champion of the downtrodden and winning a seat as a member for St John's West. When Whiteway, Bond, and Alfred Morine reinvigorated the Liberal party in 1887, Morris joined their party for the 1889 election. After their victory in this election, Whiteway appointed Morris to the executive council.

In 1907, Morris split from Bond's Liberal Party and announced the formation of his People's Party. Morris timed his announcement to coincide with the arrival of many sealers from the ice, ensuring the news spread rapidly through rural Newfoundland. In the People's Party manifesto, Morris maintained that he did not abandon his commitment to liberal politics. He declared that his People's Party would unite Liberals and Conservatives to advance the interests of all Newfoundlanders. The 1908 election resulted in a tie between Bond and Morris, each winning eighteen seats. In 1909, Morris achieved a majority government, winning twenty-six out of thirty-six seats in the house of assembly.[17]

The final party to dominate politics during the war years was the Fisherman's Protective Union (FPU). Born and educated in St John's, William Coaker formed the FPU in 1908. The original goal of the Union was to ensure that fishers got a fair share of the wealth that their labour produced. Initially, the FPU intended to avoid getting involved directly in politics. They planned on supporting whichever party best furthered their goals. Most of the initial efforts of the FPU were focused on reforming how fishers sold their fish to merchants, including demands for government intervention to ensure the fair grading of fish. Despite their desire to avoid direct political involvement, William Coaker believed the FPU would have to become politically active to secure fishery reforms. It ran for the first time as a party in the 1913 election.[18]

During the 1913 election, Coaker formed an uneasy alliance with Robert Bond's Liberals. Coaker believed that political affiliations were necessary for the FPU to achieve any of its political goals, such as fisheries regulations, old-age pensions, reduced tariffs, and a legislative change that would allow unpopular MHAs to be recalled. The result of the 1913 election, which would be the last election until 1919, was a majority for Morris' People's Party. Morris won twenty-one seats, Bond won seven, and Coaker took eight seats. The geographical divide in support between the Liberal-Union coalition and the People's Party is worth noting. Morris was most popular in areas with large populations of Catholics (Ferryland, Harbour Main, Placentia, and St Mary's), the south, and southwest (Burin, Burgeo, La Poile, Fortune, St George's, and most of St John's). The Liberal-Union coalition, however, won all seats from the northern districts of St Barbe, Twillingate, Fogo, Bonavista, and Trinity. With Morris having the support of the South and Bond/Coaker having the North, the district of Conception Bay North ultimately decided the election, returning five seats for the People's Party.[19]

Following this election, Bond resigned his leadership of the Liberal party and would never return to politics. J.M. Kent, a lawyer and MHA for St John's East took over leadership of the Liberal Party. He would remain the party's leader until 1916, when Kent was appointed to the Supreme Court, and W.F. Lloyd, the English-born MHA for Trinity Bay, became leader.

For most of the war, two major factions dominated politics in Newfoundland. Morris, his People's Party, and their supporters were classically liberal in orientation. They believed that social problems were the individual's responsibility and that the only assistance afforded to them should come in the form of charity. They also believed in laissez-faire economics and that the government had no right to interfere in free markets. On the other side of the political divide was the progressive alliance between the FPU and the Liberals. Coaker firmly believed that social problems were the state's responsibility and that it was obligated to regulate markets to ensure that producers earned a greater share from their labour. In many ways, while the British Empire was fighting the Germans on the front lines, the progressives were fighting liberals on the home front.

In September 1914, the government met for an emergency war session to pass legislation supporting Newfoundland's war effort. One of the bills, the War Measures Act, gave the Newfoundland government wide-ranging powers to curtail the rights of citizens in the name of security. This bill allowed the government to impose censorship on newspapers and private correspondence, arrest anyone deemed a threat to the war effort, and seize personal property considered essential to the war effort.[20]

Another bill, the Volunteer Force Act, created the legislative framework for the Newfoundland Regiment. Before the war, Newfoundland had no government department or cabinet position responsible for a militia or national defence. Comparatively, Canada, Australia, New Zealand, and South Africa all had either a department of defence or a minister of defence when the war started.

In a genuinely bizarre arrangement, instead of creating an official government department to control Newfoundland's war effort, the Volunteer Force Act gave the responsibility of raising and maintaining the regiment personally to Walter Davidson and his newly founded Newfoundland Patriotic Association (NPA), a civilian organization. It comprised Davidson as the chairman and twenty-five other citizen volunteers. Davidson told the local press that the government handed responsibility for Newfoundland's war effort to a civilian organization to keep it free from the messiness of party politics.

The NPA held its inaugural meeting on 17 August and split itself into six subcommittees to organize the fundraising, recruitment, equipment, training, and transportation for the Newfoundland Regiment. The NPA would have forty-five branches across the island and over three hundred members by the end of September. Throughout the war, the Newfoundland Patriotic Association would grow into an organization with the size and scope of a fully-fledged militia department. In 1917, following the departure of Walter Davidson as governor of Newfoundland and widespread displeasure with Newfoundland's war effort, the NPA was disbanded and replaced with a government-run militia department.[21]

Edward Morris served as the prime minister for the majority of the war. By 1917, his administration was having great difficulty maintaining the Newfoundland Regiment, and it seemed that conscription was necessary. The public was also outraged at the rapidly increasing cost of living. Morris knew that he would need the support of all political parties to solve these issues and that he would likely lose an election focusing on conscription. In 1917, Morris approached W.F. Lloyd and William Coaker about forming a national government of all parties.

Initially, Lloyd and Coaker rejected Morris's proposal for an all-party government. They argued that it was a shameless attempt at prolonging Morris's administration by delaying the election scheduled for 1918. The *Evening Advocate* routinely attacked Morris's proposal, saying that postponing the election would be a gross violation of Newfoundlanders' rights. Despite their initial objections, Lloyd and Coaker eventually accepted this deal. On 17 July 1917, Morris announced he would dissolve the People's Party, form a national government, and appoint cabinet positions from all three major parties.[22]

Shortly after the formation of the national government, Morris left for London, supposedly to work with the Imperial War Conference. It has been widely speculated that his impending resignation was crucial to the negotiations between Morris, Lloyd, and Coaker that made the national government possible. Morris appointed W.F. Lloyd as the acting prime minister. On 31 December 1917, Morris officially resigned as prime minister and was awarded a peerage five days later for his service to the empire.[23]

A NOTE ON TERMINOLOGY

Throughout this book, I use the term "progressive" to refer to a heterogeneous political view that saw social problems as having social rather than individual causes. Progressives often advocated that a collective state response was the only way to address these problems. Progressivism in twentieth-century Newfoundland was best represented by the Fisherman's Protective Union, which sought to secure a more equitable distribution of wealth in the fishery and to improve the lives of the producing class in Newfoundland.

I use the terms "producer" and "producing class" to refer to "working class" Newfoundlanders. I have chosen to use the term producer instead of working class because the latter has traditionally been used to describe wage labourers in industrialized centres. Without a large-scale industrialized economy, the experience of producers in Newfoundland, the majority of whom were fishers, vastly differed from the experience of the working class in Canada and Britain. The terms producer and toiler were contemporary terms that referred to Newfoundland's working class.

Throughout this book, I use the term "recruiter" to refer to anybody engaged in recruiting efforts, whether they were officially associated with the Newfoundland Patriotic Association or not. I have chosen this term because most of the recruiting efforts in Newfoundland were not directly organized by the NPA. Many private citizens, newspapers, religious officials, and politicians gave speeches, wrote letters, published articles, and worked towards the same goal. While there was no central authority for much of this recruiting material, very distinct trends can be seen among recruiters.

1

Prohibition

In Newfoundland, like the rest of the Western world, the temperance movement began in the mid-nineteenth century. The campaign to prohibit the sale and consumption of alcohol was part of the broader moral reform movement, which sought to revitalize society by eliminating prostitution, poverty, and increasing child welfare. It was the result of a growing fear that a modern, industrialized society brought moral decay to the world. The temperance movement was not just about the well-being of the individual but the health of the nation.

The international temperance movement crystallized in Newfoundland in several groups such as the Church of England Temperance Society, Sons of the Order of Temperance, the Methodist Standing Committee for Evangelism and Social Service, and most importantly, the Women's Christian Temperance Union (WCTU). The oldest and longest running group in Newfoundland was the Total Abstinence and Benefit Society that was formed in 1858.[1] These organizations saw great successes in the nineteenth century. As a result of their activity, the house of assembly passed the first Local Option legislation in 1870. This bill allowed for each district to decide whether or not merchants could sell alcohol within their borders. By 1899, every region in Newfoundland had voted for Local Option except for St John's East and St John's West.[2] From then on, anyone wishing to purchase alcohol had to order it by mail or telegraph and have it delivered to their community from St John's.

Despite the support for Local Option, merchants in St John's shipped a considerable quantity of alcohol to the rest of the dominion. In 1873, people consumed 62,000 gallons of beer, 14,000 gallons of wine, and 167,000 gallons of liquor. The quantity of alcohol shipped from St John's to rural Newfoundland outraged temperance workers. They urged the government to stem the flow. In 1899, a bill was submitted in the house of assembly to create a plebiscite on the prohibition issue.[3] When the house of assembly voted on it, many members felt that prohibiting alcohol would infringe on the rights of those who drank responsibly. It failed by a large majority.

Temperance groups made another attempt to enact prohibition through a Local Option vote in St John's in 1909. If it passed, it would have prevented the sale of alcohol in the last two remaining districts in St John's. This would have prevented the capital city from providing alcohol to the rest of the island. The vote failed, and this was the last serious attempt to pass prohibition before the war.

Even though temperance workers were able to pass Local Option laws in nearly every district, they were unable to get enough support for prohibition. The disparity in support between Local Option and prohibition stemmed from the desire of many citizens to ban public drinking establishments while allowing residents the freedom to drink in the privacy of their own homes. During the First World War, the temperance movement received a tremendous boost as the language of sacrifice and patriotism that emerged from the war transformed notions of masculinity, portrayed alcohol as a threat to the war effort, and prioritized the rights of the community over the rights of the individual.

LIQUOR AND LOCAL OPTION

The campaign for prohibition began on 3 March 1914 when Prime Minister Morris presented two petitions in the house of assembly. The first was from five hundred residents of St John's West, who were outraged by how easily people could order liquor from St John's and have it transported into Local Option districts. The second petition, from the WCTU, called for the government to pass a bill to take a plebiscite on the prohibition issue.

Morris was skeptical about these petitions. He insisted that the house of assembly take the time to give the matter serious consideration before the house could vote on a prohibition bill. He also found the petitions to be extreme because they called for a prohibition on the sale, manufacture, and possession of alcohol. As far as he was aware, no country had entirely banned alcohol. Despite his skepticism, Morris acknowledged that Local Option had effectively reduced alcohol abuse.

Unlike Morris, William Coaker expressed unwavering support for the petitions. He took issue with Morris's suggestion that a complete prohibition of alcohol would be too extreme. Instead, Coaker said he would only support a prohibition bill if it banned the manufacture, sale, and importation of alcohol. Coaker argued that allowing citizens to ship in spirits for personal use would only prevent the poor people from purchasing it because they would not have enough money to import it for themselves. Attacking the prime minister's stance on the importation of alcohol, Coaker compared drink to poison. He reminded the prime minister that Newfoundland had already passed strict regulations on who could possess toxic substances to protect the people. He swore that alcohol was worse than poison and argued the government should treat it as such.[4]

J.M Kent, a member for St John's East, spoke against the prohibition petitions. He said that the house would be shirking its duty if it put prohibition to a public vote. The people elected the members of the house of assembly to create laws, and it should decide on the prohibition issue. Kent also warned that by prohibiting liquor, the government would compel those who wanted to drink to consume things that were far worse for them than regulated alcohol. Instead of coercing citizens into sobriety, Kent advised that the government focus on "moral suasion" to discourage citizens from drinking to excess. He also suggested that the house forward any further petitions for prohibition to the colonial secretary so he could investigate the prohibition issue and revisit it if necessary when the house meets next year.[5]

Following the speeches of Coaker and Kent, eleven members presented petitions to the house from Burin, Twillingate, Harbour Grace, Burgeo–La Poile, Bonavista, Trinity, Fogo, Placentia–St Mary's, and Bay de Verde. The majority of these petitions called for an end to the shipment of alcohol from St John's to Local Option districts instead of prohibition. They were all forwarded to the colonial secretary for further consideration and discussion in the next meeting of the legislature.[6]

PONDERING PROHIBITION

When the house of assembly resumed in 1915, it was clear the war effort had invigorated the campaign against alcohol. Albert Hickman, a Liberal MHA for Bay de Verde, introduced a resolution to prohibit the importation, sale, and manufacture of spirituous liquors and wines. He reminded the house that alcohol had been responsible for a host of problems ranging from increased crime, deteriorating mental health, a lethargic labour force, and poverty. Hickman informed the house that France and Russia had already taken steps to ban alcohol because it damaged their war effort. While Hickman admitted that some would argue the government did not have the mandate to strip away the rights of the individual to drink, he argued that the countless petitions demonstrated that the people wanted the government to put the needs of the community before those of the individual. Walter Jennings, an FPU MHA for Twillingate, agreed with Hickman. He argued that alcohol posed a more serious threat to Newfoundland than the German army did. He claimed that in the first six months of the war, Germans killed over 20,000 British soldiers, while in the same period, alcohol killed over 25,000 British civilians.[7]

Not all members of parliament agreed that alcohol was a threat to the war effort. William Higgins, a People's Party member for St John's East, explained that Britain did not deem it necessary to ban liquor because of the war. Higgins indicated that he would vote against these resolutions because he believed that the only way to enforce prohibition was to have the support of the people through a vote. Similarly, the prime minister opposed enacting prohibition without consulting the people with a plebiscite. He attacked Hickman's notion that the government did not need a mandate from the people to ban alcohol. He reminded the house that Canada had a national referendum on prohibition. Morris explained that prohibition would not succeed without the assurance of public support provided by a plebiscite.[8]

After a lengthy debate on Hickman's resolution, Morris introduced a bill to the house of assembly that would allow citizens to vote on a ban on the importation, manufacture, and sale of all alcoholic beverages in Newfoundland. After some discussion over the manner of polling, the house of assembly and legislative council passed the bill. The Prohibition Plebiscite Act stated that the people of Newfoundland would be able to vote on the following question: "Are you in favour of prohibiting the importation, manufacture and sale of spirits, wine, ale, beer, cider and all other alcoholic liquors for use as beverages?" The bill required a majority of at least 40 per cent of the registered voters to vote for prohibition to pass.[9]

If this bill passed, it would require the government to introduce legislation that wholly prohibited all forms of alcoholic beverages over 2 per cent alcohol by volume. It made exceptions allowing for the use of intoxicating drinks for religious, medical, and manufacturing purposes. Anyone found to be in violation of the act and illegally imported, manufactured, sold, or possessed alcohol would face a potential fine ranging from a fine of $50 to $500 and up to three months in prison.[10]

THE PROHIBITION CAMPAIGN

The campaign for prohibition found support in a wide variety of groups. Nearly every major religious denomination in Newfoundland publicly supported banning alcohol. As Sheila Roberts Lukins points out, some of the earliest temperance advocates came from the Congregational and Methodist churches. Similarly, the early temperance movement found an ally in Roman Catholic Bishop Michael Fleming. Religious organizations such as the Methodist Sons of Temperance and the Church of England Temperance society laid the groundwork on which the 1915 campaign was built. In the months leading up to the prohibition plebiscite, various Methodist, Catholic, Anglican, Presbyterian, and Congregational religious leaders gave sermons, held meetings, and wrote letters of support for prohibition to their local newspapers.[11]

Greg Marquis has shown that the prohibition movement in Canada started was initially led by Christian churches in the early nineteenth century. By the late 1800s, the Canadian temperance movement became increasingly secularized as various organizations blamed liquor for a wide variety of societal problems. The campaign against alcohol developed in a markedly similar way in Newfoundland. Despite the Religious support for prohibition, secular organizations were responsible for most war-time temperance work. The largest temperance group in Newfoundland was the non-denominational Women's Christian Temperance Union. Across the island, communities established small local committees and groups to support the ban on alcohol. The Prohibition movement also received solid political support, particularly from William Coaker, an ardent prohibitionist.[12]

Once the government passed the Prohibition Plebiscite Act, the temperance movement in Newfoundland had a great deal of work ahead of it. While temperance advocates welcomed the chance to vote on the issue, many believed that getting 40 per cent of registered voters to vote for prohibition was impossible. John St John, the editor of the Fisherman's Protective Union newspaper, the *Mail and Advocate,* accused the government of deliberately setting the percentage so high that the vote would fail. Similarly, Theobald, a regular columnist for the *Evening Telegram*, believed that prohibitionists would have an uphill battle to achieve the 40 per cent (24,581 votes) needed to pass the bill.[13]

Knowing that they were facing a challenge, prohibitionists and temperance workers began a great campaign to convince voters to support prohibition. The prohibitionists' campaign comprised traditional arguments about the impact of alcohol on health, the family, and the nation. Notably, the wartime campaign for prohibition differed from previous attempts by adopting the language of war, presenting alcohol as a threat to the war effort, and drawing on Newfoundland's wartime focus on collectivist values.

ALCOHOL AND HEALTH

One of the primary arguments of the prohibition campaign was that alcohol was poisonous and harmed everyone who consumed it. In a letter to the editor of the *Mail and Advocate*, "Triton" expressed concern that alcohol was damaging to the health. Triton argued that alcohol sapped the strength, reduced endurance, and made it harder to deal with the everyday hardships of life. They also claimed that heavy drinkers lived, on average, four fewer years than those who did not drink. While Triton admitted that moderate drinkers did not suffer from shorter lives, they said that for many, it was impossible to drink with moderation. Given the negative impact on public health, Triton recommended that the government ban alcohol.[14]

To convince Newfoundlanders that alcohol was a public health threat, the WCTU hired Dr Carolyn Geisel of the World Women's Christian Temperance Union to do a speaking tour across the dominion. Newspapers presented Dr Geisel as an "Apostle of Health." They highlighted her successful career, which included working with the Women's Christian Temperance Union, the Michigan Federation of Woman's Clubs and the Anti-Cigarette League. Dr Geisel presented a series of lectures on a wide range of topics related to individual and community health. Her belief that alcohol harmed the individual, deteriorated the health of society, and hindered the war effort tied all of these lectures together.[15]

The WCTU timed Dr Geisel's visit to Newfoundland perfectly. One month before the prohibition vote, she travelled across the dominion, giving lectures about the dangers of alcohol. On 5 October, during a talk in St John's titled "A Blot on Your Brain," Dr Geisel told her audience that alcohol damaged brain cells. She showed statistics that supposedly proved that in Munich, where drinking was commonplace, 72 per cent of babies were born "imperfect." She compared this to Maine, a dry state, where 72 per cent of all babies were born "perfect." She explained that alcohol caused a "blot on the brain, " which resulted in mental deficiency that parents could pass on to their children. In another lecture in St John's titled "Race Betterment," Dr Geisel argued that alcohol represented a considerable risk to the race and resulted in degeneracy, imbecility, and criminality. While the content of Dr Geisel's lectures outside St John's were not recorded, newspaper reports make it clear that Dr Geisel was successful in convincing people that alcohol was dangerous.[16]

While the content of Dr Geisel's lectures was much the same as traditional temperance talks, her message about the health impacts of alcohol found an incredibly willing audience on the home front. When the entirety of Newfoundland society was dedicated to the war effort, the health of the nation was paramount.

ALCOHOL AND THE FAMILY

The impact of alcohol on the family was another tradition theme that was prominent in the prohibition campaign. The importance of family to the prohibition debate became clear in April of 1915 when the WCTU organized a march that comprised over 2,500 women and children, making it one of the largest demonstrations organized by women in Newfoundland history. This march was a powerful symbolic act by the women of the WCTU demonstrating their belief that alcohol posed a grave danger to the family. Mrs Howland, a WCTU organizer from Boston, expressed the same sentiment at a temperance meeting at the Total Abstinence Hall in Torbay. In her speech, she explained that women across the world were banding together to protect women and children and that drunken cruelty towards women and children caused the WCTU to campaign to rid Newfoundland of alcohol.[17]

The argument that prohibition would benefit families was not limited to the WCTU. Many male prohibitionists argued men could not live up to their full potential as providers and protectors of their families because of the constant temptation of alcohol. An open letter from Andrew Broaders, Vice President of the FPU, to William Coaker, stated his belief that prohibition was the best way for a man to safeguard the future for his children. He argued that too many fathers spent their money on rum instead of food and clothing for their families: "I know of many homes even in outports that have been made desolate through liquor and will never recover from the blow received on account of same. I myself would never have a feeling of security for the future welfare of my children even if I gave them the best education the world could produce. Human nature is prone to temptation and liquor is the greatest this world has ever seen, for it cuts with a two-edged sword and slays both body and soul together."[18]

Similarly, in a letter to the editor of the *Mail and Advocate*, a supposed Roman Catholic student under the pseudonym "School Boy" said that every man had a duty to leave the world a better place than he found it. He suggested that one or two drinks at the local saloon often lured young men into a life of alcoholism. He said that while young men were drinking their money away, their wives and children were suffering at home: "The time wears on, but oh! what a change has taken place, the babe which a few months ago was so beautiful and was its mother's pride is now buried in the pauper's grave and the wife – what has become of her? She is waiting again to-night a mere skeleton of what she was, waiting for him who is the curse of her life. He comes home and tells her that he is discharged but through no fault of his, then he curses and raves and wonders where he will get money now. At last he commits some crime or something and is imprisoned for life, thus ending a promising career." "School Boy" finished his letter by imploring every self-respecting father to vote for prohibition, not only for the good of his own family but for the good of his neighbour's family.[19]

PROHIBITION, PATRIOTISM, AND SACRIFICE

Arguments about the impact of alcohol on health and family were part of the temperance movement from the very beginning. Prohibitionists traditionally portrayed alcohol as the antithesis of the family as it destroyed men both mentally and physically while drawing them away from their families and into the saloon.[20] The importance of maintaining good health, combined with the powerful language of sacrifice amplified calls for prohibition during the war. Adrian Gregory has shown that the language of sacrifice was pervasive during the war in Britain. Those who remained on the home front constantly compared their sacrifices to soldiers who paid the "blood tax." Comparatively, there was no sacrifice too large for those on the home front. The societal importance placed on sacrifice profoundly altered the debate for prohibition. It prioritized the needs of the community over the freedom of the individual. During the war, advocates often described prohibition as a patriotic movement and insisted that anyone who loved their country would support it. Given the wartime importance placed on patriotism and sacrifice, this shift in language was very beneficial for the prohibition campaign.[21]

A *Daily News* article from August 1915 shows the importance of sacrifice to the prohibition campaign. In this piece, the editor told his readers that the prohibition plebiscite would allow citizens to decide if "Newfoundland will be better without [alcohol]; whether her people will be happier if it is abolished; whether the social and economic gain will not far out-balance the loss, whether it will not pay to remove what to thousands is a relentless enemy and a snare they cannot escape." He further explained that citizens would have happier, more prosperous lives if they would be manly enough to give up alcohol. He called upon every male citizen to "show his manhood, his sense of responsibility, and his spirit of self-sacrifice," and join the movement to end the liquor traffic.[22]

Sir Joseph Outerbridge, a St John's businessman, philanthropist, and vice president of the Newfoundland Patriotic Association expressed a similar sentiment at a large Prohibition Committee meeting at the Board of Trade Rooms in St John's. During this meeting, Outerbridge admitted that he was a moderate drinker. Despite this, as a patriotic citizen, he was willing to give up any enjoyment or gratification he received from drinking so that the greater community could benefit from prohibition. When the president of the Prohibition Committee spoke at this meeting, he admitted that he also enjoyed an occasional drink. He said that those who already abstained from alcohol were not sacrificing anything by voting for prohibition. For those like him, who drank moderately, voting for prohibition would be a serious act of self-denial.[23]

In a sermon to St Thomas Anglican Church, Reverend Edgar Jones addressed the issue of individual rights and liberty that prohibition would impact. He told his parishioners that a fundamental part of living in a community was voluntarily sacrificing individual rights for the sake of the greater good. He said that while citizens may have great liberty to do as they please in their home, any activity that impacts life outside their home must not be harmful or detrimental to the interests of the greater community. Jones also reminded his audience that the government had passed legislation to close unsanitary markets, move foul-smelling factories away from the city, and require milk to meet purity regulations. He said that society had increasingly demanded that the rights of the community take priority over the rights of the individual, and all citizens must be willing to sacrifice their right to consume alcohol for the greater good of the community.[24]

Perhaps the most compelling example of the importance of the language of sacrifice to the prohibition campaign came from the editor of the *Daily News*, John Robinson. On 14 September 1915, Robinson argued that during the war, sacrifice for the greater good was paramount and prohibition was a small sacrifice to rid Newfoundland of liquor's grave threat. Drawing on wartime conceptions of sacrifice and masculinity, he wrote:

> These are the days of self-sacrifice. All that is best and manliest in the nation is surrendering comfort and safety, imperilling, and in many instances, losing life or limb. And why? In order that others may be protected; that tyranny may be overthrown; that women may be protected from outrage and children from brutality. And surely the overthrow of the traffic in intoxicants has a similar object in view. Is there a harsher tyrant than rum? ... The infamies of zeppelins dropping bombs that bring death to women and children; the awful butchery of the babies of the Lusitania; the outrages committed upon defenceless womanhood and childhood in Belgium and elsewhere, stir to white hot indignation the soul of every decent man. Is there one who can honestly deny that equal horrors daily result from the drinking customs of the age?[25]

Another powerful tool for the prohibition campaign was the tremendous importance placed on patriotism during the war. The temperance movement used Newfoundland's wartime patriotic craze to advance the prohibition campaign. It argued that voting for prohibition was the most patriotic thing that a citizen could do as it would have profound benefits for the nation.

In 1915, temperance advocates began portraying prohibition as a revitalizing force for the dominion. They argued that people were spending over $1,000,000 on alcohol each year. Temperance workers said that once drinkers could no longer spend money on spirits, they would either put that money into savings or spend more on food and clothing, resulting in a healthier population and more taxes for the government.[26] Given the supposed benefits of prohibition for the nation, temperance workers argued that voting for it was a supremely patriotic act. In a column in the *Mail and Advocate*, the editor extolled the patriotism, principle, and masculinity of prohibitionists: "The man in the Assembly who votes for prohibition will be forever enrolled amongst our greatest men. For only strong men possessing a confidence grounded upon principles that will always defend right against wrong and place country first and always be found ready to strangle an evil that requires no arguments to convince the most stupid, that it is the one studendous [*sic*] curse of Christian civilization, responsible for more crime, misery and destruction of life than all other agencies of evil that exist."[27]

In the *Mail and Advocate*, William Coaker warned that people in the outports were suffering because of the sale of alcohol in St John's. He said that workers drinking liquor in town were reducing their workplace efficiency, increasing the cost to transport fish out of St John's. Coaker argued that stopping the liquor traffic in St John's would cause a rise in the price of fish by 20¢ per quintal. He said that any man who loved his country would be ready to vote for prohibition and "make such sacrifices gladly and willingly to advance the public welfare and make their native land prosperous and happy."[28]

By describing prohibition as an example of patriotic self-sacrifice, temperance advocated were tapping into a powerful wartime idea that the primary responsibility of all citizens was to make personal sacrifices for the good of the nation. The inclusion of the language of sacrifice provided a tremendous boost for the temperance movement. While soldiers were sacrificing their lives for the greater good, temperance campaigners argued that civilians could also make sacrifices by ridding the dominion of alcohol.[29]

PROHIBITION AND THE WAR

During the war, citizens and governments around the world began to worry that alcohol was damaging the war effort. In an in-depth examination of the history of alcohol, Rod Phillips concludes that the pressure of the First World War increased concerns about the health effects of alcohol. Consequently, he argues that citizens demanded their governments pass legislation that they would have never supported in peacetime.[30] Phillips says that alcohol consumption was not compatible with wartime ideas of masculine military service:

> If alcohol had a negative effect on health, then it had the potential to be particularly serious in the case of soldiers. They were expected to be fit and robust models of manhood, rather than weak, hollow-chested, and mentally deficient specimens that temperance literature general portrayed drinkers as being. If alcohol undermined moral order and the stability of civilian society – which became crucially important as the "home front" during the war – it threatened havoc and defeat in military society, where men had to be in peak physical and emotional form, unquestioningly patriotic, and ready to obey orders, no matter what the consequences.[31]

While Phillips's work does not examine prohibition in Newfoundland, these debates that were occurring in Britain, Canada, France, Russia, and other nations, were developing in similar ways in the Dominion of Newfoundland.

As a result of the concerns over wartime consumption of alcohol, Temperance workers utilized the wartime language of sacrifice and service to describe the prohibition campaign. To harness the powerful language of war, prohibitionists described the campaign to ban alcohol as a national struggle and as critical to the future of Newfoundland as was defeating Germany. They portrayed the prohibition campaign as a battle of good versus evil, sobriety versus drunkenness.

A prominent example of this came from Britain. In March of 1915, David Lloyd George, the British minister of munitions at the time, told the Shipbuilding Employers Federation, "we are fighting Germany, Austria, and drink, and as far as I can see the greatest of these three deadly foes is drink."[32] Lloyd George's spread like wildfire across Newfoundland and was repeated in newspapers and public speeches, resonating among local people. Those who used this quote sought to convince Newfoundlanders that alcohol was as dangerous to the dominion as the German army.

Methodist Reverend N.M. Guy expressed this sentiment at a Temperance Rally at the Methodist College Hall in St John's. He told his audience that alcohol was destroying the masculinity of Newfoundland

and the whole of the British Empire. Reverend Guy explained that alcohol damaged men's ability to live up to their traditional roles as providers for their families and protectors of the nation. He explained that alcohol hindered the efficiency of men, whether they were soldiers, fishers, or loggers, saying that "the liquor traffic destroyed the homes and made wrecks of the cradles of those who should perpetuate the country." Guy argued that alcohol was a far graver risk to Newfoundland than the war. He said: "many mothers in this Island to-day would rather see their sons face the German bayonets than the open saloon doors which constantly tempt them to destruction."[33]

Reverend W.H. Thomas also portrayed alcohol as a grave threat to Newfoundland. In a sermon at the Congregational Church in St John's, Thomas told his parishioners that the enemies outside of Newfoundland (Germany and Austria) were much less dangerous than the threat of liquor that resided in every household: "Prussian militarism is bad but British alcoholism is worse. The cruelest German or Turk can but temporarily outrage the bodies and slay the lives of his victims. He cannot deprive them of their manhood and womanhood, nor cut them off from everlasting bliss. But alcohol murders the God-like in man and the angelic in woman, dooming them to enternal [*sic*] destruction." Thomas implored people to support prohibition because he believed that it was far worse for young men to die from drinking than it was for them to die in the trenches.[34]

Theobald also believed that the campaign for prohibition was as vital for the future of Newfoundland as the war was. He said that force was necessary for both causes; the war used "physical force" while prohibition used the "force of the law" to accomplish its goals. He said that if Newfoundland was justified in using force to stop Germany, then it was justified in using force to stop the drink traffic. In both cases, Theobald argued that moral suasion was not enough, and direct action was necessary. He explained that Britain was fighting the war so that "freedom may be born in the world, and a lasting peace may come," while prohibition was "cleaning out an evil of the physical appetite in order that good may come to us and to future generations." Given the incredible similarities, Theobald argued that it would be hypocritical for anyone who supports the war to oppose prohibition.[35]

Comparing the work of the prohibitionists to the work of soldiers, the editor of the *Evening Telegram* argued both soldiers and prohibitionists were doing their patriotic duty. He praised soldiers serving in the Dardanelles and the North Sea, who were patriotically fighting the enemies of the British Empire. He also praised temperance workers: "at home the friends of these [soldiers] are also engaged in patriotic service in endeavouring to cleanse the Ancient Colony of the cursed drink." By maintaining that the prohibition campaign was a battle of good against evil, prohibitionists tapped into the powerful language of war that pervaded public discourse during the war years. In doing so, prohibitionists augmented their traditional arguments for prohibition by suggesting that the battle against alcohol was every bit as important as the war against Germany.

One final argument made for prohibition was practical in nature. Shortly after the war began, many people started to suggest that Newfoundland needed to ban alcohol to support the war effort. The driving force behind this argument was the claim that Russia had banned the manufacture and sale of vodka, and France had prohibited the sale of Absinth.[36] Those making this argument claimed that both France and Russia had put restrictions on alcohol because of the detrimental impact it had on the economy and the demoralizing effect on soldiers. Journalists, politicians, and temperance workers began to cite examples of wartime restrictions on alcohol from France, Russia, Germany, Switzerland, Denmark, Austria, Italy, Britain, and Canada. This argument was so persuasive that upon hearing that France and Russia had restricted alcohol, the Twillingate division of the Sons of Temperance forwarded a petition to the government demanding that Newfoundland prohibit alcohol for the duration of the war.[37]

Others argued that alcohol was a waste of resources that the government needed for the war effort. In a letter to the editor of the *Daily News*, a writer under the pseudonym "Citizen" said that alcohol was an unnecessary drain on a household's resources that would worsen the standard of living for women and children. Given the increased cost of living, "Citizen" said that the government and the people had to do everything they could to save money. They advised that preventing men from wasting their money on alcohol was a good start.[38] Similarly, in the *Evening Telegram,* Theobald pointed to Russia as a shining example of how prohibition could improve the economic standing of a country. He told his readers that following the banning of alcohol, the Russian government saw an increase in tax revenue and an increase of money in citizens' savings accounts. Through prohibition, Theobald maintained Newfoundland would see an increase in the standard of living, a decrease in crime and poverty, and a general increase in health.[39]

The editor of the *Mail and Advocate* also called on citizens to support the war effort by conserving and economizing. He advocated for societal thrift because he believed the war would end either with a decisive victory or with the complete exhaustion of resources of Britain or Germany. The editor argued that Germany had already reduced waste and was therefore in a better position to sustain a long-term war effort because it had eliminated alcohol. He accused drinkers of being less patriotic than their German counterparts and loving alcohol more than they loved Newfoundland. In calling on Newfoundlanders to eliminate wasteful spending on alcohol, the editor made a direct connection between temperance and the war effort.[40]

The argument that alcohol was a waste of scarce wartime resources was not unique to Newfoundland. Craig Heron has shown that many Canadians viewed drinking as an unnecessary indulgence. When every citizen was expected to sacrifice, conserve, and save, it was unthinkable to waste food and money on the production and consumption of booze. In Canada, prohibitionists argued that citizens should save their money and purchase Victory Bonds instead.[41]

In addition to economic reasons for prohibiting alcohol, prohibitionists argued that alcohol was detrimental to the health of men and particularly to the ability of soldiers to fight. This theme was evident in the lectures of Dr Geisel on her speaking tour of Newfoundland. At an address in the Grenfell Hall, in St John's, Dr Geisel told the audience that because of the war, every Britisher owed a duty to God and King to be the very best that they could be. Men, in particular, had a responsibility to prepare themselves both physically and mentally for the rigours of war. She preached that only abstinence from alcoholic beverages could ensure that men had the strength to win the war and "rebuild the race" after the war was over. She warned her audience that liquor could be the downfall of their society, arguing that Rome was a healthy society until Romans began drinking wine, which resulted in the decline of Roman manhood and, eventually, the fall of Rome. During her time in Newfoundland, Dr Geisel focused her speeches on what she claimed was the debilitating impact of alcohol on soldiers, including a loss of strength, the deterioration of muscles, a reduction in cognitive ability, and a decrease in accuracy when firing a rifle.[42]

The relationship between sobriety and combat effectiveness was apparent in the minds of those who advocated for prohibition. In a letter to the editor of the *Daily News*, Reverend Daniel O'Callaghan of St Bride's extolled the importance of temperance on a soldier's ability to fight: "But in these days when our Empire is fighting for its very life, when all that are best and pluckiest and hardiest amongst us are appealed to by King and Country to go forth and fight a grim and dogged fight that will test the mettle of the best – what do we find? We find that the greatest organiser and soldier, upon whom and in whom every heart of every child of Empire has pinned its absolute trust, Kitchener of Khartoum strongly advocating his great Army to entirely refrain from intoxicants of any sort." O'Callaghan continued to say that it was far more than a coincidence that the German army, who supplied their soldiers with liquor, were suffering appalling losses. At the same time, the armies of France and Russia, who did not receive alcohol, were winning battle after battle.[43]

Some supporters of prohibition felt so strongly that alcohol was a threat to the British war effort that they attacked anyone who sold liquor. In a letter to the editor of the *Evening Telegram,* an author writing under the pseudonym "Reason" argued that 50 per cent of all rejected volunteers showed evidence that drinking had caused their health to deteriorate. They claimed that a significant number of men were discharged for drunkenness after they had passed the medical screening.[44] The belief that alcohol was hindering Newfoundlanders' ability to fight the war was so strong that the editor of the *Daily News* declared that anyone who sold alcohol to soldiers was committing treason by weakening British soldiers and aiding the German war effort.

The importance of the Great War on the prohibition debate in Newfoundland cannot be understated. The discourse of patriotism, sacrifice, and the practical implications of prohibition during the war impacted the temperance movement. Contemporary temperance workers were well aware of the impact that the war was having on public support for prohibition. Some claimed that the horrors of war were causing the public to see the terrible effects that liquor had on society. Others argued that the war increased support for prohibition because of the need for sober soldiers. What is clear is that all temperance workers acknowledged that across the world, the war had advanced the cause of prohibition.[45]

On 4 November 1915, citizens across the dominion went to the polls to vote either for or against prohibition. For prohibition to pass, 40 per cent of registered voters had to vote for prohibition, which meant 24,581 votes. On 26 November 1915, after the polls closed and the votes were counted, the government announced that prohibition had been successful. The plebiscite passed by the slimmest of margins, receiving just 381 votes over what was required. While the plebiscite barely passed the threshold of 40 per cent of registered voters, a vast majority of those who showed up at polls voted for prohibition. 24,956 people voted for, and 5,348 voted against. Port de Grave, Carbonear, Harbour Main, Harbour Grace, Bay de Verde, St John's West, St John's East, Trinity, Bonavista, St George's, Burgeo, Fogo, Burin, Fortune, Twillingate, and St Barbe districts all overwhelmingly voted for prohibition. The only districts that voted against prohibition were Ferryland and Placentia.[46]

CONCLUSION

The First World War changed the prohibition debate in Newfoundland. During the war, the emerging priority placed on the needs of the community above the individual amplified traditional arguments about alcohol's effect on health and families. In addition, temperance workers used the wartime language of sacrifice and patriotism to convince people that the government should prohibit alcohol. They argued that drinking was hurting Newfoundland and the war effort. Temperance advocates lectured that banning alcohol would help Newfoundland contribute to the war by preventing the waste of resources, improving men's health and increasing combat effectiveness. They persuaded people that prohibition was in the best interest of the nation and that every citizen had a duty to make personal sacrifices for such a benefit and to help the British Empire win the war.

The wartime temperance movement in Newfoundland developed in many similar ways to other wartime campaigns for prohibition around the world. Britain, France, Russia, and other countries worried about the impact that alcohol was having on the home front and on soldiers who were fighting in the trenches. What separated Newfoundland from other countries was how far the dominion government was willing to go to eliminate the consumption of alcohol. In Russia, the government prohibited vodka shops from operating for the duration of the war and banned soldiers on active duty from consuming alcohol. They continued to allow civilians to consume beer and wine. France banned the production and sale of absinthe in 1914 and attempted to discourage its soldiers from drinking strong liquor by providing them with wine. Britain had comparatively fewer restrictions on alcohol, only limiting the hours that bars and restaurants could sell alcohol.[47]

Throughout the war, the majority of Canadian provinces voted themselves dry. In 1918, the Canadian government passed an order-in-council banning the manufacture and transport of alcohol across the country. This order only targeted public drinking. The law still permitted the consumption of alcohol in private residences.[48] Comparatively, Newfoundland's prohibition of alcohol was drastically different from that of Britain, France, Russia, and Canada. By criminalizing the sale, consumption, manufacture, and possession of recreational alcohol, the Newfoundland government took more drastic steps to prohibit the use of alcohol than any other state involved in the war. In many ways, Newfoundland's prohibition of alcohol closely resembled prohibition in the United States imposed by the Volstead Act in 1919.

The prohibition debate highlights the wartime changes in the liberal order. Before the war, Local Option prohibited the sale of alcohol in specific districts but did not prevent individuals from ordering liquor from St John's. Those who believed that the government had no business telling individuals that they could not consume alcohol hindered prewar attempts to prohibit alcohol. During the war, very few people argued that the rights of the individual to drink outweighed the rights of the community. In essence, the rights of the individual took precedence over the benefits of the community.

During the war, the language of sacrifice altered discussions on prohibition. The societal focus on the good of the community was so powerful, that very few people dared to speak out against prohibition or the right of the individual to choose to drink. Instead, the temperance conversation was dominated by citizens demanding that the government protect communities, families, and soldiers from the scourge of alcohol. This time around, the good of the community outweighed the rights of those who wanted to drink.

2

Food Rationing and Price Control

An important aspect of total war is the control of economies and markets to ensure that citizens have enough food and other necessities to last for the duration of the war. During the First World War, international demand for food and coal caused the cost of living in Newfoundland to skyrocket. While the rest of the British Empire faced increases in the cost of living, Newfoundland was in a uniquely challenging situation because it heavily relied on food imports. Without the ability to significantly increase domestic production of food, the government struggled to respond to rising prices and the plummeting availability of the necessities of life. As a result, there was considerable public debate over what the government should do to ensure citizens had access to affordable nutrition. On one side of this debate were supporters of liberal state policies, who aligned themselves with Prime Minister Edward Morris. This group believed in free markets and felt that social problems were the responsibility of the individual to solve. On the other side were the progressives, who aligned themselves with William Coaker. They advocated for state regulation of the economy and supply chains and believed that society had collective responsibility for social problems.

THE COAL CRISIS

Shortly after the outbreak of the war, Newfoundland had difficulty securing enough coal for its industrial and residential needs. The cause of the shortage was twofold: the British war effort required vast amounts, which increased prices and created shortages; and a lack of tonnage in Newfoundland, which left merchants unable to import sufficient quantities. While the war's impact on the cost of coal was outside the government's control, the decisions of several businesses to sell their vessels to the Russian government exacerbated the situation.

In 1914, the Russian government was critically short of steel-hulled steamships suitable for use as icebreakers in the White Sea. In search of vessels for this task, the Russian government approached Newfoundland shipowners and offered them exceptionally high prices, often double the vessel's true value. Most of the vessels the Russians wanted were used in Newfoundland for importing goods from Canada. The government in Newfoundland quickly approved the sale of these ships. The first ships to be sold were the Reid Company's *Lintrose* and *Bruce*, which the company used to ferry freight and passengers between North Sydney and Port Aux Basques. By 1916, five more ships had been sold, including A.J. Harvey's *Bellaventure, Bonaventure,* and *Adventure*; Job Brother's *Beothic;* and Baine Johnson's *Iceland.*[1]

While the sale of these steamers was incredibly profitable for the vessel's owners, it was disastrous for the people of Newfoundland. The loss of these ships caused a severe shortage of tonnage that merchants could use to carry imported goods. Many of the owners attempted to replace the vessels they had sold, but their new ships were often much too small. By 1915, freight was building up in Sydney as companies had trouble securing tonnage to get their goods to Newfoundland. Importers could not obtain enough coal to satisfy the requirements of the dominion's industrial and residential demands. This coal shortage became serious by the winter of 1915 when many began to worry that the dominion would not have enough coal to last the winter.[2]

Given the limited stocks of coal held in Newfoundland, prices began to rise dramatically. As a result of the rising cost, some people demanded coal dealers limit their profits and lowering the price for everyone. In a letter to the *Daily News*, Reverend Canon Noel informed the coal dealers that their counterparts in England had agreed to limit their profits on the sale of coal for residential use. Reverend Noel suggested that the actions of these coal dealers were the pinnacle of patriotism: "Here is a splendid example of patriotism. Merchants who cannot leave the country and shoulder a rifle, can 'do their bit' to keep up their end of the plank and help others to do the same. Are there not some in this country who can emulate them?"

Noel's letter was an attempt to regulate coal prices not through government intervention but through appeals for voluntarism that would meet wartime conceptions of patriotism and sacrifice.[3]

In June of 1915, the *Evening Telegram* published a letter to the editor by an author under the pseudonym "Importer." It argued that supply and demand was the only thing that could regulate coal prices, not the coal merchants themselves. Theobald responded to this letter. He asked "Importer" if he could square his faith in supply and demand with Christian ethics. He then quoted Proverbs 22:16, implying that those who make their wealth by oppressing the poor would inevitably end in poverty. Theobald implored the coal dealers to regulate prices themselves, telling them that using the excuse of supply and demand was disgraceful to the human intellect.[4]

While writers for the *Daily News* and *Evening Telegram* tried to convince coal dealers to lower their coal prices, the government was far more concerned with ensuring that the dominion had adequate stocks of coal. On 4 December, Prime Minister Morris sent a telegraph to seven coal dealers in Newfoundland asking if there was any truth to the rumours of coal shortages. Morris demanded to know if there was any risk of a coal famine over the winter and spring and what coal dealers were doing to rectify the situation. He also cautioned them that if the rumours he heard were true, then the government would have no other choice but to take drastic measures to prevent a scarcity of coal and prevent increases in price.[5]

In response to Morris's inquiries, J.J. Mullaly of J.J. Mullaly and Co. told him that coal supplies in the dominion were unusually low due to the lack of tonnage available. He warned Morris that he was not aware of any concerted efforts on behalf of the coal dealers to bring in more coal, and he did not think there was much they could do unless dealers could secure additional tonnage.[6]

A.J. Harvey, the owner of a sizeable import and export operation, also wrote the prime minister, informing him that Newfoundland was approximately 22,000 tonnes short of what they needed for the winter. Harvey told Morris that his company was bringing in as much coal as possible, but they had not been able to fill their stores due to the lack of tonnage. On a positive note, Harvey told Morris that he had sent out many telegraphs and letters trying to obtain another steamer of approximately 5,000 tonnes to bring coal to the island.[7]

A.H. Murray, another coal dealer, also agreed the lack of tonnage resulted in the depletion of stocks and warned that a famine was likely.

He informed the prime minister that prices would rise if merchants had to purchase new ships. Instead, Murray recommended the government hire a 2,000-tonne steamer to get coal from Sydney and distribute it to the various dealers who would sell it to consumers. He admitted that this would cost the government some money, but he told Morris that it was the only way to prevent merchants from passing the cost of new ships on to the consumer.[8]

While Morris weighed his options, progressives in Newfoundland attacked the prime minister for his failure to take decisive action to prevent either a coal famine or a surge in prices. They believed the prime minister had a duty to ensure that merchants were putting people's needs over profits. On 7 December, the *Mail and Advocate* demanded to know why Morris had waited until December to determine if the dominion had enough coal to get through the winter. John St John argued that if Morris had been proactive in looking out for the needs of the people, he could have induced the owners of the several sealing vessels, in October, to sail back and forth from Sydney with loads of coal.[9]

On 10 December, the *Mail and Advocate* again attacked Morris for failing to ensure that there would be enough coal to last the winter. St John argued the prime minister had a duty to ensure that merchants had adequate stocks of the necessities of life. The *Advocate* further criticized Morris for trusting that local merchants and the capitalist free market would provide people with enough coal to sustain them through the winter. Instead, the newspaper advocated that Morris interfere with the free market by forcing the owners of sealing vessels to travel to Sydney for coal, even though there were more profitable uses for their ships.[10]

Unlike the *Mail and Advocate*, the *Evening Telegram* did not blame the shortage on Morris's inaction. Instead, Theobald said the real reason for the rise in prices was the lack of tonnage. He pointed out that once businesses sold their large steamers to the Russian government, the only ships available to bring coal to Newfoundland were much smaller sealing vessels. To make their small loads profitable enough to justify the journey to Sydney, they charged a freight rate of $4.00 a tonne, whereas the previous vessels charged $1.80. For this reason, he concluded that citizens could not blame the dealers for the high price of coal. In the eyes of Theobald, the only way to reduce the price was for Morris to place a limit on freight rates, thereby bringing down the price.[11] While the *Evening Telegram* and the *Mail and Advocate* disagreed on what the government should do, one thing was clear: the government had to ensure adequate stocks of coal for a reasonable price.

Despite the criticism Morris received in the news, once he determined a coal shortage existed, he set to work to ensure the dominion would have enough coal to last the winter and spring. To secure more vessels, Morris telegraphed several ship owners to request they bring back partial loads of anthracite for merchants while their sealing vessels were in Sydney to pick up coal for the seal fishery. Robert Job, the owner of Job Brothers & Co., replied to Morris and said that he could send the *Neptune* to Sydney. The vessel could not carry much coal outside the needs of the company. To turn a profit, the freight rates on that coal would be exceptionally high.[12]

The prime minister understood that without adequate tonnage, merchants would neither be able to get sufficient stocks of coal nor sell that coal for a price that most citizens could afford. He wrote to D.H. MacDougall, manager of the Dominion Coal Company in Sydney, to request assistance in securing stocks of coal. MacDougall told Morris that he would do everything in his power to ensure that Newfoundland had enough, but Morris would have to supply the ships to bring the coal to St John's.[13]

To secure more tonnage for the dominion, Morris wrote to Governor Davidson. He confessed to Davidson that the dominion was facing a critical coal shortage, and there would likely be a famine in February if he did not obtain an additional 20,000 tonnes. He told Davidson that Morey & Co. had recently sold the *Beatrice* to the Imperial government. This ship was routinely used by Morey & Co. to bring in coal. Morris requested that the governor contact Arthur Long, secretary of state for the colonies, and request that the Admiralty loan the Newfoundland government the *Beatrice*, or another vessel, to bring coal to the dominion. After some negotiations, Davidson was able to secure another vessel, the *Alconda*, from the Admiralty. It was not available to leave London until 12 January and would not arrive in Newfoundland until 12 February.[14]

While waiting for coal to arrive on the *Alconda*, the people of Newfoundland had two main concerns. First, they were worried that there would not be enough to last until the *Alconda* arrived and second that the cost of the *Alconda*'s coal would be higher than fishers could afford. The *Evening Telegram* showed that before the war, soft coal cost around $8.00 a tonne. By 1915, it soared as high as $10.80.

Given the circumstances of the war, the *Evening Telegram* attacked the government for failing to control prices and recommended it cancel all duties on coal immediately. The *Telegram* also suggested that the government use the *War Measures Act to* seize all stocks from dealers in the dominion and sell it directly to the people. Their recommendation was a drastic abandonment of the liberal principle of free markets. The newspaper argued that the war justified such government interference.[15]

Unlike the *Evening Telegram,* the *Daily News* did not blame the government for the price of coal. On 4 January, the newly appointed editor of the *Daily News*, John Currie (a People's Party MHA for Burin) reported that high coal prices were unavoidable. He argued that the cost had risen because of conditions created by the war, namely the high cost of labour, high freight rates, and a lack of tonnage. Instead, Currie defended Morris, asserting that he was doing everything in his power to fix the situation. He congratulated Morris for his efforts to bring in several large shipments of coal. Currie's position on the coal issue highlights changing liberal views on free markets. While he objected to government interference in coal pricing, he had no issue with government intervention in the procurement of coal for dealers to sell.[16]

In response to the *Daily News'* article, the *Evening Telegram* published a rebuttal. In this article, W.F. Lloyd, who also served as the editor for the *Telegram*, defended his position that the government had a duty to regulate coal prices. He said that even though there was a limited amount of coal in St John's, many homeowners could not afford to buy any because it was too expensive. As a member of the opposition, Lloyd pledged the support of his party to "any reasonable measure or measures which will bring down the price of coal to the normal one." Lloyd understood dealers were contractually obligated to provide coal to factories and industrial concerns at a set rate. Despite this, he found it unacceptable for the dealers to raise their rates for domestic coal to offset flat rates for industries. Given the extreme necessity of coal during the winter, Lloyd declared that the government desperately needed to intervene in the market to keep prices down.[17]

On 4 January, the *Mail and Advocate* also weighed in on this controversy. John St John called the rise in the price of soft coal to $10.80 "barefaced robbery." He opined that the rapid increase targeted low-income families, who had to purchase their coal every week. At the same time, wealthier citizens were able to buy enough for the whole winter. This insulated wealthier citizens from the rapid increases in price. Given the conditions of the war, St John wholly agreed with the *Evening Telegram's* call for the government to seize all stocks of coal and sell it to the public for a maximum of $6.50 a tonne.[18]

The *Daily News* responded to these articles by the *Mail and Advocate* and the *Evening Telegram* on 5 January. In response, John Currie reminded readers that a backlash was inevitable any time dealers raised prices. He admitted the *Telegram* and *Advocate*'s outrage would be justified if merchants manufactured the advance in prices to increase profits. Currie argued that the rise in price was only natural, given the increase in freight rates and the decrease of available tonnage. He explained that the key to solving the coal famine in Newfoundland was to worry less about the price of coal and more about ensuring that there were adequate quantities.[19]

In addition to the *Daily News*, P.T. McGrath, editor of the *Evening Herald*, also defended the government against charges of failing to control the price of coal. McGrath maintained that there was nothing the government could do to control international prices. Instead of focusing on price, McGrath argued that people should focusing on using as little coal as possible. On 4 January 1916, the *Evening Herald* published an interview with several coal dealers that explained the high coal prices. A.J. Harvey said that he raised prices to encourage people to use less coal. J.C. Crosbie explained that the lack of tonnage resulted in higher freight rates, which drove up the price. J. Morey reasoned that much of the coal being sold to customers was taken from stocks reserved for fixed-price industrial contracts. To replace these stocks, Morey had to purchase more coal at inflated rates.[20]

The protests of the *Daily News*, the *Evening Herald*, and the coal dealers did not convince the *Mail and Advocate*. In response, St John referred to McGrath as a "rascal" and suggested that any attempts at justifying the high coal prices were nothing more than excuses to rob the poorest citizens of their hard-earned money. Furthermore, the *Mail and Advocate* did not believe that coal dealers had to raise prices to break even. He viciously accused coal dealers of being unpatriotic by trying to line their pockets during a time of war:

> Get off your despicable roosts and try to be men once during your miserable existence, and get coal for the poor at $6.50 per ton, and give up excusing the rascality of men who

> on Monday demanded $10.80 for what they were selling on Friday at $8.00. What is the use of Governments in war times if a ship owner can ask $5.00 for [freight that was] worth $1.50 six months ago? If the enemies' warships had captured our carriers or gained mastery over our seas then all would calmly submit to the inevitable, but the only enemy encountered is the grabber of gold filtered from the miseries of the people under war conditions, when hundreds of the sons of those who are severest sufferers are dying for their King on foreign soil, thousands of miles from Home and Country.

St John declared that only an idiot would believe that a rise in coal prices was necessary.[21]

While the *Evening Telegram* and *Mail and Advocate* were debating with the *Daily News* and *Evening Herald*, the prime minister was busy meeting with coal dealers and arranging enough affordable coal to sustain Newfoundland for the winter. Morris's plan began with the 3,000 tonnes of coal held in the stocks of various companies, which he would allow dealers to sell for no more than $8 a tonne. He tasked the government with importing 6,000 tonnes of coal at a net cost of $6.36 per tonne. He arranged for the Newfoundland Produce Company (a division of Crosbie & Co.) to import 6,000 tonnes. Finally, he requested that all other coal dealers work together to bring in an additional 6,000 tonnes of coal.[22]

In addition to importing coal, Morris attempted to regulate its price. He stipulated that all stocks in the dominion, as of January 1916, would be sold to the public at $8.00 per tonne, in half tonne lots, to people in need. The wholesale cost of the incoming coal was, on average, $7.23 per tonne. To this price, Morris allowed dealers to add $2.13 to the sale price to cover the cost of landing, storage, cartage, and duty, bringing the total to $9.36. On top of this price, Morris also allowed dealers to add 50¢ for them to make a "reasonable profit." The government would split the 18,000 tonnes between each of the companies for sale to the public.[23]

Once Morris had solved the immediate issue of obtaining coal for the dominion and fixing its price, he formed several committees to oversee its importation and sale for the duration of the war. To ensure that Newfoundland had an ample supply of coal and to control its price, Morris appointed William Coaker and Michael Cashin, the People's Party MHA for Ferryland, to sit on a Coal Committee to determine the best way to keep the dominion supplied with coal. Morris was also eager to ensure that dealers distributed the limited supply evenly and to prevent hoarding. The Coal Committee required any person wishing to buy coal to make an application to the Coal Committee, outlining their reason for needing coal. If approved, the Coal Committee would only allow each household to purchase a half tonne for domestic purposes.[24]

While progressives in the dominion were pleased that Morris had set a maximum price, the dealers were not. On 8 January, J.R. Bennett, the colonial secretary, sent a letter to the major coal dealers in Newfoundland, informing them that they were required to sell their current stocks of coal for no less than $8 per tonne. If they were not willing to agree to these prices, the government would seize all coal in the dominion and sell it to the public for a reasonable price. Several of the coal dealers complained that they were not able to sell their current stocks at such a low price.[25]

A.H. Murray, a purveyor of coal, wrote to the prime minister to express his anger over the interference in coal prices. Murray told Morris he was outraged that the government neither included him in the discussion about obtaining coal nor the talks about fixing the price. Murray insisted his company had always treated people fairly and never withheld coal from the market to get a better price. He also informed Morris that it was impossible to sell his inventory at $8.00 a tonne and make a profit. He criticized the prime minister for failing to provide coal to smaller dealers who often charged less than the larger firms.[26]

Murray was not the only merchant who felt that he was unable to sell coal for $8.00. Many other dealers refused to sell coal for the price the government required and refused to lower their prices. As a result, the executive council met on 10 January and decided to seize all the existing stocks of coal from all dealers in the dominion and sell it at $8.00 a tonne.[27]

The response to the coal situation in Newfoundland was dependent on the political leanings of the individual newspaper. Progressive papers, like the *Mail and Advocate* and the *Evening Telegram*, argued that the conditions created by the war gave the government a responsibility to interfere in the coal market to ensure citizens had ample supplies of affordable coal. They believed this would provide low-income citizens with a basic standard of living on par with the rest of the British Empire. These newspapers and their readers advocated that the government not only take an active role in importing coal but that they also regulate prices and even seize coal stocks to ensure that people had the necessities of life.

On the other hand, liberal newspapers like the *Daily News* and the *Evening Herald*, which represented business-class interests, demanded a much more limited response by the government. They contended the price of coal was not high because of the dealers' greed but because of the conditions of the war. A lack of tonnage and increased freight rates required merchants to sell at higher prices to earn a profit on their investments. They believed it was unproductive for the government to attempt to regulate prices when the conditions causing the high prices were out of its control. These newspapers advocated that the government focus less on the cost of coal and more on importing sufficient quantities for merchants to sell.

THE PRICE OF FLOUR

The First World War affected more than just the price of coal. By early 1915, the cost of food had risen dramatically. The price of potatoes, vegetables, salt, sugar, molasses, fresh meat, salted meat, milk, margarine, tea, bread, and flour skyrocketed. While all foodstuffs became more expensive, the cost of flour caused the most indignation amongst the public. The sensitivity over the price of flour was due to the reliance of many Newfoundlanders on white flour. Without the ability to produce flour or large quantities of vegetables, imported white flour was an essential staple in the diets of most people.[28]

From the outset of the war, the government realized that the conflict would impact the cost of living. In 1914, the house of assembly held an emergency war session to pass legislation to support the war effort. One bill passed in this session was the *Act to Enable to Governor in Council, During the Existence of a State of War, to take Possession of Food Stuffs Unreasonably Withheld,* otherwise known as the *Foodstuffs Act*. This bill allowed the prime minister to seize any stocks of food that merchants unreasonably withheld from the market and permitted him to set a maximum price on all food to keep the cost of living down. While Morris's administration had the tools to control prices in Newfoundland as early as 1914, it lacked the desire to do so.[29]

In early 1914, merchants sold flour for approximately $5.00 a barrel. Within eight days of the declaration of war, residents worried that the war would cause flour shortages. To obtain enough for their families, people across the dominion rushed to purchase as much flour as they could afford. Due to the increased demand and the fear of rising prices on the international market, merchants increased their prices. By 12 August, merchants in St John's were selling flour for $7.20 a barrel. The editor of the *Mail and Advocate* pleaded with people not to hoard flour as this caused prices to rise. He estimated that the increased cost would land flour merchants up to an additional $60,000 in profits above what they would typically make. He called on the prime minister to intervene and prevent the flour dealers from getting rich by bleeding the poor dry during a time of war.[30]

Despite the calls of the *Mail and Advocate*, reports came in across Newfoundland about flour hoarding. The increasing price of flour caused many wealthier citizens to purchase as much as they could afford, in fear of another price hike. In some communities, no flour was available because several wealthy residents had purchased all of the local merchant's stock. In other places, where the government was distributing flour to the poor, several men repeatedly visited to collect pans full of flour and had amassed several barrels for themselves.[31]

In some ways, it is understandable that those who could afford to stock up would do so. In January 1915, the price of flour was $7.50 a barrel, and by February, it had increased to $8.50. Theobald condemned merchants for this increase. He said that they were not basing the selling price on what they paid but on what it would cost to replace the flour. Theobald surmised merchants were motivated by greed and argued that there was no reason they should increase prices on inventory they already possessed. He further criticized merchants for their generous donations to the Newfoundland Patriotic Association. He asked his readers: "What sacrifice is there in giving $2,000 to the Patriotic Fund and making $5,000 on flour purchased before the advance?"[32]

The *Evening Telegram* was not the only newspaper to chastise merchants for making large donations to the NPA while increasing flour prices. On 16 February, the *Mail and Advocate* published an article condemning the "so called patriots" who were giving to the NPA with one hand, while robbing the poor with the other. St John said if the government was full of real patriots than it would not allow unscrupulous merchants to make excessive profits by increasing the price of flour during a national turmoil. By challenging the patriotism of flour merchants, the *Evening Telegram* and the *Mail and Advocate* let them know that society expected all citizens to provide service during the war. For merchants, that service was providing affordable food to the people of Newfoundland.[33]

Throughout 1916, the price of flour continued to rise, reaching an unprecedented level of $16 a barrel by the spring of 1917. Given the high cost of living, the *Mail and Advocate* urged the government to control food prices. St John told his readers that the advent of unrestricted submarine warfare was the reason for the massive increase in the cost of flour from Canada. He recommended that the government take inventory of all flour in the dominion, make plans to ensure that supplies were adequate, and take measures to guarantee merchants sold it at a price that Newfoundlanders could afford. The *Mail and Advocate* also recommended the formation of a new social contract between citizens and the state, whereby the military service of male citizens would be repaid by the state looking after the welfare of their families. He urged the government to accept this contract, to ensure that soldiers knew that in their absence, the government would take care of their dependents.[34]

While the *Evening Telegram* agreed the price of flour was a problem, it did not believe there was much the government could do to regulate the price of food. H.A. Winter, the newly appointed editor of the *Evening Telegram*, contended that while the conditions of the war would naturally increase the price of food, merchants in Newfoundland could charge lower prices and still make a healthy profit. He advised the government to pass a War Profits Tax, which would ensure that the more profit merchants made, the more taxes they paid. He also suggested a government commission to investigate the cause of the rapid increase in the cost of living and potential methods for lowering it.[35]

As the price of flour increased, many people began to question the patriotism of the merchants. In a time when society expected every person to sacrifice in support of the war effort, many viewed it as a disgrace that the dealers were not willing to sacrifice some of their profits to ensure that flour was affordable. The editor of the *Evening Advocate*, for instance, questioned why merchants were buying flour for $11 a barrel and selling it for $16. He accused the merchants of being unpatriotic and damaging the war effort. He said: "we care not who the merchant is that will ask $16.00 for the flour that cost him at the most $12.00 – we challenge his patriotism, and class him in the same category as the German who ruthlessly ill-treats his enemies."[36]

Following the *Evening Advocate*'s attack on the flour merchants, it turned its sights on the government. A.W. Mews, the newly appointed editor of the *Evening Advocate*, cautioned the government that the price of flour was very likely to rise to $18 or $20 a barrel by the summer. Mews was adamant that the state had a duty to the people of Newfoundland that required them to step in and set a maximum price for flour. Mews argued that because the government asked young men to fight for the empire, it must protect their parents and dependents from merchant profiteering: "This is not a time when the interests of business can be considered. The practice of unholy profits must give way to the call of the sacrifice that the young men are making to-day in Europe. If we ask them to give their lives for the Empire, the least that we can do is to prevent their parents from suffering hardships by reason of men who will not give up their monetary gains. It looks dangerously as if material interests were preferred to flesh and blood. People talk as if monetary loss were something worse than to risk the lives of our boys."[37]

Most sections of Newfoundland society deemed the rise in the price of flour to be unacceptable. In the wartime ideology of patriotism, sacrifice, and service, all citizens were required to make sacrifices for the greater good of the community. With merchants seemingly unwilling to reduce their profits to make flour more affordable, citizens turned to the state to regulate the economy for the benefit of everyone on the home front.

THE HIGH COST OF LIVING COMMISSION AND THE FOOD CONTROL BOARD

Even though consumers in Newfoundland agreed that the price of flour was too high, they debated the cause of and solution to these prices. The *Mail and Advocate*, for instance, believed the increase in the cost of flour was due to flour merchants trying to capitalize on the war to make record profits. It believed the only solution was for the government to set a maximum price. On the other hand, the *Evening Telegram* thought that regulating prices was unproductive, and the government could prevent merchants from price gouging by establishing a tax on war profits. The *Telegram* worried that if the government attempted to control the price of food strictly, merchants would simply abandon their efforts to supply Newfoundland. The *Daily News* believed that the merchants were receiving unwarranted abuse in the press because the war caused the price of the foodstuffs to rise, and that was outside the government's control.[38]

Despite public outrage, Prime Minister Morris seemed unconvinced that the cost of food was a problem. Speaking in the house of assembly, Morris stated that the high price of coal, flour, and salt showed that the economy was booming. Oblivious to Newfoundland's reliance on white flour, Morris reasoned that if people could not afford flour at current prices, then they would not buy it, and the merchants would not import it. Morris reminded the house that before the war, fishers were getting, on average, $6 per quintal of fish, whereas during the war, they were getting $9. He said the increased price fishers received for their fish balanced out the increased price that merchants were charging for the necessities of life.[39]

Morris's argument did not convince William Coaker. While Coaker acknowledged that the price of fish had risen considerably, he maintained that it had not increased enough to offset the ballooning cost of food. Coaker estimated the value of fish would have to go up another $3 per quintal, for a total of $12 per quintal, if the people were to maintain an acceptable standard of living. He further attacked Morris for being more than willing to fix the price of coal in 1916, while being far too lenient with merchants who, in his estimation, had made $2,000,000–$3,000,000 from raising food prices. Coaker called on Morris to do his duty as prime minister and defend the people against a rapidly rising cost of living. Finally, Coaker warned the house of assembly that young men would not come forward and do their duty by enlisting in the regiment or naval reserve if the government was not taking care of their wives and children.[40]

Despite Coaker's arguments, and the outrage of the public, Morris remained unconvinced that the cost of living in Newfoundland was an issue. To get to the bottom of the matter, Morris appointed a High Cost of Living Commission (HCLC) to investigate the cause of the increased prices of all foodstuffs and other necessities. P.T. McGrath (the owner of the *Evening Herald* and a friend of Morris) led the five-member HCLC. Morris tasked the HCLC with investigating the high prices of food, taking stock of the quantity of food in the dominion, and making any recommendations it believed were necessary to ensure Newfoundland's food security.[41]

By June of 1917, the HCLC had released three reports. The first two were related to coal, and the third was associated with the price of flour. Following its investigation, the HCLC determined that there were three main reasons for the drastic increase in flour prices. The first was that the increase was part of a general rise in prices due to a global wheat shortage. The HCLC acknowledged that neither the merchants nor the government could do anything in this regard. However, the commission also found that there were more local causes within the power of government to change: freight rates and mercantile price-fixing. The HCLC reported that before the war, the Reid Company was charging roughly 20¢ in the summer and 30¢ in the winter to bring flour from North Sydney to various locations in Newfoundland. In 1917 that rate had risen to $1.28 per barrel.

Similarly, the Red Cross Line was charging 25¢ to bring flour from Halifax and 26¢ from New York. By 1917 it was charging $1.30 a barrel from Halifax and $1.32 from New York. Despite these companies claiming that they had higher than average operational expenses because of the war, the HCLC concluded that there was no justifiable reason for a 300 per cent increase in shipping rates for flour. It further found that local merchants were setting the price of flour by current international prices rather than what they paid for their inventory. The HCLC determined that prices set by merchants had begun to exceed the global market and were earning them unprecedented profits. It reported that before the war, merchants were happy with making a profit of $1 per barrel of flour. By 1916, it was not unusual for dealers to make $4 or $5 per barrel, which amounted to a 4–500 per cent increase in profits.[42]

In addition to the report, the HCLC recommended that the government appoint a Food Control Board (FCB) to examine not only the prices and stocks of flour but the prices and stocks of all food in the dominion. It suggested that the FCB's mandate should include fixing prices; "conserving and distributing food during the progress of the war; making a complete and detailed survey of the whole food situation in the Colony; adopting measures prohibiting the storage of large quantities of food during the war; licensing distributors of all kinds of food; and establishing stands for flour to be imported." Finally, the HCLC recommended that the government adopt an Excess Profits Tax to discourage mercantile price gouging.[43]

Newspapers in the dominion reacted with mixed reviews to the findings and recommendations of the HCLC. The *Evening Telegram* congratulated the HCLC for exposing the causes for the increase in flour prices, but the newspaper was critical of the report's recommendations.

H.A. Winter criticized the proposal to construct a Food Control Board. He thought there was little an FCB could do to control prices without legislative power. Winter also criticized the HCLC for recommending steps to prevent the storage of large quantities of flour. He advised that large stores of flour would be the only thing that could insulate Newfoundland from rapidly increasing flour prices on the international market.

Furthermore, Winter argued that the HCLC had bent to public opinion and focused most of its efforts on the price of flour. He contended that supply and demand were causing the increased cost, and the government could do nothing to combat that. Winter told his readers that the people were able to absorb the additional cost of flour, and the biggest concern was maintaining a steady supply. He believed that the key to solving the problem was to consume less flour. For Winter and the *Evening Telegram*, the issue of flour was one of sacrifice, economy, and restraint. He was far more concerned with ensuring that every person had access to limited stocks of flour than in making sure that everybody could afford as much flour as they did before the war.[44]

The editorial stance of the *Evening Telegram* differed on the issue of flour prices in 1917 than it did on the subject of coal prices in 1916. This is due to the change in editors in June 1916 from W.F. Lloyd to H.A. Winter. While W.F. Lloyd was editor of the newspaper, the *Evening Telegram* displayed a progressive bias. Advocating for low-income citizens, Lloyd's *Telegram* called for the government to interfere in the coal market to regulate prices. Under H.A. Winter, the *Telegram* took on a liberal bias. In a reversal of its editorial opinion on coal, the *Evening Telegram* argued that the government was powerless to control flour prices and instead called for rationing to maintain adequate stocks.

The stance of liberal newspapers, such as the *Evening Telegram*, represented traditional views of liberal democracy. They reaffirmed their belief in free markets and argued that the government could and should not interfere in the food pricing. They prioritized conserving flour so that all individuals had equal access to the limited stocks. On the other hand, Progressives were very concerned about the price. The *Mail and Advocated* demanded equitable access to food and attacked liberal papers, arguing that having ample stocks of flour was pointless unless every citizen could afford it.

The *Mail and Advocate* praised the HCLC for exposing the massive increases in profits charged by flour dealers. The newspaper censured merchants, arguing it was unpatriotic for flour dealers to make record-breaking profits while Newfoundland soldiers and sailors were being killed in the war. To fix this situation, the editor called on the government to regulate the prices of flour so that the producers could afford to feed their families.[45]

In addition to the FPU, another organization expressed its concerns to the government over the price of food. On 15 June 1917, the Newfoundland Industrial Workers Association (NIWA) met at the Longshoremen's Protective Union (LSPU) Hall in St John's and drafted a resolution for Prime Minister Morris.[46] The NIWA informed the government that enormous increases in the cost of living were harming its members. The Association admonished the government for having the ability to regulate prices for the past two years but refusing to do so. The NIWA unanimously resolved to request that the government follow the recommendations of the HCLC and form a Food Control Board (FCB) to oversee the food situation and utilize the *Foodstuffs Act*. Fearing that the business class would overrun any potential FCB, it further recommended that the board consist of fifteen members, with no less than two-thirds coming from trades, labour, fishing, and industrial organizations. The NIWA admitted that some representation of the flour merchants was necessary on the FCB. Still, it recommended that the flour merchants distance themselves from the "lepers and pariahs" who were seeking excessive profits and making life harder for families who had already sacrificed their sons and brothers so that others could live in peace and freedom.[47]

While the Morris administration was reluctant to interfere in the flour markets, the formation of a national government in 1917 stimulated government interest in tackling the issue of the rising cost of living. On 20 July, Morris introduced the *Trading in the Necessaries of Life Bill*. The prime minister told the house of assembly that he intended this bill to control the prices of any commodities that might be considered a necessity of life, including food, coal, salt, fuels, and animal feed.

Morris also followed the recommendations of the HCLC and created a Food Control Board. Morris told the house that the FCB would be responsible for several things: they would have the authority to set maximum prices on necessities of life; prevent wastage; encourage the production of food; and seize stocks of food if necessary. In discussing his rationale for creating the FCB, Morris joined with public sentiment and condemned merchants who had been earning excess profits during the war. He accused profiteers of being every bit as evil as the Germans. In concluding his speech on the high cost of living Morris explained that his government had previously wanted to take action on this issue. Still, he felt it was necessary to investigate what measures other countries had taken before drafting policy for Newfoundland. Despite this, Morris maintained that he was now ready to do anything to advance the interest of the public.[48]

Although the house of assembly universally supported this bill, there was opposition in the legislative council. During the council's second reading of the bill, A.J. Harvey attempted to defend the high prices that merchants had been charging for flour. Harvey argued that they were necessary to ensure that Newfoundland had adequate supplies of food. Furthermore, he told the council that flour merchants were using their increased profits on flour to reinvest in the dominion. In particular, he said the high profits were necessary to replace tonnage that merchants sold to the Russian government.[49] Harvey's argument that flour profits were required to replace steamers sold to the Russian government was bizarre. His Company, A.J. Harvey & Co., sold three of its ships to the Russian government for a hefty profit. It seems unusual that Harvey would try and convince the legislative council that he required to charge more for flour to offset the sale of his steamers, on which he made a tremendous profit. In essence, Harvey wanted the taxpayers to pay for new ships for his company.

Harvey's protest did not convince the legislative council. On the final reading of the bill, P.T. McGrath argued that a Food Control Board was necessary to ensure that Newfoundland had sufficient stocks of food for the duration of the war. He also told the council he believed the role of the FCB would be to focus much more on obtaining adequate supplies of food and encouraging people to conserve what food is available, than on fixing prices.[50] The bill was passed in both houses and became law in August of 1917. Much to the disappointment of the NIWA, the board only consisted of three people, none of whom came from any labour organization. The FCB would consist of P.T. McGrath, as the chairman, Henry Le Messurier, a former Reform Party MHA for Burin, and George Grimes, an FPU MHA for Port de Grave.[51]

FLOUR RATIONING AND SUBSTITUTES

Once the prime minister appointed the FCB, it quickly set about determining Newfoundland's requirements for flour to ensure merchants could purchase enough to feed the dominion. Many residents believed there was going to be a considerable shortage of flour in the winter. In August, the *Evening Telegram* reported that the United States and Canada were 400,000,000 bushels of wheat short of what they agreed to supply to their allies. Winter told his readers that every other Allied country had either voluntary or compulsory rationing programs while Newfoundland had nothing. He expressed dismay that the dominion should be eating more than its share of flour, while all other countries were eating less to ensure soldiers in the trenches were well fed. Winter implored the FCB to start a program of rationing. He hypothesized that if Newfoundland did not control its flour consumption, William Hanna (the Canadian Food Controller) and Herbert Hoover (head of the United States Food Administration) would restrict the amount of flour they would export to Newfoundland. Winter believed Hanna and Hoover could reduce Newfoundland's flour imports from 400,000 barrels to 320,000 barrels a year. In Winter's mind, rationing was not just a practical method for saving flour but a patriotic duty required of every citizen in the British Empire.[52]

P.T. McGrath confirmed Winter's fears that the United States and Canada would restrict the amount of flour available to Newfoundland when he travelled to Ottawa to meet with William Hanna to arrange for the winter stock. Hanna told McGrath that Canada had set a goal of reducing flour consumption from 6.25 bushels per person a year to 4.75. He recommended that Newfoundland embrace similar reductions. McGrath told Hanna that such a substantial reduction would be impossible in Newfoundland. Still, the dominion could reduce consumption by 10 per cent if it increased potato production to offset the decrease in flour. McGrath informed Governor Davidson that even such a moderate reduction would be very unpopular.[53]

Once McGrath had relayed this information to the governor, Davidson requested that W.F. Lloyd appeal to the people of Newfoundland to conserve flour. Davidson hoped that the government could encourage people to consume less by making them realize how their sacrifice would make life easier for allied soldiers fighting in Europe. He hoped the people of Newfoundland would follow the lead of the

United States and substitute a pound of potatoes for a pound of flour per week for every person in a household. He was confident that the wheat saved through these substitutes could better feed soldiers and help win the war. The focus on food as a method of winning the war is evidence of the pervasive nature of total war. With the entirety of Newfoundland society dedicated to the war effort, even flour became part of the machine of war.[54]

To encourage Newfoundlanders to substitute potatoes for flour, the Agricultural Board made loaves of potato bread and sent them around to local businesses and newspapers to prove that it was not only a great way to save flour but was delicious as well. The Agricultural Board's recipe replaced either a third or a quarter of the flour in the recipe with potato. A.W. Mews was not impressed with the board's potato bread. In the *Evening Advocate,* he described it as dense and heavier than most people like. Mews was measured in his promotion for it, suggesting, "it may not be advisable for all to use this bread, but those who are healthy can certainly adopt it with profit to themselves, and bring assistance to the more economic use of flour."[55]

H.A. Winter gave a much more positive review of the bread in the *Evening Telegram.* Winter described it as only slightly heavier than ordinary bread and tasting different to whole wheat. He further described the bread as "very palatable" and suggested that many would prefer potato to whole wheat. He said that replacing flour with potato was an excellent way to conserve flour. Winter concluded this article by calling on the women of Newfoundland to improve potato bread recipes because it was a way for women to "exhibit a most useful and practical patriotism."[56]

Despite the efforts of the Agricultural Board, Newfoundlanders did not reduce their flour consumption by any meaningful amount. As a result, the government put additional pressure on citizens to reduce their flour consumption. On 12 October 1917, newspapers across the dominion published the following announcement on behalf of the Governor Davidson and W.F. Lloyd (now the acting prime minister). It informed the people that Canada and the United States would be 400,000,000 bushels short of the requirements for the war effort. They implored everyone to reduce flour consumption and rely on potatoes crops that citizens could grow at home. Furthermore, Lloyd and Davidson insisted that every pound of flour that Newfoundland saved would help win the war effort. This message tapped into powerful wartime conceptions of sacrifice and patriotism to convince people that they had a duty to conserve flour to help bring about the end of the war by ensuring that allied soldiers were well fed.

As the situation worsened over the winter of 1917, and many believed supplies would not last until the summer, local newspapers supported the government's plea for Newfoundlanders to conserve flour. A.W Mews implored readers of the *Evening Advocate* to cut down on flour consumption, stating that those on the home front had a duty to conserve just as young men had a duty to enlist with the regiment. He warned that if people did not cut their flour usage by a quarter, it was very likely that there would be none from May to October. Frustrated with people's refusal to eat less flour, Mews labelled anyone who failed to do so as a traitor, not only to Newfoundland but to the basic principles of Christianity.[57]

The editor of the *Evening Telegram* also seemed concerned that the people of Newfoundland were ignorant of the global wheat shortage. Winter recommended that everyone should endeavour to substitute a portion of potato or other grains for a portion of their flour, to dedicate one day a week to abstain from eating any food that contained wheat, and to have one meal per day that was free of flour. He reminded his readers that the United States had already made these sacrifices to ensure that soldiers had enough food on the front lines. Winter expressed disgust with the waste and extravagance of food in the dominion and called on the FCB to enforce rationing if people could not control their consumption.[58]

In a last-ditch effort to encourage Newfoundlanders to substitute other grains for wheat, the FCB held a Victory War Bread Show at the British Hall in St John's. The objective of this show was to "encourage the baking by the housewives of St John's of bread, cake, buns, etc. containing substitutes for wheat flour, to lessen the consumption of the latter and thereby release more for the use of the Allies." There were four categories to this competition. The prizes comprised a barrel of flour for first place in each category and a half-barrel of flour for second place in each category.[59]

The Victory War Bread Show was quite popular, and over 350 contestants entered the competition. Despite the popularity of the show, it did not motivate many people to reduce the amount of flour they used. Throughout the latter part of 1917 and early 1918, there were various reports of hoarding across the dominion. The *Evening Advocate* received reports that many women were hiding their hoarding by purchasing large amounts of flour from many different stores.

The *Twillingate Sun* reported that government officials on the West Coast had stashed vast quantities in their basements. Similarly, the *Harbour Grace Standard* said that some people in the Conception Bay area were hoarding multiple barrels of flour.[60]

Wartime changes to the liberal order resulted from negotiations between citizens and the state. These conversations went back and forth. In this instance, the state wanted to conserve flour for the war effort. On the other hand, citizens had no intention of voluntarily reducing their flour consumption. Despite this, the government was determined to join forces with the United States and Canada in lowering per capita flour consumption.

On 1 July, the FCB enacted new regulations designed to reduce the use of wheat flour. Foremost amongst these was the legal requirement for every vendor of flour to sell one pound of substitutes (oatmeal, cornmeal, etc.) to a customer for every four pounds of wheat flour (20 per cent). Similarly, the FCB also required everyone to use 20 per cent substitutes to 80 per cent wheat flour in all their baking. To ensure that merchants were indeed selling the required substitutes with flour, the FCB prohibited any merchant from selling flour if they did not have enough substitutes to go with it. If the Newfoundland constabulary, a peace officer, or an agent of the FCB caught anyone with baked goods containing less than 20 per cent substitutes, they would seize and destroy the offending food. The penalty for baking without substitutes or for selling flour without substitutes was an excessive fine of up to $1000, imprisonment for a period not exceeding three months, or both.[61]

The Substitutes Act enraged citizens across the island by forcing them to consume substitutes. Just five days after the regulation became law, the *Evening Advocate* expressed dismay that people were complaining about the government requiring them to purchase flour substitutes. Mews said that Newfoundlanders had never understood the seriousness of the food situation. He argued that the people were so accustomed to a life of luxury that even small sacrifices for the war effort seemed like starvation rations. He reminded his readers that authorities in Canada and the United States limited the amount of flour that could be exported to Newfoundland and would not allow any exportation of wheat flour without the importation of flour substitutes. He concluded his article by stating that if people want to blame anyone for having to purchase substitutes, they should blame the Kaiser.[62]

The *Harbour Grace Standard* also took umbrage with the flour regulations. On 11 October 1918, the editor of the *Standard* wrote an article explaining the trouble with the law. He reported that many in Newfoundland realized that saving flour was necessary, patriotic, and sensible but were having difficulty giving up old habits. Furthermore, the editor explained that even though many people knew saving flour would benefit them, they despised the government for forcing them to eat food that was traditionally fed to animals. Showing how unpopular substitutes like cornmeal and oatmeal were, the editor explained that it was a widespread practice for people to eat the white flour and feed the substitutes to their animals.[63]

During the war, Canada and the United States began to include more wheat bran and germ with the endosperm to create a more economical whole wheat flour. The majority of the flour imported into Newfoundland during the war was of this variety. It was variously called Standard Flour, Victory Flour, or War Flour. The *Harbour Grace* standard complained that Standard Flour was not well suited for making palatable bread and required an expert baker to turn it into suitable loaves. When people added substitutes to the standard flour, the editor argued that it became even worse. He said that if the government knew how to make edible bread with a flour substitute than it should educate the population on how to make it and only allow merchants to sell substitutes that make acceptable bread.[64]

Having received the *Harbour Grace Standard*'s criticisms, the FCB wrote a response. In response to the claim that Standard Flour did not make good bread, the FCB reminded the *Standard*, that pre-war white flour included 72 per cent of the wheat berry, while war flour contained only 76 per cent, which only amounted to a 4 per cent increase in bran and germ. Meanwhile, the editor informed the *Standard* that in Britain, war flour comprised 83 per cent of the wheat germ and bran to which 20 per cent of flour substitute was added, and this did not cause the British people any harm. He said that the Americans, Canadians, and British were all using the same flour that Newfoundlanders had access to, they were all mixing in the same amount of substitute, and the bread in each country was perfectly edible.[65]

The unpopular requirement to purchase and use 20 per cent substitutes with every portion of flour remained in place until February of 1919. Though citizens despised the regulation they begrudgingly followed it. When the war concluded, much to the anger of the majority of Newfoundland, the FCB required citizens to continue to purchase substitutes. As a result, opposition to the policy reached a fever pitch as citizens wrote many angry letters to their newspaper editors. The strongest opponent of the substitute's regulation was H.M. Mosdell, editor of the *Daily Star*. In December 1918, Mosdell published a series of articles calling on the government to end the much-hated law. When he received no reply, he attacked the government, demanding to know why it would force Newfoundlanders to eat grain that he claimed was unfit for human consumption:

> The people of Newfoundland are still forced by the local authorities to use twenty per cent of this hog food with all the flour they consume. Some flour importers assert that the people of this country will still be using this HOG FEED when another Christmas season rolls around. The [*Evening Advocate*] can tell us where this is a true presentation of the food outlook ahead for this country. It can tell us when we are likely to be relieved of the irksome regulations calling for the use of HOG FEED with our flour. It can tell us if supplies of flour will be issued next spring to outport customers and to city householders without the twenty per cent accompaniment of HOG FEED.[66]

It seems that while Mosdell may have deemed it necessary to eat what he considered animal food during the war, such food was no longer tolerable when the fighting was over.

In response to Mosdell's attacks, a member of the FCB, Geoff Grimes, published a rebuttal in the *Evening Advocate*. Addressing the accusation that flour substitutes were only fit for pigs to eat, Grimes informed Mosdell, in a most cheeky tone, that he had eaten substitutes for the duration of the war to no ill effects: "Sir, – I have noticed in recent editorials that you have much to say about hog feed, and having eaten more than one meal of this feed (rolled oats, corn meal, etc.) as a breakfast food, and as a constituent part for bread to the extent of one part to four, I find that it did not produce within me any of the hog propensities for wallowing in mire. I do not know what kind you may be using, but I am inclined to think from your editorials that if you are using any you must have struck a bad barrel or sack somewhere." Grimes told Mosdell that the only reason the substitute regulations prevailed was that merchants were unable to obtain enough white flour to feed the dominion. As soon as they received adequate supplies, the FCB would lift the regulation. On 1 February 1919, the *Evening Advocate* shared the news that the substitute regulations were over and rejoiced in the fact that Mosdell no longer had to share a meal with his pigs.[67]

The arguments over flour rationing and substitutes prove that wartime alterations to the liberal order were negotiations between the citizens and the state. While the government was able to impose many war measures on the people of Newfoundland, the citizens would not always accept these measures. Flour substitutes are a good example. While the government could force citizens to buy the substitutes, they could not force them to eat them, and many found a loophole by simply using the substitutes as animal feed.

FOODS FOR A WORLD WAR: SEAL MEAT, CODS' HEADS, AND POTATOES

Given the scarcity of flour during the war, many residents argued that it was the patriotic duty of citizens to economize in every way possible. They urged people to eliminate waste, grow as much of their food as possible, and investigate foods that were unpopular or uneaten before the war. The food economy was part of a reciprocal relationship between citizens and the state, whereby the government would provide citizens with as much flour as they could obtain, while the citizens would do their bit to rely on that flour as little as possible.

One of the first methods of economizing, suggested by citizens, was to eliminate waste from the cod fishery.[68] In October of 1914, the editor of the *Western Star* reported that it was common practice for fishers on the west coast of Newfoundland to throw away the cods' heads, sounds (the swim bladder), and tongues after the fish had been split. Andrew Barrett, the editor for the *Western Star*, advised that the global market would accept large volumes of heads, tongues, and cheeks and condemned the waste of this food. He estimated that if a fisher caught 360 pounds, which would produce a quintal of salt cod, the value of the quintal would be $6.50, while heads, tongues, sounds, backbones, roe, and liver would be worth $1.41. Given Newfoundland's rough catch of 1,500,000 quintals a year, Barrett estimated that fishers dumped over $2,000,000 worth of fish into the water each year, an unacceptable waste during the war.[69]

Despite the pleas of the *Western Star*, it does not seem that many fishers began retaining the by-products of the fishery. Throughout the war, the *Western Star* published several articles declaring that Newfoundlanders were among the most wasteful people on the planet for discarding so much of the cod. At the end of the war, Barrett published an account of a boy named Harvey Sharp from Cow Head who made $65.50, in the summer of 1918, by cutting out and selling cod heads and tongues before fishers threw them in the water. He argued that women and children could do the work of saving these valuable resources to create more food and bring in more money for the family.[70]

While the *Western Star* called on fishers to save less desirable parts of the cod, others were calling for fishers to bring back another abundant source of meat: seal flippers and carcasses. The seal hunt was an important part of Newfoundland's economy. Fishers set out every spring to hunt seals and harvest their valuable fat (which was rendered into seal oil) and pelts. The meat, however, was of little value. Even though some flippers were brought back for human consumption, the overwhelming majority of seal meat was left on the ice.

The campaign to bring back seal meat began in 1915 when an author writing under the pseudonym "Economy" wrote a letter to the editor of the *Evening Telegram* to complain about the amount of seal meat wasted every year. "Economy" pointed out that during the last season, fishers harvested 250,000 seals. They used the average weight of a seal (fifty pounds) to estimate that 12,500,000 pounds of "fresh wholesome food" was destroyed. During a time when food prices were skyrocketing, and food was getting scarce, they believed it should be illegal to waste such vast quantities of food: "we are guilty of one of the greatest human crimes, destroying such lots of fresh wholesome food, when millions of poor people are crying for bread. What a difference it would make in the homes of the poor in this country during the next year, if one million pounds of fresh meat were brought in before the 1st of April and distributed for a few cents a pound to those who needed it. If there was once an excuse for such criminal waste, it has ceased now, when bread and meat are so dear, and when we hear so much of the poverty prevailing." "Economy" called on the government to intervene in the seal fishery and find some way for the sealing fleets to bring back the valuable meat they left on the ice.[71]

Theobald agreed with "Economy" and said that fishers were wasting a tremendous amount of wholesome food on the ice. He interviewed a local sealer who reported that seal meat was "splendid" and said that he took some home every year and fried it with onions.

Theobald believed that if the government could arrange for cold storage in St John's, seal carcasses could be a valuable source of food to sustain the dominion and make it more self-reliant.[72]

In 1918, the rapidly increasing cost of food caused the demand for seal meat to increase. In February, "Patriot," a columnist for the *Evening Telegram*, praised the United States for supposedly attempting to substitute whale meat for beef, pork, and chicken. Given that the US was looking for new sources of food, Patriot asked why nobody had attempted to bring in the nutritious flippers and carcasses from the ice. In particular, Patriot praised the flippers of whitecoat seals for being the most palatable of all seal meat. They recommended that a ship, fitted with a canning operation, follow the sealing fleet so it could pick up and can Whitecoat flippers for human consumption.[73]

The editor of the *Western Star* also expressed concern that Newfoundland was not utilizing all of its natural resources. Barret claimed that the US was doing everything it could to reduce beef consumption, including eating whale, shark, and dogfish. No fish was more hated and reviled in Newfoundland than the dogfish. The spiny dogfish, a small shark species, was notorious for eating bait, getting tangled in and destroying fishing gear. Its poisonous dorsal spines make the dogfish particularly hard to remove from nets. By suggesting that the Americans were resorted to eating such a despised fish, Barrett highlighted how important food conservation was.

Barrett reminded his readers that while the US was resorting to eating dogfish, Newfoundland was leaving roughly 250,000 seal carcasses and flippers on the ice every year. Enough seals were left on the ice to provide every household with multiple carcasses. Barrett urged the government to use the War Measures Act to compel sealing vessels to bring seal carcasses back along with the pelts. He admitted that such compulsion would be an inconvenience for the sealing industry but reminded readers that many the government was asking soldiers to make the ultimate sacrifice. Finally, Barrett said that the $50 cost per barrel of salt beef would make fresh seal meat a welcome addition to many people's diets. He believed the taste of seal meat was far preferable to the "salt junk" that merchants imported from the United States.[74]

On 15 February, the *Harbour Grace Standard* added its voice to the list of newspapers calling for fishers to bring seal meat back from the ice. The editor recommended the FCB work with the owners of sealing vessels to arrange for the harvest of meat. He said that having a cheap source of fresh meat was important because salt beef and pork had become so expensive that many could not afford to eat meat. The editor said that it was a sin to waste food and a greater sin "against God and man" to waste food during war.

In March, the *Evening Telegram* also called on the government to arrange for sealing vessels to bring meat to St John's. He admitted that seal was not a popular food in Newfoundland but added that everyone in the dominion had tasted seal flippers at least once in their lives. He insisted that despite the unpopularity of seal, people did not have a choice, and citizens had to utilize all food sources to prevent starvation.[75]

Despite the optimism of the *Evening Telegram*, *Western Star*, and *Harbour Grace Standard*, the *Evening Advocate* remained skeptical that seal meat was a solution to Newfoundland's food situation. Mews said that even if sealers could bring back meat from the ice, nobody would eat it unless they could not afford any other food. The editor argued that if sealers could bring back meat from the ice, of which he was also skeptical, it would be difficult to secure sufficient cold storage to store enough meat to feed the dominion.[76]

Given all of the press coverage on the issue of seal meat, the FCB decided to investigate. It interviewed Captain Abram Kean about the possibility of harvesting seal meat. Kean informed the FCB that it was out of the question to bring in carcasses. Firstly, Kean told the FCB that sealers could earn far more money from the pelts than they could the carcasses. To compensate sealers for their time, the price of meat would be prohibitively high. Kean also said that keeping the meat from spoiling until it could be landed in St John's would also be impossible. Following Kean's interview, the FCB considered harvesting seal meat unfeasible, and newspapers dropped the matter.[77]

Even though public calls for the use of cod heads, sounds, tongues, seal flippers and carcasses were largely unsuccessful, the conversation surrounding these issues was meaningful. The change in discourse shows that some Newfoundlanders were beginning to take a collectivist view of food production and consumption that placed the community's needs over the desires of the individual. They argued that every citizen was responsible for using all forms of food available on the island to reduce food imports, thereby saving food for soldiers in the trenches.

Despite the failure of calls to use other "new" sources of food, there was one successful initiative: the planting of potatoes. While potatoes were traditionally a part of Newfoundlanders diets, the high price of flour created a movement that urged everyone to increase potato production to reduce the need for food imports to the dominion. The first calls to increase potato planting came from the *Mail and Advocate* in 1915. It urged the government to encourage and support Newfoundlanders in planting as many potatoes as possible. It argued that the soldiers could not fight unless they were well fed with food grown by producers on the home front. Therefore, the *Mail and Advocate* argued that men who stayed home to produce for the war effort were just as vital to the war effort as soldiers. It also argued that because the government required citizens to enlist, make financial contributions and otherwise support the war, the government had a duty to help Newfoundlanders feed themselves.[78]

As the war progressed, farming became wrapped up in the concept of a total war effort. In 1916, the *Mail and Advocate* argued that everyone must find a way to contribute to the war effort. The newspaper said that young men must come forward to enlist, merchants and shipping concerns must not seek excess profits, and the government must compel anyone owning land to plant as many vegetables as they could. He believed that if people planted enough vegetables, Newfoundland would require fewer food imports. By using the language of a total war effort, the editor implied that the state needed every single person to work together to win the war.[79]

In 1917, the fear of U-Boat attacks against Newfoundland caused an increase in calls for increased potato production. As a result, the Agricultural Board began to urge all Newfoundlanders to plant potatoes. In an advertisement appearing in the *Evening Telegram*, the Agricultural Board argued Newfoundland's dependence on food imports made it vulnerable to a blockade by German U-boats, which could result in starvation. It implored citizens to plant as many potatoes as they could, believing that a surplus was the only thing that could protect the dominion from a U-Boat blockade.[80]

Governor Davidson also joined in the efforts to encourage the production of potatoes. In March of 1917, Davidson wrote letters to religious leaders across the island, requesting that they convince their parishioners to plant potatoes. He informed them that the Agricultural Board was doing everything it could. Still, he believed that its efforts would fall short of its goal unless Newfoundland's religious leadership, who were in regular contact with the people, stressed the importance of the dominion growing its food.[81]

As the war progressed, the Agricultural Board emphasized that planting potatoes was a patriotic duty. It said Newfoundlanders owed a duty to God and the British Empire to help win the war and ensure "the triumph of Christian ideals and of justice over the inhuman and semi-barbarous procedures of our enemies." The Agricultural Board also suggested that if Newfoundlanders did not grow enough food, they could bring shame to the dominion by requiring support from Britain. One ad from the Agricultural Board stressed the importance of potatoes to the war effort: "Let us, therefore, make a united and supreme effort to protect Newfoundland from becoming a weak link in the Empire's chain of war cares, as this will result if, by our indifference, we allow starvation to threaten us. With our God-given abundant fish supply and the requisite quantity of potatoes we cannot be made to suffer very acutely from hunger, and we can afford to await the time when, in the wisdom of the Divine Providence, it shall be fitting to crown the heroic struggle we are making with a victorious and lasting peace." The Agricultural Board and Governor Davidson drew on the language of both piety and patriotism to encourage Newfoundlanders to become self-sufficient.[82]

By 1917, it was clear that the effort of the Agricultural Board was successful. In June, Mr Devereaux announced to the house of assembly that, because of the work of the Agricultural Board, between 1916 and 1917, Newfoundland's potato crop had grown by 400,000 barrels.[83] In addition to the increase in the quantity of locally grown potatoes, there was an increase in price. Devereaux explained that the price went up as people began to rely on them as a larger part of their diet, as a replacement for expensive flour. On the whole, the Agricultural Board was able to convince Newfoundlanders that they not only had a patriotic duty to plant potatoes, but that flour rationing by the FCB was effective in replacing a portion of the dominion's flour consumption with the consumption of potatoes.

CONCLUSION

Before the First World War, Newfoundland relied on free-market capitalism to provide food and the necessities of life. Conditions created by the First World War resulted in the abandonment of the liberal ideal of free markets, resulting in a new demand for the government to become involved in the provision of the necessities of life. Before the war, two major political movements dominated Newfoundland politics. Liberal-oriented newspapers and politicians believed in laissez-faire economics and felt that the government had no right, or was unable to, interfere in free markets. On the other hand, progressives argued for government intervention in free markets to alleviate social problems. During the war, both groups called on the government to intervene in the free market in vastly different ways.

On the issue of coal, liberals in the dominion thought it was useless for the government to intervene in coal prices. They argued the conditions of the war created the high cost of coal, and the government of Newfoundland could do precious little to control them. Many liberals argued that coal merchants had to raise their prices to turn a profit and make the effort of importing coal worth their while. They suggested that increased profits were also necessary due to the risk of wartime shipping. In the eyes of liberals, the government was responsible for ensuring the dominion had enough coal, regardless of the price, and advocated for Morris's administration to obtain coal for merchants to sell.

Conversely, progressives in the dominion focused entirely on the price of coal. They accused the coal merchants of taking advantage of the war by charging inflated prices to line their pockets. They maintained that the government was responsible for protecting the people against merchant greed. Progressives argued that merchants had a patriotic duty to provide Newfoundlanders with the necessities of life at a price they could afford. They advocated that the government could do this by setting coal prices, and if necessary, seizing all coal stocks in the dominion to ensure that merchants sold coal for a fair price. Ultimately, the progressives came out on top of the coal issue when the government set a maximum price for coal in 1917 and seized coal stocks when merchants exceeded this price.

On the issue of flour prices and availability, liberals argued, as they did on the coal issue, that flour prices were the product of the international market and that flour prices were rising because of the conditions of the war. Instead of meddling with flour markets, liberals argued that the government should focus on rationing flour. They suggested that Newfoundland were gluttons for flour and were shirking their duty while the rest of the British Empire and the United States were cutting back on their flour consumption. Progressives, on the other hand, were outraged at the price of flour. They admitted that the war caused part of the price increase but maintained that a large portion of the rise in the cost of living was the result of merchants attempting to make as large a profit as possible. They advocated that the government had a responsibility to ensure that every citizen could afford flour and advocated that the government step in to regulate flour prices.

While the government pleased the progressives by creating the Food Control Board, which had the power to regulate food prices and seize stocks of food, its actions aligned more with the wishes of the liberals. Instead of controlling the price of flour, the FCB sought to reduce Newfoundland's reliance on flour by forcing people to use flour substitutes, which were often much cheaper than wheat flour.

The issue of new sources of food, on the other hand, saw limited traction. Many progressives and liberals argued that Newfoundlanders should rely on cod heads, tongues, cheeks, and seal flippers and carcasses as a wartime alternative to fresh or salted meat. Despite their calls on the government to encourage the consumption of these foods, Newfoundlanders did not readily add them to their diets. The government was effective, however, at persuading people to increase the quantity of potatoes in their diets. By informing the people that potatoes were a patriotic and economical option, the government was able to increase the dominion's potato production by over 400,000 barrels a year.

At the heart of the issue of food rationing and price control was a shifting focus on the rights of individuals versus the rights of the community. During the war, progressives and liberals renegotiated the social contract between citizens and the state. They argued that in return for the service of soldiers, who were fighting and dying for their country, the government had an obligation to ensure that those on the home front were provided with the necessities of life. Like any negotiation, the liberals, progressives, and the government had different agendas and different ideas about what should be done. Despite their disagreements, both sides agreed that the government had a duty to focus on the basic needs of the community and become more involved in both free markets and the everyday lives of citizens.

3

Taxation

The collection of taxes is perhaps the most fundamental characteristic of the relationship between citizens and the state. While taxation can be a contentious issue during peacetime, the added expense of a total war effort can exacerbate existing tensions over discussions about what citizens owe to the state. In 1914, the Newfoundland government initially committed to providing a regiment of five hundred soldiers for the British Expeditionary Force. This number eventually ballooned to over 12,000 soldiers and sailors by the time the war ended in 1918. The cost of training, paying, lodging, equipping, and caring for these soldiers required a substantial expenditure on behalf of the Newfoundland government. The cost of Newfoundland's war effort led to a debate over how the government should pay for the regiment and on whose shoulders the burden should fall. Fundamental to this debate were shifting understandings of class and what responsibilities the liberal individual owed to the state.[1]

Historically, the Newfoundland government's revenue came from indirect methods of taxation, primarily import tariffs. In 1911–12, for example, the government took in $3,736,455 in total revenue. Eighty-five per cent of this ($3,142,491) came from import tariffs. Merchants paid import tariffs on the importation of goods. They generally charged these taxes back to the consumer by raising their prices accordingly. Other forms of income included natural resource royalties, profits from the postal service, and light dues. While direct taxation (income tax) had been implemented or attempted in Britain and other British colonies, Newfoundland had never attempted direct taxation before the war.[2]

The government's first attempt at collecting the money required for Newfoundland's war effort comprised increasing existing tariffs on the staples of everyday life such as flour, sugar, pork, tea, and kerosene. In September of 1914, Edward Morris told the house of assembly that he was loathe to impose on increase on general taxation, but the government needed additional revenue to support the war effort. He then introduced a bill that would increase existing taxes to include a tariff of 25¢ per pound of flour, 5¢ per gallon of kerosene, 5¢ per pound of tea, 3¢ per pound of sugar, and $1.50 per barrel of salt pork and beef. The editor of the *Mail and Advocate* estimated that this burden would be so unpopular that producers would force Morris out of office.[3]

In many ways, Morris's increase in taxation followed traditionally liberal principles of the equality of the individual. In this school of thought, each individual should pay roughly the same amount of sales taxes, no matter how much they made. While wealthier Newfoundlanders could afford to purchase more food, it would only result in a marginally larger tax load than poor fishers.

The rise in the cost of living caused by this increase in taxation caused widespread resentment. Rural Newfoundlanders felt that the government was making the poorest of the dominion pay for the war effort by increasing tariffs on food. In a letter to the editor of the *Mail and Advocate*, "Ready for Action" expressed their anger. In this letter, the author wondered whether or not Morris was trying to starve outport residents through excess taxation. They suggested that if Morris was attempting to kill fishers, he might as well send them all to the front. Ready for Action expressed their condemnation of Morris's administration and those who supported it: "If I voted for the Morris Party in 1913 I would try to get to Germany and ask the Kaiser to accept me for a wad for his big guns for I would not count myself worthy to be a wad for a British Gun."[4]

As the tariffs increased, so too did producers' discontent. As time went on, many began to believe that the fishers were primarily responsible for paying for the war effort. Fred Ollerand, a resident of St Anthony, made this sentiment clear in a letter he wrote to the editor of the *Mail and Advocate*. Ollerand complained that producers were responsible for providing the men needed for the Newfoundland Regiment. Meanwhile, Ollerand explained that both the government and the business community were taking money from the fishers through taxation and profiteering: "It seems to me there is two types of patriotism in Newfoundland to-day, one which we have seen manifested in the offering up of our young men for active service, the other a patriotism shown in the contribution of large sums of money gained through the deprivation of the poorer classes."[5]

This feeling of unfairness escalated in 1916 when Morris's administration increased tariffs on supplies needed to prosecute the fishery. Fishers were insulted when a new gasoline tax increased the cost of gas from 27¢ to 48¢ a gallon, which meant that many poorer fishing crews could not afford the fuel needed to get to fertile fishing grounds. William Coaker estimated that the tariff on gasoline caused the loss of over 25,000 quintals of fish with a potential value of $125,000 and only resulted in $5,000 in tax revenue for the government. He decried this tax in the house of assembly and protested the unequal tax burden the government placed on the shoulders of fishers.[6]

While the *Mail and Advocate* and its readers were concerned about taxation, other newspapers were not. The *Evening Telegram* pointed out that Britain had much higher levels of tax on a broader range of goods. Similarly, in a speech given in 1916, W.F. Lloyd admitted that Newfoundland was falling behind the other British dominions in its financial contribution to the war effort. He suggested that the dominion had to raise this money through taxes or other means.[7] Where this money would come from would turn out to be one of the most controversial political issues during 1916 and 1917.[8]

BUSINESS PROFITS TAX

By 1916, one thing was clear: both liberals and progressives agreed that the government could not rely on import tariffs to pay for the war effort, but they disagreed on the best way to raise the funds. Progressive elements leaned towards lower tariffs and a business profits tax, while the liberals preferred high tariffs and an income tax. Both of these methods of taxation would result in more money in the government's coffers. The difference was who would shoulder the burden of this taxation. Proponents of the income tax argued that taxing every citizen's income would be a fair way to ensure every individual paid an equal share. Those who supported a business profits tax suggested that taxing the income of fishers would unfairly place the responsibility of paying for the war on those who could least afford it. Instead, progressives urged the government to place a higher tax burden on those who could best afford it: the business community.

The first calls for a profits tax came from John St John, the editor of the *Mail and Advocate*, in 1915, when he accused business owners of profiting from the war effort while producers were burdened with heavy taxation and a rising cost of living. He criticized the 40 per cent increase in freight rates, which were driving up the cost of living, while the wealthy drove motor cars through the streets of St John's. Instead, he suggested that the government owed a responsibility to the citizens to place the burden of taxation on the shoulders of those who are best able to support it: "Let us tax the people who scoop in the huge profits, and there will be no reason for taxing the commodities of the poor and the industrious."[9]

The rising cost of living and the widespread belief that merchants were using the war to justify earning excess profits was a prime motivation for those who wanted a tax on profits. The feeling that merchants were taking advantage of war conditions increased in 1916 after the sale of steamers to the Russian government. The sale of these ships was seen as a betrayal by many Newfoundlanders. They believed, on account of the war, that merchants had a civic duty to put the needs of the community over their profits. By selling these ships, they were breaking their civic responsibility. Their actions led to many calls for these companies to pay hefty retroactive taxes on the sale of their vessels. The *Mail and Advocate* demanded such a tax: "We insist further that the Shylocks who have had their pound of flesh should be made to disgorge some of their ducats and compelled to aid the cause of the Empire by digging down into their jeans and passing into the Exchequer some of their easily gotten coin ... We say, tax the monied interests; and do not lay greater burdens on the shoulders of the fishers and the daily wage earner." In the eyes of many producers, the business owners who sold these ships were wholly unpatriotic, and the government needed to protect fishers by enacting a profits tax.[10]

The *Evening Telegram* also called for the shipowners to pay a substantial tax on the sale of their vessels. Unlike the *Mail and Advocate*, the *Evening Telegram* was very concerned about Newfoundland failing to live up to the financial contributions of other dominions. The editor pointed out that Newfoundland was lagging behind Britain and Canada in its contribution to the war effort. To raise more money for the war, he demanded that vessel owners turn over a substantial portion of their profits to help offset the cost of the war. While the *Evening Telegram* was quick to call for a specific tax on the sale of steamers, it did not advocate for a tax on profits.[11]

The sale of these vessels began a conversation across Newfoundland about the responsibilities of producers and business-class citizens. For progressives, the widespread belief that merchants were making record-breaking profits convinced them that the government should require businesses to pay a tax on all profits. The editor of the *Evening Advocate* cautioned the government that, without such a profits tax, it was placing the burdens of war on the shoulders least able to bear them. He warned that during the Napoleonic Wars, the government put the burden of the war on producers instead of commerce and industry. Working-class Britons suffered and resorted to riots, mutinies, and conspiracies. He asked the government if it would learn from the mistakes of previous wars and place a greater burden on Newfoundland's wealthiest citizens.[12]

A major issue driving the campaign for tax reform was ongoing discussions of conscription. Liberals initially led a drive for compulsory service that progressives opposed. For progressives, it was a perverse idea that the government would conscript men into the military before the government conscripted the wealth of the business community through taxation. They demanded that the conscription of wealth preceded any conscription of labour for the trenches. According to the *Evening Advocate*: "The war has demanded the service and life of every young man, and it is manifestly absurd that when money can be of such service in the war, that it should be exempt." For those who advocated for the conscription of wealth, it was unimaginable that the state men to give their lives before it would ask the business community to give a portion of their profits.[13]

MP Cashin presented a business profits tax bill to the house of assembly on 26 July 1917. It proposed a tax of 25 per cent on the net profits on all trades and businesses in the dominion. Business owners would only be taxed if they made over $2,000 profit and were also granted a deduction of 6 per cent of their capital before the tax was calculated. For example: if a company was valued at $100,000 and made $20,000, they would subtract $6,000 (6 per cent of $100,000) from their profits. They would be left with a total taxable profit of $14,000, of which the government would take $3,500. For progressives, this was a reasonable and equitable way of raising money for the war effort as it only impacted the wealthiest people in the dominion. Importantly, business owners could not charge this tax back to the consumer.[14]

For liberals and those friendly to the business community, the business profits tax represented a grave threat to the dominion. H.A. Winter, the editor of the *Evening Telegram,* accused the government of pushing this tax through the house of assembly without considering its impact on the dominion. He argued that this legislation was a joke: "if the genius responsible for the scheme wished to include his humour in a more popular manner, we advise him to try the stage – comedy or light opera – or the comic papers. He will find it also a more happy outset for his talent." Winter believed this bill would negatively affect the dominion by hindering businesses from reinvesting their abnormally high profits back into the local economy. He also accused this legislation of unfairly targeting the upper class, while leaving the middle class, who were seeing unprecedented prosperity, free from taxation.[15]

The debate over the business profits tax very quickly became divided by classes. After the *Evening Telegram* said that the tax would unfairly target business owners and cripple Newfoundland's economy, the *Evening Advocate* provided rebuttal. It argued that the same business circles that decried the profits tax showed no concern while they crippled the producers by raising the cost of living to maximize profits. The editor pointed out that a similar tax had been instituted across the British Empire and did not result in the destroy economies. Instead, he suggested that their opposition to this tax was based on unpatriotic greed.[16]

In reply to the *Advocate,* the *Telegram* published an article claiming that the *Advocate* was attempting to mislead the people into accepting the profits tax. Winter suggested that the bill would not be a tax on "excess" profits but all business profits. Furthermore, he said that the tax would not impact profiteering, as the *Advocate* claimed, but instead would cripple small businesses that were just managing to stay afloat. Similarly, in a letter to the editor, a writer under the pseudonym "Commerce" questioned whether the tax would impact the importation of food. He highlighted that the dominion was 40,000 barrels of flour short of what was needed to get through the year, and questioned whether this tax would impede the merchants' ability to bring in the necessities of life.[17]

Local newspapers and politicians were not the only entities to express opposition to the profits tax. After the announcement that banking institutions would not be exempt from the tax, Minister of

Finance Michael Cashin received several letters from the managers of banks. Concerned that an additional tax on banking could have unforeseen consequences on the issuing of credit, the manager of the Bank of Nova Scotia wrote to Cashin requesting that the government defer the bill. The Bank of Montreal wrote a similar letter suggesting that banks already paid a high tax for the privilege of doing business in Newfoundland. He pointed out that the Bank of Montreal already paid $5,000 a year to the government and $2,000 to the City of St John's. Due to the high taxes already incurred by banks, he requested that they receive the same exemption as life insurance companies. Similarly, the Canadian Bank of Commerce and the Bank of Canada also wrote to Cashin expressing their concern. The Manager of the Bank of Canada also made it clear that Canada has a similar excess profits tax, and banks were exempt from it.[18]

Shortly after the introduction of the business profits tax in the house of assembly, the bill became one of the primary points of the renegotiation of class in wartime Newfoundland. This debate was centred on what society should expect from its citizens of various classes during the war. On the one hand, producers felt that it was the patriotic duty of wealthier citizens to pay a larger share of the war debt to support the greater community. On the other hand, those of the upper class felt that this legislation unfairly targeted them and that government interference could damage Newfoundland's economy. This debate boiled down to liberal ideas about the equality of the individual under the law. Liberals believed that the state should treat all individuals equally, and a tax targeting a specific class was unconscionable. Instead, they wanted the government to spread the tax burden evenly across all citizens. On the other hand, progressives felt that an equal tax burden prioritized the rights of the wealthy over the rights of the greater community.[19]

When the house of assembly met on 2 August 1917 to discuss the profits tax, the authors of the bill made some amendments to make the act more palatable for the business community. P.T. McGrath explained that the bill had been altered, so the deduction of 6 per cent on capital was removed. Instead of allowing a per cent on capital, the bill would increase the minimum amount for taxation from $2,000 to $3,000, and the tax rate was lowered from 25 per cent to 20 per cent. The house of assembly passed this bill on 2 August 1917 and then passed it onto the legislative council.[20]

While the business profits tax passed through the house of assembly with minimal discussion, things were quite different when it reached the legislative council, where council members censured it. The first to attack the bill was Samuel Milley, a prominent importer of dry goods. He felt that the house of assembly did not give a passing thought to its impact. He told the council that if the house had seriously considered the bill, then it would have realized it was absurd and rejected it outright.[21]

Though he opposed the bill, Milley made it clear that his opposition did not arise out of his distaste for paying taxes. Instead, he suggested that Britain and Canada focussed their taxes on excess profits from war production, which was absent in Newfoundland. Instead, Milley recommended that the government put a tax of between 20–40 per cent on every quintal of fish exported from Newfoundland because the war had caused the price of fish to rise abnormally high. Milley's suggestion to tax the exportation of fish was deeply unpopular among fishers as it could be easily passed along from merchants to the fishers by lowering the price offered to fishers by an amount equal to the export tax.[22]

The next member of the legislative council to attack the profits tax was John Harvey of Harvey & Co, a powerful import/export company. Harvey argued that the amendments made to the profits tax would result in a dramatic increase in taxation. He explained that under the old scheme, a business with $1,000,000 in capital and $100,000 profit would pay $10,000 in taxes. Under the new amendments, Harvey calculated that the same business would pay $19,400. In addition to the increase in taxes, he argued that the profits tax would have a detrimental impact on the shipping industry. He claimed that Canadian and American vessels would avoid doing business in Newfoundland because they would not want to pay the tax. Similarly, Harvey pointed out that the Canadian government waved the profits tax for any business capitalized under $50,000. He suggested that many vessels could operate tax-free in Canadian waters, encouraging them to leave Newfoundland, resulting in a worse shortage of tonnage than the dominion was currently facing.[23]

While Harvey's calculations are correct, he used an extreme example of a business with high capital and a low-profit margin. The following would be a much more realistic example: a company that had $100,000 in capital and $20,000 in profits would pay $3,500 under the first iteration of the bill. Under the amended version, the same business would be taxed 20 per cent on all their profits after $3,000, which would amount to $3,400. While the amendments to the initial bill would raise the taxes paid by large companies with high capital, it would reduce the tax burden on small and medium-sized firms.[24]

A common theme in the criticism of this bill in the legislative council was that it unfairly targeted one class of Newfoundland society. John Anderson, the owner of a large dry goods firm, said that he believed in the conscription of wealth, but he did not "believe in partisan and unjust taxation of those who are doing whatever they can to help win this righteous and great war." Similarly, Edgar Bowring, a partner in the large Bowring Brothers firm, posited that this bill targeted only one class, the business class. He said that Newfoundland's business community were as patriotic as any other section of Newfoundland society and were willing to pay their fair share of taxes. Still, they felt that the bill discriminated against them. Bowring reminded his colleagues that business owners were taking substantial risks by operating in the dominion, and they needed to be able to rely on large profits to justify the increased risk of wartime shipping.[25]

Despite the harsh criticism of the bill by some members of the legislative council, not all members opposed the bill. J.J. Murphy, the majority shareholder of the United Towns Electric Company, told the council that he had some reservations. He thought it was of the utmost importance that the government get the money it needed to fight the war effort, but he believed that some elements of society were giving generously of their sons and money while others were not. Murphy said that it was only "right and proper" that the law compelled slackers to pay their fair share. William Ellis, a building contractor from Ferryland, also supported the bill. He contended that patriotism and self-sacrifice should motivate every member of the legislative council to vote for it. He told the house that passing this bill was the first step to ensuring that every citizen was doing their bit.[26]

After allowing for a protracted debate, the president of the legislative council, P.T. McGrath, refused to allow members to speak more than once on the first reading of this bill. To prevent an interminable debate on the matter, he made a motion to vote on a second reading. The resulting vote was divided. John Harvey, Michael Gibbs, Marmaduke Winter, Michael Power, William Ellis, Richard Squires, and S.D. Blandford voted for another reading. George Knowling, John Anderson, J.D. Ryan, A.F. Goodridge, Dr G. Skelton, James Ryan, and Samuel Milley voted against it. Following the divided vote, P.T. McGrath used his powers as the president to cast a vote in favour of a second reading.[27]

The opposition to a second reading of the business profits tax drew widespread condemnation from progressive citizens. The *Evening Advocate* told its readers that "those who voted against the second reading virtually threw the bill out and wrote themselves down as opposed to the bill – a most unreasonable and unpatriotic stand that is not worthy of them." The editor accused the members who opposed the second reading of prioritizing their profits over the good of the dominion.

Similarly, after the legislative council members cast their votes, P.T. McGrath told the council that this vote was the most regrettable occurrence in the history of the legislative council. He declared that members' rejection of this bill had done more to increase hostility between fishers and merchants, between urban and rural, than any event in Newfoundland history. Given the historical tensions between fishers and merchants caused by the truck system, McGrath's statement was a scathing attack on those who voted against the bill.[28]

The comments by McGrath and the *Advocate* represented outrage that was common in some sections of society that viewed this vote as a selfish and unpatriotic act, designed to put the needs of the business community over the needs of the dominion. Those who supported the business profits tax believed that all economic classes had to make equitable sacrifices, and those with more money should make larger contributions. To them, this vote showed that the Newfoundland's business community prioritized money over human life.

When the legislative council returned for a second reading of the bill, the debate intensified. The first to speak after the second reading was Marmaduke Winter, a member of the Newfoundland Patriotic Association and owner of T&M Winter, a provisions dealer. He argued that this bill would result in Newfoundland businesses investing money outside of the dominion. He asserted that investors would seek opportunities outside of the dominion so they could avoid the unfairly high taxes. John Harvey agreed with Winter and counselled that the only way to make this tax fair was to introduce an amendment that would reinstitute the 6 per cent deduction on capital that was included in the first bill. J.D. Ryan, an owner of a grocery store in St John's, told the council that he believed it was discriminatory to force business owners to pay the vast majority of taxes while professionals with high salaries paid nothing. As a result of all this criticism, Mr Harvey motioned for the legislative council to rise, which would kill the bill if successful.[29]

In response to Mr Harvey's motion, P.T. McGrath implored the council to think about how the people would view the failure of this bill in the legislative council. McGrath told the members that the majority of Newfoundlanders would not understand their opposition to the bill and assume that the legislative council voted against it simply because its members did not want to pay the tax. He reminded the members of the grave situation of the war and how desperately the government needed money. He chided those who supported conscripting labour for the trenches but balked at the suggestion that they surrender a portion of the excess profits they earned since the war started. McGrath warned the council members that if they expected the masses to give up their children to fight and die for the British Empire and everything it stood for, then the wealthy members of society had an obligation to give a reasonable amount to support the war effort.[30]

Before the house took a vote on Harvey's motion, Richard Squires, the justice minister, urged the other members of the council to vote in favour of this bill. Squires reminded the council that this was a financial measure, which was the sole responsibility of the House of Commons. Under the constitution, the legislative council was not able to amend it. Squires also noted that because the bill was a financial matter, the council should not summarily reject it. In addition to highlighting the constitutional issues of killing the bill, Squires attacked those who claimed it unfairly targeted specific individuals:

> From one home a son goes forth to live one glorious hour before the foe, and then with his life's blood to inscribe his name upon the roll of Britain's honour. Another lad goes forth, fights as valiantly, spares himself no risk, and after years of conflict returns bearing upon his unscathed breast the honors of military achievement. Viewing these things as we do, at one moment through the mist of sorrow over the snuffing out of heroic life, and at another moment looking upon the scene with the sunshine of honor, victory and life about us, we see apparent inequalities so great that inequality representing a mere difference in dollars suggested by the honorable members as resulting from the operation of this Act is as a dead level and as insignificant as the straws upon a mud puddle on a country road.

Squires appealed to the council to accept the sacrifices required in this bill and give up a reasonable portion of their income while others sacrificed their flesh and blood to stop the juggernaut of war.[31]

Following Squires's speech, the council took a vote on the motion to rise. Despite the efforts of Squires and McGrath, the motion succeeded. Harvey, Bowring, Anderson, Milley, Winter, Goodridge, J.D. Ryan, J. Ryan, and Knowling voted in favour and Squires, Gibbs, Power, Ellis, Murphy, Blandford, and McGrath voted against it. By rejecting a financial bill, the legislative council drew the ire of the producers and created a constitutional crisis.

The reaction to the failure of the business profits tax was predominately negative. Miranda, a regular columnist for the *Evening Advocate*, expressed outrage that the members of the legislative council would be unwilling to part with a portion of the profits they were making from the grossly inflated prices they were charging for the necessities of life. Miranda also remarked that the business community would live on in eternal shame because of their unpatriotic greed that prioritized money over human life.

The editor of the *Evening Telegram* suggested that the legislative council's refusal to accept the profits tax would hurt the recruiting effort. Winter explained that the legislative council had supported the raising of troops for the war effort, and now it had a social obligation to sacrifice a portion of their profits so the government could care for soldiers upon their return.[32]

Outrage over the legislative council's actions was not limited to the pages of the *Evening Advocate*. The editor of the *Daily News* attacked the council for its unjustifiable opposition to the bill. He reminded the readers that the house of assembly, which was elected and represented the people, passed the bill. He argued that a council made up of unelected members had no right to kill a financial bill, that was a war measure, and one that many other parts of the British Empire had already passed. He further criticized John Anderson's argument that the bill was an example of unfair class legislation. He pointed out that the house routinely passed class legislation that benefitted wealthy citizens. Anderson's comments highlight a primary aspect of pre-war Newfoundland liberalism. Pre-war liberal thinkers continually defended free markets yet took no umbrage with government intervention on behalf of the narrowly defined liberal individual: the wealthy male capitalist. By campaigning for a profits tax, Anderson argued that society should afford Newfoundlanders of all economic classes the rights of the liberal individual.[33]

Like the *Evening Advocate*, the editor of the *Daily News* also believed that the rejection of the business profits tax would hurt recruiting, as it would discourage people from enlisting to defend those who refused to pay their fair share. Similarly, the *Twillingate Sun* viewed the criticism of the business profits tax as a smokescreen. "Observer," a regular columnist for the *Twillingate Sun*, compared opposition to the business profits tax to opposition to William Coaker's Seal Fishery Act. This bill contained a series of regulations designed to keep seal fishers safe. These regulations included a prohibition on sealers being on the ice after dark, compensation for death and injury for any sealers who were left on the ice after dark, a standardization of signalling equipment, limits on the number of pelts a ship could carry, and a requirement to have trained navigators and a doctor. Some merchants claimed this bill would destroy the sealing industry and leave Newfoundland in ruins. Despite the extreme pessimism surrounding the Sealing Bill, the sealing industry continued to thrive. Observer predicted that the merchants of St John's were making a similar bluff in the hopes of killing a bill that would force them to give up a portion of the profits they squeezed from the colony in a time of war.[34]

Having unanimously passed the bill, the members of the house of assembly were also outraged that the legislative council killed it. On 8 August, the house had a special meeting to discuss this issue. Morris was incensed at the actions of the Upper House. He told the house of assembly, "the Legislative Council are living in a fool's paradise if they imagine that public opinion will tamely submit to a body such as they are, irresponsible to the people, throwing out a measure calculated to provide the means of carrying on the war."[35]

Following this meeting, Edward Morris sent a letter to Governor Walter Davidson, informing him that he had the unanimous support of the House of Commons to submit a request that he prorogue parliament for one week. Morris also requested that Davidson seek permission from Secretary of State for the Colonies Arthur Long to increase the size of the legislative council from twenty-four to twenty-eight. With four already vacant seats, this move would allow the government to appoint eight new members. Morris planned to fill these seats with members who supported the business profits tax to stack the council with supporters before Parliament resumed, and the business profits tax was reintroduced to the legislature.[36]

The reaction to Morris's prorogation of parliament was polarized. The *Evening Advocate* lauded the prime minister's decision as a defence against a flagrant violation of the constitutional rights of Newfoundlanders. Both Morris and the *Evening Advocate* argued that the house of assembly alone had the responsibility to create and administer taxes because it was elected by and responsible to the people. While Morris admitted that the legislative council could technically throw out a "money bill," he thought it was unconstitutional for an unelected council to throw out a taxation bill put forward by the representatives of the people. For the *Evening Advocate*, the actions of the legislative council amounted to an affront on democracy and citizens' rights.[37]

The editor and readers of the *Evening Telegram* were on the other side of this debate. In the eyes of H.A. Winter, Morris requested a prorogation of Parliament so he could "carry out a trick, a gross abuse of parliamentary privilege, which would enable it to impose its arbitrary will upon the country." He further said that Morris's attempt to appoint several new "government puppets" to the legislative council was nothing more an authoritarian ploy to force the will of the government on the people. He was adamant that the legislative council had every right to reject a financial bill that was rife with inequities and targeted a specific class.[38]

In addition to Winter's commentary, the *Evening Telegram* received many letters to the editor from concerned citizens. One letter, written under the pseudonym "Cross Roads," argued that it was Morris who was violating the constitutional rights of the people by attempting to meddle with the legislative council's decision, using public antipathy towards merchants as a way of garnering support for another term. "Cross Roads" also said that the legislative council was right in blocking the bill because this tax would only result in higher prices. Another letter by "One of Yourselves" accused Morris of using Germanism and Kaiserism to push through the profits tax. Furthermore, they anticipated that no man would sell "his manhood" to Morris and accept a position on the legislative council as a "hireling."[39]

Despite the prediction of "One of Yourselves," and the outrage of individual business owners, when a special session of the house and assembly and legislative council began on 16 August, there were four new members of the legislative council: Samuel Bell, a shipwright and marine contractor originally from Grand Bank; Francis McNamara, owner of a wholesale grocery firm; Tasker Cook, a politician and business owner who served as vice-consul for Norway and consul for Denmark; and A.W. Mews. When the special session resumed debates on the business profits tax, the tone of the discussion had changed from the previous session. One of the first to speak on this bill was Mr Ellis. He confessed that he believed the failure of the profits tax in the legislative council made the majority of Newfoundland believe that the members of the council had put their business interests over the interests of the dominion and empire, which provoked class division. He advised the special session that the only way to change public perception was to pass the bill quickly and unanimously.[40]

The next to speak on this bill was a new member, Francis McNamara. He told the session that after studying it at length, he did not believe that it was as unfair or obnoxious as its detractors claimed. In McNamara's opinion, a profits tax was a fair way to raise money for the war effort, because increased profits were directly attributable to the war. He also responded to Mr Milley's suggested tax on all fish exports instead of imposing a profits tax. McNamara informed the house that he was opposed to this, as the merchants could manipulate the price they paid for fish to pass that cost along to the fishers. He also challenged the notion that requiring business owners to pay a tax on their profits was unfair. Comparing the sacrifices of the business community to the sacrifices of soldiers, McNamara said:

> We are talking about class legislation, – unfair contributions. Look around our streets to-day and what will you see? You will find returned soldiers, some of them with one leg, others with one arm, still others helpless cripples, and I say, what contribution can the wealthiest man in Newfoundland give to equal the contribution or sacrifice given by these returned heroes to the Empire? We are singing patriotic songs; our bands are playing patriotic airs; we stand up and uncover our heads when "God Save the King" is announced, but as soon as our pockets are touched, we forget our patriotism, and by quibbling and raising objections try to evade the duty we owe the Empire in its darkest hour.[41]

The final member to speak on this issue was another newly appointed council member, A.W. Mews, one of the most vocal supporters of the profits tax before his appointment to the legislative council. Mews argued that import tariffs had unfairly targeted producers because under import taxes a citizen would pay roughly the same amount of tax whether they made $500 a year or $5,000 a year. He admitted that the bill was an example of class legislation but said that it was targeting a class that has traditionally benefited from tax legislation.[42]

Following Mr Mews' speech, the legislative council voted and the Business Profits Tax Act passed unanimously without amendment. The majority of newspapers in Newfoundland celebrated the act. The editor of the *Evening Advocate* praised the legislative council. The *Harbour Grace Standard* suggested that the tax was fair but regretted the acrimonious debate over the issue. The editor of the *Western Star* shared the same sentiment. He was pleased that the profits tax was passed but deemed it unfortunate that the two houses were fighting when the empire required a unity of purpose.[43]

In the end, the people of Newfoundland decided that the war effort required class legislation that put the burden of supporting the war effort on the dominion's wealthiest citizens. Under the new social covenant between citizens and the liberal state, the vast majority of citizens believed that all social classes should make sacrifices that supported the war effort and benefitted the greater community. Despite the protestations of business owners who argued that the bill would be a failure and depress Newfoundland's economy, business continued as usual. Eight months after parliament passed the Business Profits Tax Act, the government had generated over $400,000, making the tax even more successful than its most ardent supports had hoped.[44]

INCOME TAX

In addition to increases to general taxation and the business profits tax, the topic of an income tax was introduced to the house of assembly in April of 1918. While some provincial and municipal governments in Canada had enacted direct income taxation prior to 1917, this was uncharted territory in Newfoundland.[45] Alongside the profits tax, the income tax was part of the movement to find a fair method of taxation that ensured every citizen supported the war effort in accordance with their wealth. The first discussions of an income tax followed shortly after Morris's increase in general taxation. While the editor of the *Evening Telegram* continually argued against a profits tax, Theobald supported taxation on income. He maintained that the cost of living had already risen to unprecedented levels, and adding additional import duties on food and clothing would mean that many Newfoundlanders would not be able to afford to feed their families.[46]

Similarly, in a letter to the editor from "Junius," the author expressed concern that as a result of prohibition, other goods would have to be taxed an additional 12 per cent to make up the difference in revenue for the government. He argued that it would be an injustice to make rural people (who he believed were teetotallers) pay additional taxation to make up for the lack of money coming in from alcohol purchases. Junius recommended the government put a tax of 50 per cent on incomes over $2,500 and an extra 5 per cent for each additional $500 a person earned.[47]

Many of those who supported the income tax act believed the government was negligent for not establishing an income tax shortly after the war started. In the *Evening Telegram,* Theobald expressed his frustration at the government's reluctance to institute an income tax. He reminded his readers that "almost every civilized country" had some sort of income tax. In another article, Theobald told his readers that by taking out war loans, instead of raising money locally, Newfoundland would be paying back the cost of the war effort long after the war is over. He proceeded to criticize the government for failing to impose an income tax while England, Scotland, Canada, and Australia had already done so.[48]

Unlike the profits tax, there was no widespread opposition to income taxation. The first discussion of an income tax occurred in April of 1918 when George Grimes complained that many professionals did not own businesses, earned over $3,000 a year, and were not required to pay taxes under the business profits tax. He informed the house that there was a bill in Canada that required every citizen, who earned over a set income, to pay a tax. He endorsed the creation of an income tax to ensure that everyone was paying their share.[49]

On 13 May 1918, Michael Cashin made a motion for the house to form a committee to examine income taxation. He told the house that despite predictions that the business profits tax would cost more to enforce than it would bring in, it succeeded in generating $400,000 while only costing $10,000 to implement. Despite this success, the finance minister said that in enforcing the bill, he noticed that many professionals and some fishers were earning over $3,000 a year and not paying taxes on their incomes. He said that these people were not doing their bit to help the war effort.[50]

Cashin suggested that Newfoundland follow the lead set by England and Canada and established taxation on some incomes. He introduced a bill titled "An Act to Authorize the Levying of a War Tax on Certain Incomes." It proposed that unmarried men pay a 5 per cent tax on all incomes above $1,000, and $2,000 for married men. Any citizen making over $6000 a year would have to pay an additional "super tax" that would be issued on a sliding scale from 5–50 per cent depending on how much the person made. He estimated that this bill would result in eight times as many citizens paying taxes as they did under the Business Profits Tax Act. Following Cashin's introduction of the bill, the Income Tax Act received only a few questions and passed the second and third readings, and the house passed it without amendments.[51]

The ease with which the house of assembly and legislative council passed the income tax bill is evidence of the impact that a renegotiation of class had on the liberal state. When Cashin presented the business profits tax in the house of assembly, it drew widespread debate among politicians and the people. It brought Newfoundland to the brink of a constitutional crisis. In comparison, the income tax bill faced next to no opposition and drew minimal discussion in local newspapers. By the time that the government introduced an income tax bill, most Newfoundlanders had already acknowledged that wealthy citizens had a duty to their country and fellow citizens to sacrifice a portion of their wealth for the greater good.

The development of taxation in Newfoundland closely paralleled the development of taxation in Canada. Both dominions passed a business profits tax in 1916. The Canadian profits tax collected a 25 per cent tax on all profits while allowing for 7 per cent profits on capital. This placed roughly the same tax burden on Canadians as Newfoundland. The main difference between the two taxes was an exemption on Canadian businesses with less than $50,000 capital that was not offered in Newfoundland.

In 1917, the Canadian government passed an income tax. Canada's thresholds for taxation were slightly higher at $1500 for single men and $3000 for married men, but the tax rate was slightly lower at 4 per cent. Altogether, the two dominions had incredibly similar taxation schemes. This is largely because Newfoundland legislators closely monitored developments in Canada and used Canadian legislation as a benchmark for what Newfoundland should be doing.

Though the taxation schemes were quite similar, citizen's reactions to them were quite different. Shirley Tillotson points out that progressives in Canada were not satisfied with Canada's tax schemes after the implementation of income taxation. *L'Avenir du Nord*, a progressive paper from St Jerome, felt that taxation in Canada hardly affected the wealthiest citizens in Canada while putting the burden on skilled workers who earned enough to break the threshold for taxation. Similarly, the *Winnipeg Free Press* argued that income taxation would do little to solve the unequal tax burden.[52]

Progressives in Newfoundland were much more satisfied than their counterparts in Canada. The *Daily News*, for example, praised the implementation of income taxation because it believed the tax ensured that the burden of supporting the war effort was equitably spread across all citizens. The *Evening Advocate*, took things a step further, arguing that the implementation of equitable taxation was proof that a new day was dawning in Newfoundland where the government would put the needs of the people before the needs of the mercantile elite.[53]

THE VICTORY LOAN

In addition to the money raised locally, the government took out a series of loans to help fund its contribution to the war effort. In 1914, the government received $2,000,000 in loans from the British government and the Bank of Montreal. The government agreed to pay these loans back in two years. With the war still raging in 1916, the government passed "An Act to Authorize the Raising of a Sum of Money by Loan for Naval, Military, Railway, and other Public Purposes." This act authorized Morris to raise a loan of $5,000,000 with an interest rate not higher than 5.5 per cent. The government used this money for several different purposes: $1,000,000 went toward the completion of sections of the railway, the government used another $1,000,000 to start paying off other existing loans, and it used the remaining $3,000,000 to support Newfoundland's war effort.[54]

In the fall of 1916, Morris visited the United States and secured a loan of $5,000,000. By early 1917 this loan was exhausted. Morris then turned to Britain for an additional loan of $1,500,000 that was meant to keep the war effort going until the government could find additional revenue. Knowing the loan from the British government would not last, the house of assembly passed another bill in 1917 titled "An Act to Authorize the Raising of a Sum of Money for Naval and Military Purposes," which allowed Morris to seek an additional $3,000,000 with an interest rate of not more than 5.5 per cent.[55]

Unlike Morris's previous trip to the U.S, when he sought a second loan, he was informed that American banks would no longer be loaning money to foreign governments. When Morris surveyed market interest rates in Canada and Europe, he found that if the government acquired a loan in Europe, it would have to pay 7 per cent to 7.25 per cent interest at a minimum, and the rates could go as high as 9 per cent.[56]

Inspired by Victory Loan programs in the United States, Michael Cashin suggested that instead of paying a large amount of interest to a foreign country, the state should offer citizens the opportunity to finance the country's war effort. Cashin informed the house that there was approximately $16,000,000 in savings accounts in the dominion that was only earning 3 per cent interest. He said that with an interest of 6.5 per cent on their investment, both practicality and patriotism might persuade people to purchase Victory Loans. In many ways, both citizens and the state could benefit from the Victory Loan. Citizens would get an investment at much higher rates than offered at local banks, and the government would get a loan at a lower rate than the international market offered.[57]

Cashin told the house of assembly that if it passed the Victory Loan Bill, it would be the duty of every citizen to loan money to the government. He said that it was just as important for the wealthy man to donate to the war effort as it was for women to sacrifice their sons on the battlefields of Europe. By making a comparison between enlisting to fight and lending money to the war effort, Cashin was drawing on the wartime idealization of soldiers to encourage the sale of Victory Bonds.[58]

After Cashin introduced the victory loan bill to the house of assembly on 4 May, there was little discussion, and both the house of assembly and the legislative council passed the bill by 13 May. It allowed the government to raise $6,000,000 in loans at a rate of 6.5 per cent interest. The government would not have to repay this loan until 1928, at which time it would make payments twice a year to all bondholders.[59]

Before the government announced the Victory Bond drive, it sought loans from Canada and was able to get $4,000,000. The goal for the Victory Bond drive was set at $2,000,000. Now the government had to convince people to take their savings out of the banks and purchase Victory Bonds. To do this, it began an advertising blitz in newspapers across the island. Together, the newspaper editors and the government used two main themes to sell Victory Bonds: that it was the duty of every citizen to purchase Victory Bonds to support the troops overseas and that buying Victory Bonds was a way for those who could not serve to defend Newfoundland.

The first advertising strategy was straightforward. It relied on the wartime obligation of citizens and the state to provide for those who enlisted in the Newfoundland Royal Naval Reserve or the Newfoundland Regiment. In an *Evening Telegram* article titled "How A Newfoundland Victory Loan Can Help Win the War," the editor told his readers that the government would use money from the Victory Loan to equip and arm soldiers and sailors from Newfoundland who were risking their lives. He said: "No matter how brave our soldiers may be they cannot contend against the enemy unless they are fully equipped, and arms, equipment, etc., cannot be obtained without money." Given the dire need for money to support the war effort, the editor told his readers that it was their "duty as citizens and lovers of our country to see that Newfoundland does not fall behind in this struggle."[60]

In addition to practical arguments about arming and equipping soldiers, some advertisements reminded that Newfoundlanders owed an unpayable debt to the soldiers who gave their lives. The editor of the *Evening Advocate* asked his readers if they ever gave a passing thought to how they would repay, even in the smallest amount, those soldiers and sailors who were giving their lives in the fight against tyranny and oppression so Newfoundland could live in peace and security. He told his readers that the only way they could begin to repay that sacrifice was to purchase Victory Bonds. The editor of the *Evening Telegram* agreed that citizens owed a debt to the soldiers that could only be repaid through Victory Bonds. In another letter several days later he reminded his readers that they were "in debt to the valiant living and the glorious dead who have fought YOUR battles, who have suffered while YOU lived in comfort, who have watched while YOU slept, who have died that YOU might live."[61]

On 10 July, the editor of the *Western Star* encouraged his readers to think about soldiers in French hospitals who had been lying in agony for months on end and would return to the front once they had healed. He said that Newfoundlanders should be ashamed of how little they were doing for those who had risked their lives and suffered in the trenches. The editor claimed that the dominion could make itself worthy of their devotion and self-sacrifice by ensuring that every citizen purchased as many Victory Bonds as they could afford.[62]

In addition to the many editorials, the government also purchased ad space for the Victory Loan. In July 1918, several Newspapers ran a full-page government ad titled "Suppose You Were Going over the Top?" The ad asked the reader to imagine themselves going into no man's land and asked if they would stop and argue over how much glory they might earn or request that someone else go over the top instead. The ad told the reader that, of course, they would go over the top without question because it was their duty. The advertisement attacked the unenlisted and told them that they could save the lives of the "real men" who enlisted by purchasing Victory Bonds.[63]

This ad was a powerful message to Newfoundland citizens. It relied on the wartime gender ideals that equated military service with masculinity. It plainly said that men who remained on the homefront were unmanly and should be ashamed. Once recruiters established that the unenlisted should feel shame, the government gave these men a way to assuage their guilt through donations that could save the "real men."

Another advertisement compared a mother sacrificing her son to a citizen purchasing Victory Bonds. The advertisement read:

> She Has Given Her All! With a proud heart and a firm smile she has made the supreme sacrifice of motherhood – her son. Her patriotism, her loyalty, cannot be measured by mere dollars – she has given her heart's blood, of her very soul. Her boy is "Over There." He is on the firing line, risking his life that you may live in safety; watching through the night that you may sleep; suffering untold hardships that you may live at home in ease. She Would Give the World to Have him Back. What sorrow is like unto her sorrow! What sacrifice can compare with that which she is offering upon the Altar of Freedom! And YOU are but asked to lend! If you have every dollar you have or hope to have, your sacrifice would be as nothing compared to hers. And YOU are merely asked to LEND.

While the previous ad attacked idealized wartime masculinity, this ad played on wartime ideals of femininity which prioritized sacrifice. If patriotic women were sacrificing their children to the war, it was unconscionable for others to refuse to give willingly of their money.[64]

Another powerful advertising strategy told readers that their Victory Loan subscriptions could help defend the dominion and the empire from Germany. In an editorial from the *Evening Telegram* titled

"Support Your Country," the editor proclaimed that it was the duty of every citizen to buy Victory Bonds. He said that if Newfoundlanders neglected this duty, then Germany would defeat the British Empire and replace democratic institutions with autocracy. He implored his readers to enlist for service or subscribe to the Victory Loan because "blood and money must be poured out in never-ending streams ere the rights of the people are made safe."[65]

An ad with a similar theme appeared in several newspapers on 6 July 1918. The advertisement, titled "Your Home Is on Path of the Hun," warned citizens that Newfoundland faced great danger from the German army. It drew on a common belief that if Germany were to defeat Britain on the battlefields of Europe, then Germany would seek to annex British Colonies. The advertisement said that the only thing standing between Newfoundlanders and a German invasion was soldiers and sailors who volunteered to defend their country. It continued to say that the only way these soldiers and sailors could be successful was with the support of the Victory Loan. Therefore, if individuals failed to subscribe, they would be at the mercy of German soldiers. A similar advertisement titled "Must You Be Begged" reminded readers of the atrocities that occurred in Belgium and told them that if they failed to subscribe to the Victory Loan, they would face the same fate that befell the Belgians.[66]

Some editorials and advertisements equated Victory Loan subscription to volunteering for the regiment or naval reserve. In an article titled "Two Alternatives," the editor of the *Evening Advocate* articulated that every male citizen has one of two options: enlist in the Newfoundland Regiment or subscribe to the Victory Loan. He reminded his readers that the state asked soldiers to risk their lives, while the state only asked citizens to loan their money. He reiterated that there was no risk involved in the Victory Loan, so every citizen had to purchase as many Victory Bonds as they were able to afford.[67]

The *Western Star* also equated Victory Loan subscription with military service. In an article titled "They Also Serve," the editor argued that Victory Loan subscribers were as important to the war effort as those who were doing the fighting.[68] The *Western Star* told its readers that the Victory Loan was a form of national service open to every man and woman:

> "All men and women are liable for service to their country. They are bound to serve their native land and Empire in such capacity

> as they may be fitted for in the present crisis. All who have money to invest are in duty bound to now lend it to their country. This is a form of service to which all can respond. This is a call which each one can answer. This is a duty which none can escape, and which all are bound to obey. Any man or woman who can afford to invest in Newfoundland Victory Bonds, and who does not do so, is a SLACKER, to just as great an extent as the man who shirks his military service. Are you a Slacker?"[69]

The discourse surrounding the Victory Loan campaign, especially in advertising, tapped into the potent language of sacrifice and service. For men in the British Empire, society upheld military service as the very essence of masculinity. The language of sacrifice put tremendous pressure on men to prove their masculinity by volunteering to fight in Europe. Being unable to serve was often a profound embarrassment for men, which white feather campaigns and the near-constant label of "slacker" that circulated in newspapers exacerbated. By equating the Victory Loan to military service, these articles told men that they could reclaim their masculinity by purchasing Victory Bonds.

The intense two-month advertising campaign for the Victory Loan proved to be incredibly effective. The government initially hoped to sell $2,000,000 worth, and in less than two weeks following the start of the campaign on 14 June it had achieved its goal. To ensure that all citizens were able to purchase Victory Bonds, Michael Cashin sought and received an Order in Council to sell as many bonds as possible until 27 July.[70] When the final deadline passed, the government had sold over $3,590,000 in Victory Bonds to 1,838 people.

CONCLUSION

The raising of enough money to support Newfoundland's war effort took a gargantuan effort. Though the Newfoundland government relied on loans from the British, Canadian, and American governments, it wanted an increase in taxation to offset the debt that accrued from successive loans. To pass taxation measures such as profit taxation, income taxation, and a Victory Loan, citizens and the state renegotiated conceptions of class, and the liberal order accepted that wealthy citizens had a duty to the community to make financial contributions to the war effort.

Before the war, the only method of taxation in the dominion was the collection of tariffs paid by consumers on imported goods. With the financial demands of the war effort, the Newfoundland government required more money from its citizens; this need became the centre of a great debate over what citizens of each class owed their government. According to the business class, every citizen in the dominion should pay an equal amount to the war effort. They opposed income taxation because they believed the liberal state should not expect greater contributions from one class as opposed to another. They believed in equality of contributions from each class. The working and middle classes, however, thought that their contributions should be equitable, and each citizen should give in accordance with their wealth.

The liberal-minded business community put up an intense fight with the support of the legislative council. Ultimately, however, the language of sacrifice, patriotism, and service was more potent than the power and privilege of the business class. As a result, anyone who opposed the profits tax was labelled as unpatriotic and selfish, and their worth as citizens was questioned as they were labelled traitors, shirkers, and slackers. The public condemnation of the legislative council's vote on the profits tax was so powerful that when they returned for a second vote, not a single member voted against the bill.

The issue of taxation was part of a new social covenant that citizens and the liberal state negotiated during the First World War. As part of this covenant, every citizen in the dominion had a patriotic duty to make financial contributions to the war effort. As a result, former methods of taxation, such as import taxation, were seen as insufficient because they allowed businesses to pass the cost of taxation onto the consumer. The introduction of a business profits tax, an income tax, and a Victory Bond drive ensured that those who could best afford to support the war effort did so.

4
Enemy Aliens

INTRODUCTION

During the First World War, Newfoundland had a rather homogeneous society. The vast majority of Newfoundlanders were either of British or Indigenous heritage. Despite this, there were minority groups in communities across the dominion. The two largest minority groups were Chinese and Syrian, but there were also individuals from Germany, France, Russia, Italy, Norway, Sweden, and the United States.

When the war broke out, Newfoundlanders found themselves thrust into a global conflict. As a result, the dominion drew closer to Britain's allies (France, Russia, Bulgaria, and Japan). At the same time, the war created new animosities with belligerent nations (Germany, the Austro-Hungarian Empire, and the Ottoman Empire). The complicated international relations of the war forced Newfoundlanders to rethink pre-war conceptions of ethnicity as they attempted to determine who their enemy was.

The renegotiation of ethnic conceptions altered the liberal order. Before the war, all Germans and Austro-Hungarian men had achieved the status the liberal individual. During the war, as Newfoundlanders demanded protection from alleged German spies, the liberal order shifted from prioritizing the rights of the individual to the rights of the community and stripped these citizens of equal treatment under the law. People, once considered valued members of the community, were stripped of their basic rights and denied the status of a liberal individual.

GERMANS AND AUSTRO-HUNGARIANS

Before the First World War, most people held Germany in high regard. Newspapers often portrayed Germany as a clean, efficient country filled with cultured, intelligent people. Similarly, newspapers often praised Germans for their military prowess. The positive view of Germans manifested in Newfoundlanders travelling to Germany and the Nickel Theatre in St John's hosting many German-themed evenings with a combination of educational and entertaining films about Germany. When two German vessels visited Newfoundland in 1903 and 1907, they received widespread praise from local newspapers, and many travelled to see the ships.[1]

Despite pre-war positive perceptions, public opinion began to change after Britain declared war on Germany. Following the outbreak of war, editorials did not immediately demonize Germans. An article by the editor of the *Mail and Advocate* described Germany as a brilliant nation that needed rehabilitation. He said that Germans had made significant advancements in science and industry and stated that Britain had no quarrel with the German people. Instead, the editor suggested that Britain's fight was with the government autocrats who were leading Germany down the wrong path. He described the war as "a war to free the people of [Germany] from the shackles of military despotism and secure for them a place in the grand brotherhood of democratic nations." In another article, the editor argued that intelligent, civilized Germans were downtrodden by the violent barbarians who supported the Kaiser.[2]

Some readers of the *Mail and Advocate* expressed outrage over news cables from Britain demonizing German people. In a letter to the editor, an author writing under the pseudonym "A. English" expressed his shock at the outrageous anti-German slander published in Newfoundland newspapers. "English" said that these newspapers were publishing vile calumny, slander, and lies that painted Germans as fiends and savages. He refused to stand idly by while his German friends were attacked in the daily papers. "English" implored Newfoundlanders not to make German citizens pay for a political quarrel between the German and British governments. "A. English's" letter shows that despite the anti-German propaganda in Newfoundland newspapers, some could resist the powerful messages telling them to hate Germans.[3]

While the editor and readers of the *Mail and Advocate* initially resisted anti-German propaganda, it became increasingly difficult as newspapers published cables that contained lurid accounts of violence, sexual assault, cruelty, and sadism by German soldiers in Belgium. One cable accused German soldiers of dragging Belgian civilians behind horses, constructing bridges out of corpses, making priests strip naked before executing them, and cutting women's fingers off to get their rings. Another described German soldiers who arrested a group of Red Cross nurses and amputated their hands. Belgian refugees in Toronto, supposed reported of a Belgian priest who complained to German authorities about random executions of Belgian civilians. In response to his complaint, German soldiers tied him to a tree and left him to die from a combination of starvation and exposure to the elements. Another cable recounted a letter written to a priest in England by a British soldier. He told the priest of young women who ran onto the battlefield and into British trenches to escape German soldiers in the nearby village who had raped them and cut off their breasts.[4]

These atrocity stories were not entirely fictional. Between August and October 1914, the German army killed over 6,500 civilians in Belgium. Horne and Kramer have shown that Allied countries used the details of these atrocities as highly powerful tools to win over both neutral countries (the United States and Italy) and to solidify public support behind the war effort by dehumanizing the enemy. By portraying Germans as irreconcilably evil, Allied countries used atrocity stores to provide a moral justification for the war. Atrocity stories were used in Newfoundland in much the same way.[5]

Atrocity stories were highly effective, and public perception of Germans in Newfoundland changed rapidly. Initially, the editor of the *Mail and Advocate* argued that Britain was not fighting the German people but the autocratic German government. By October, the editor had abandoned all notions that Britain was not fighting a war against the German people. In a complete reversal of his previous articles, the editor of the *Mail and Advocate* wrote:

> "Time and time again one hears the expression 'We are not warring against the German people; we are warring against the military caste that has plunged the Germans into war' … the vast majority of the Germans is so decidedly enthusiastic for the war

> as any of the Allies and are just as firmly convinced that they are warring for a just caus. It is preposterous to contend that a class could permanently hoodwink the intelligent people of Germany to the extent that the charitable-souled allege ... The fact is that there exists in Germany a tremendous hatred of Great Britain and all things British."[6]

In August the editor of the *Mail and Advocate* argued that Germany was the central nexus of culture in Europe, by October he argued that German culture was nothing more than barbarism. He acknowledged that before the war, the whole world viewed Germany as an educational powerhouse, and British parents were eager to send their sons and daughters to Germany for higher education. The editor changed his stance on Germany after the war. He said, "Germany is no longer looked to as the home of 'culture'; nor after the war is it likely to be anything like the same extent of former days, the Mecca of the seeker after the highest in the educational sphere."[7] This article highlights the power that conflict has to reshape conceptions of ethnicity. In it, the author admitted that Germany was once known for culture and higher education but acknowledged that the war shifted public perceptions of Germans.

German unrestricted submarine warfare was also responsible for turning public opinion. In particular, the sinking of the RMS *Lusitania* changed how Newfoundlanders thought about Germany. Shortly after the incident, the *Daily News* admitted that before the attack, people did not hate Germans. According to the editor, the murder of 1,198 civilians, including 150 children, was the last straw. He condemned anti-German rioting in Britain but admitted that restraint was challenging when German soldiers were murdering women and children. Instead of attacking Germans living in the dominion, he recommended that Newfoundlanders express their anger towards Germany by flooding the recruiting stations.[8]

When Germany resumed unrestricted submarine warfare in 1917, the *Daily News* expressed its outrage. In an article titled "Shoot the Brute," John Currie contended that Germany forfeited its right to be considered among the civilized nations of the world. He wrote: "[Germany] has cast on one side, as a cloak, her humanity, and stands revealed as a merciless and cruel monster. Hereafter she can only be classed with the brute and treated as such." He argued that you could not attribute Germany's war crimes to the lawless actions of some soldiers but instead to a planned campaign of the government, the military leaders, and the German people. Currie believed that the conduct of German sailors was so egregious that British sailors should execute any German submariners taken prisoner.[9]

The invasion of Belgium and unrestricted submarine warfare altered the ethnic concepts of Germans in Newfoundland. While some people clung to pre-war stereotypes, at the beginning of the war, by 1915, the language of war recast public representations of the Germans. Writing in 1915, the editor of the *Mail and Advocate* said that under a thin veneer of intelligence and culture, the German race was "rotten to the core," and that "the German character was criminal in its very essence."[10]

In 1917, C.T. James replaced H.A. Winter as the editor of the *Evening Telegram*. He took a much more anti-German stance than Winter. In a 1918 article titled "The Leopards Spots" James published a vicious diatribe against Germans: "The German is brutal from birth. Savageness is ingrained in his nature and the destructive element is uppermost within him. Stealthy and treacherous in his actions, he is to-day the pariah of the world. The Red Indian in his midnight attacks on the homes of the white man and his massacring of innocent women and children has his counterpart in the 20th century Hun who glories in the dastardly work of killing, by land and sea, defenceless humanity." He said that brutality and criminality characterized the German race and that Germans could no more change their character than the leopard could change its spots. In a scathing indictment of the German Empire, James claimed that, to attain peace, Britain must annihilate Germany, plough their land with salt, and force them to stay confined within their borders, unable to trade or conduct business with the rest of the world. James also said that Britain was fighting the German people as much as it was their government because German culture only appreciated ruthlessness. He believed that German conduct during the war showed that every German citizen was devoid of any positive characteristics.[11]

C.T. James' tirade against the German people shows how radical wartime alterations to ethnicity were. Germans were generally seen as educated, cultured, clean, and efficient before the war. By 1917, atrocity stories in newspapers transformed German stereotypes into savageness, treachery, and cruelty. Furthermore, James drew on contemporary racist stereotypes of Indigenous people to cement his point.

SPY MANIA

As a result of the demonization of all things German, Newfoundland found itself in the depths of "spy mania" by the winter of 1914. Given Newfoundland's proximity to Canada and the United States, its sparse population, and isolated coastlines, many government officials believed that Germany might use the coast of Newfoundland or Labrador as a U-Boat base for attacks against allied shipping. At the beginning of the war, the British and Newfoundland governments assumed that if U-Boats were to operate off the coast of North America, then they would need a safe harbour to refuel, resupply, and re-arm. Many believed that Germany would send spies to Newfoundland to establish clandestine supply bases or operate resupply ships that would allow them to attack British, Canadian, and American shipping.[12]

Consequentially, many citizens became suspicious of any German or Austro-Hungarian people living in the dominion. The *Mail and Advocate* made one of the first public accusations of espionage against a German living in Newfoundland. In July of 1914, Robert von Stein, a mechanical engineer with the Newfoundland Railway, died. Immediately following his death, the people of St John's celebrated Von Stein as a popular figure. His obituary described him as a "prominent and popular citizen" of St John's who enjoyed fishing, hunting, and curling. It declared that denizens would remember him for his cheery voice.[13]

Despite the high esteem with which St John's remembered Robert von Stein, shortly after the war started, a front-page article in the *Mail and Advocate* accused him of being a German spy. It alleged that Von Stein infiltrated Newfoundland society and earned its confidence to obtain sensitive information and relay it back to Germany. It claimed that documents found after Von Stein's death proved he had visited many coastal and inland locations, including the Bell Island Mines, and sent maps and information about them to the Kaiser. Finally, the article suggested that Von Stein had two sons in the German army fighting against Britain.[14]

In response to this article, Von Stein's sister-in-law wrote a letter to the editor. She refuted the claims that he was a spy and was adamant that there was not a single piece of evidence that would connect Mr Von Stein with Kaiser Wilhelm. She told the editor that she went through Von Stein's belongings after his death, and there was not a shred of paperwork that suggested he was a spy. Furthermore, she said that the most insulting accusation was that Von Stein's sons were fighting for Germany. She informed the editor that Von Stein had six sons: two were in the United States, one in Canada, two in St John's, and one in Botwood. His son in Botwood was the only one of military age and was in the process of enlisting to fight with the Newfoundland Regiment.[15]

The claim that Robert Von Stein was spying for Germany in St John's was outlandish, and there is no evidence that he was working as a spy. Why someone would go through the trouble of accusing the deceased Von Stein of being a spy remains unclear. What is clear, however, is that the accusation against Von Stein sent a message to all Newfoundlanders that they needed to be vigilant because any Newfoundlander of German origin was a potential spy.

The next person to face public accusations of espionage was a man named Otto Rusch. Rusch immigrated to Newfoundland in 1896 and married a woman from the dominion. In October of 1914, an editorial in the *Evening Telegram* claimed that Rusch had come to Newfoundland at the invitation of Mr Von Stein and worked as a gardener and chicken farmer. W.F. Lloyd, the editor of the *Evening Telegram*, suggested that Rusch served in the German military before arriving in Newfoundland and accused him of telling people that he wished he was back in the German army, fighting the British Empire in the trenches. Lloyd demanded to know why the constabulary had not arrested Rusch. In response to this article, A.H. Salter wrote a letter to the editor of the *Daily News*, titled "Germans in Our Midst." He was outraged that Germans were still at large. He implored the government to round up all Germans in Newfoundland and put them behind bars.[16]

While the editor of the *Evening Telegram* and A.H. Salter agreed that the police should arrest all Germans in Newfoundland, the *Daily News* disagreed. While it admitted that the government should prevent Germans from leaving the island, it did not believe that they should intern them. Instead, it said that the court should grant all Germans bail and allow them to remain at large if they presented no security risk, on the condition of good behaviour. The *Daily News* reasoned that the British Empire should treat German citizens well because many British people were living in Germany. It said that if the British Empire wanted Germany to treat British citizens well, then they should treat German citizens well.[17]

By 1915, the tension between Germany and the United States over the transportation of ammunition and foodstuffs from the US to

Britain had exacerbated concerns that German U-Boats could visit Newfoundland waters. Things became worse in July of 1915 when Governor Walter Davidson received a secret document from Cecil Spring-Rice, the British Ambassador to Washington. This report warned that Germany planned to land soldiers and set up a U-Boat supply base on the sparsely populated North-West coast at either Pigeonnier Arm, Forchette Bay, Robineau Cove or Groais Islands. In response, the Home Defence Committee (HDC) sent a detachment of forty-three armed soldiers to defend these locations. Though no German soldiers ever materialized, many citizens were convinced that it was only a matter of time before Newfoundland was infiltrated by spies.[18]

The next group of Germans accused of spying were the Moravian missionaries in Labrador. The Moravian missions had been part of the landscape of Labrador since 1771 when Jens Haven founded a station in Nain. In the 143 years since the Moravians first came to Newfoundland, the predominately German missionaries had established eight missions (Nain, Okak, Hopedale, Hebron, Zoar, Ramah, Makkovik, and Kilinek) on the incredibly sparsely populated coast of Labrador. In the minds of many Newfoundlanders, they also established a reputation as a group of selfless Christians doing God's work converting the Inuit to Christianity. Despite their reputation, the Moravian's German heritage and their presence on any isolated coast fuelled worries that they might use the missions to supply U-Boats for attacks in the Gulf of St Lawrence.

While the *Daily News*, was initially against the detention of all German civilians living in Newfoundland, the threat of U-Boat attacks changed the editor's mind. In July 1915, the *Daily News* called on the government to protect North American trade routes by placing all German nationals in internment camps. In particular, he recommended that the government investigate Moravian missionaries living in Labrador, as he believed they were using the mission to extend German influence in North America. He claimed that the Moravians were very wealthy, "trained in German methods," and capable of inflicting great harm.[19]

Several days after this article appeared in the *Daily News*, Reverend Frank Smart, of Heart's Content, replied to the editor. He acknowledged that the Moravian missions posed a potential threat to the region and asked if the government was watching them. Smart gave two reasons why he believed the Moravians should be under surveillance. First, he drew on wartime conceptions of German ethnicity and suggested that the Moravians were Germans first and missionaries second. They could not avoid their German deviousness. Second, he believed that Germany was using its missionary work to spread German influence around the world. He said it was probable that missionaries in Labrador would pose as Norwegian whalers and rendezvous with German agents to supply U-Boats.[20]

The *Mail and Advocate* also expressed concern over the Moravians. The editor said that at one time, people believed that Germans living abroad had wanted to escape Hohenzollernism and had honestly sworn allegiance to their new countries. He argued that this belief was a delusion and that "[Germans] have evidently been sent across the sea to promote a Germanising propaganda to weaken the principles of democracy, to wreck the foundations of human liberty, and to destroy the fundaments of Christianity." He proposed that the Moravians were exerting German influence over the Inuit, teaching them the German language and turning them into spies for the German Empire.[21]

The deep suspicion of Moravian missionaries in Labrador was not limited to newspapers. In June of 1915, the Deputy Head of Agriculture and Mines, J.P. Turner, sent a letter to Captain Abraham, the intelligence officer for Newfoundland, detailing his concerns about German missionaries living on the coast of Labrador. Turner informed Abraham that he had received information that German missionaries were indoctrinating the local Inuit with pro-German propaganda, and the Inuit had split themselves into pro and anti-German factions. He also expressed concern that the Moravians could be training the Inuit to work as German agents to resupply U-Boats on the coast of Labrador.[22]

The shift in perception of Moravians in the dominion is robust evidence of changing conceptions of ethnicity. For hundreds of years, many people saw the Moravians as a benevolent group doing god's work in Labrador. Shortly after the war started, however, many citizens no longer saw the Moravians as a source of good but a subversive threat to the rest of the dominion.

In addition to reports of Moravian missionaries, the government received many reports of suspected German and Austro-Hungarian spies living in Newfoundland. One of the prime targets of these accusations was Richard Warschauer. Warschauer was born in Germany and came to Newfoundland in 1914. He worked as a representative of German Rosenstern and Company for whom he purchased and exported canned lobster. His affluent lifestyle and frequent communications with other German nationals drew the suspicion of citizens and the government, who believed his work as a lobster merchant was a cover for his spy operations.[23]

Many citizens also complained about Franz Luttge. Luttge was of German heritage but was born in Manitoba and was, therefore, a British citizen. His neighbours were highly suspicious of him because he lived near a wireless station in Placentia. Many of his neighbours believed he moved to Placentia so he could spy on the station. Luttge found himself in additional trouble after he enlisted with the Newfoundland Regiment and told the recruiters that his surname was Smith. When his fellow troops discovered that his real name was Luttge, they complained to their chain of command that "British born subjects could fight England's battles without the aid of a German bastard."[24]

The government also received many complaints about an Austro-Hungarian man named Richard Korner. Korner was born in Budapest in 1891 and worked there as a farmer. From 1910–11, he completed twelve months of compulsory military training in the Austro-Hungarian army. Fearing conscription, Korner left Budapest in 1912 for the United States. Not happy with this life in the US, he decided to move to Newfoundland after seeing an advertisement for the dominion. After arriving in 1913, he purchased a parcel of land on Major's Path and established a fox farm with his wife. Korner initially came to the attention of authorities after Richard Warschauer provided his name to the Newfoundland constabulary while complaining that he was under investigation while other enemy aliens were not. In addition to this, Korner's Austro-Hungarian birth and his former military service resulted in citizens submitting "constant stories" to the government.[25]

TREATMENT OF GERMAN CIVILIANS

Following the British declaration of war against Germany, the justice department labelled German and Austro-Hungarians "enemy aliens," and the Newfoundland constabulary subjected them to suspicion, investigation, surveillance, and arrest. One of the first measures taken against Germans living in Newfoundland was rigorous postal censorship. In September 1914, H.J.B. Woods, the Postmaster-General, banned the sending and receiving of letters to and from Germany, prohibiting

German Newfoundlanders from sending mail to their families. Additionally, any mail coming to Germans in Newfoundland was subject to inspection and censorship. In particular, government officials were worried that Richard Warschauer was a spy, and his letters to his employer were coded messages for the German government.[26]

Starting in October of 1914, the justice department arrested Germans and Austro-Hungarians for a variety of reasons. The detention of Germans began when the secretary of state for the colonies, Lewis Harcourt, told Governor Davidson that German seaman should not remain aboard neutral vessels in British ports. Harcourt was worried that these civilians could pass along information to the German government, who could use it to attack sensitive British ports. As a result, every time a neutral vessel entered a Newfoundland port, the constabulary would arrest any Germans working onboard the ship. The first person arrested was John Echurafonde. Echurafonde lived in Kiel and was working aboard a Norwegian vessel that was bringing a load of salt to Herring Neck. When his ship landed, a constable arrested him and brought him to St John's. Similarly, the constabulary arrested F.G. Lamjack on 21 October after the boat he was working on landed on the Burin peninsula to pick up a load of fish. The constabulary arrested four more German sailors: Otto Rusch, Tobias Feuerpach, Wilhelm Lembeck, and an unnamed man from Kelligrews on 26 October in Harbour Grace.[27]

Eager to weed out any more potential spies, Governor Davidson ordered Richard Squires to create a list of all "aliens" living in Newfoundland to determine who should be treated as an enemy. He instructed Squires to include anybody of foreign heritage, whether or not they were a British subject, to inquire about their education, their financial situation, and their whereabouts. Davidson believed that this list would ensure that the Newfoundland government could keep track of anyone who might be a danger to the dominion.[28]

After Richard Squires compiled the list of enemy aliens, the constabulary arrested every German of military age in the dominion. By early 1915, the constabulary had arrested sixteen Germans and Austro-Hungarians including Richard Warschauer, Wilhelm Markwardt, Richard Frohner, Klaus Heskjer, Emil Freund, Carl Rebers, Frederick Bernhart, Otto Rusch, Tobias Feuerback, Thomas Lehrer, Carl Muss, Wilhelm Lembeck, Walther Kann, Karl Jost, and Johann Drexler. All of these men, except three, were German civilians and were working as firemen or sailors. The Newfoundland constabulary arrested them off their ships. Richard Warschauer, Peter Kercher, and Otto Rusch, on the other hand, were naturalized British subjects and were detained by the constabulary after public accusations that they were spies.[29]

After the constabulary arrested these men, interning them became quite an issue. Initially, Her Majesty's Penitentiary (HMP) in St John's housed the majority of these men, but this was a source of controversy. When Governor Davidson visited these prisoners, he got the impression that they were harmless young men who were pleased that they did not have to fight in the war. Davidson wrote in his diary that he regretted having to lock them up in prison indefinitely. Many of them complained that they did not have enough space or time to exercise as they were not allowed outside prison walls, and most of their exercise came from walking the length of the halls at HMP. The prisoner's most serious complaint was that they were denied fundamental rights under Newfoundland law: they had committed no crime, were given no trial, and were housed with convicted criminals.[30]

The prisoners also complained about the quality and quantity of food, clothing, and medical treatment that HMP provided them. After Davidson ordered Richard Squires to investigate the meals served to these POWs, Squires informed him that prisoners received two meals a day: breakfast always consisted of tea, porridge, molasses, and biscuits. On Monday, Wednesday, and Friday, their second meal consisted of fish, potatoes, and biscuits; Tuesday, Thursday, and Saturday, it comprised rice soup with meat and biscuits. On Sundays, they had pea soup. This was the same diet provided for criminals serving long sentences. Following his investigation of the living conditions for POWs at HMP, Davidson found that their rations were "unpalatable and insufficient." He agreed with the prisoners' complaints and ordered the justice department to move them to other prisons across the island.[31]

The constabulary relocated the POWs following Davidson's order and sent them to small facilities in Harbour Grace, Placentia, and Curling. Most of the prisoners who moved from St John's to rural Newfoundland found their new conditions to be far superior. In these rural communities, they had more room, were seldom housed with criminals, allowed to take walks around the town without a guard supervising them, and were allowed to keep hobbies such as gardening and woodworking.[32]

In addition to better living conditions, the quality and quantity of food also increased in rural prisons. In Harbour Grace, POWs' diets comprised bread, butter, fish, potatoes, beans, corned and fresh beef, pickles, biscuits, and the occasional pudding. Prisoners in Curling were fed homemade bread, butter, eggs, pork, salt beef and fresh beef, potatoes, herring, fresh and salted fish, cabbage, beans, rice, pea soup, and tea.

Despite the improvement in food quality, some prisoners still found the food to be insufficient and of poor quality. In 1916, Tobias Feuerbach made a claim against the Newfoundland government seeking compensation for money he said he had to spend on food. He claimed that the meals provided to him were not sufficient. In a subsequent investigation, J.M. Bartlett, District Inspector for Curling, informed Squires that the only food Feuerbach purchased were cigarettes, tobacco, fancy biscuits, fruit, and confectionery. Furthermore, he stated that after prisoners were moved from HMP, there was only one complaint about food: that it was too sweet. Another prisoner, a British subject named Peter Kercher, made recommendations that would make the food more palatable for the prisoners and was allowed to assist the prison cooks in preparing their meals.[33]

Despite the improvement in living conditions through the move to rural prisons, the justice department eventually came to believe it was dangerous to disperse "enemy aliens" across the island and felt that Newfoundland was not prepared to house POWs for the duration of the war. The first step in finding permanent housing was to move all the prisoners to a central POW camp. To do this, the Newfoundland constabulary built a makeshift prison camp at the end of Topsail Road on the site of what is now Donovan's Industrial Park. At Donovan's, eight guards armed with rifles and bayonets monitored them, and a staff of four people looked after their needs.[34]

The government only intended for Donovan's to be a temporary measure. In July and August of 1915, the Home Defence Committee (HDC) began to look for a better solution for Newfoundland's POWs. Initially, the HDC thought that Britain could intern these POWs. This plan fell through because the HDC could not find a ship to transport the prisoners across the Atlantic. Instead, it set its eyes on Canada. On 29 July 1915, Governor Davidson wrote to the Duke of Connaught and Strathearn, the governor-general of Canada, and inquired if the Canadian government could intern the dominion's POWs at a camp in Amherst, Nova Scotia, at the expense of the Newfoundland government.[35]

In late October of 1915, the Newfoundland government struck a deal with the Canadian government. Newfoundland would send its POWs on the *Corsican* to North Sydney. From there, the Canadian government would transport them by rail to camps in Beauport, Québec, and Amherst, Nova Scotia, where Canadian authorities would intern them. Ten days after this agreement was struck, the Newfoundland government sent twenty-five Germans and Austro-Hungarians on board the *Corsican*, under the guard of the Newfoundland Regiment. The justice department attempted to arrange for the wives of POWs who were residing in Newfoundland to travel to Québec with their husbands. Despite their efforts, Canadian officials advised that they were not able to take female prisoners. When the *Corsican* sailed on 30 October, it had twenty-five prisoners onboard. The constabulary forced the wives of Richard Warschauer, John Pleninger, and Richard Korner to remain in Newfoundland.[36]

The government did not send Otto Rusch and Peter Kercher to Canada. Peter Kercher was born in Germany but became an American citizen in 1907 before he moved to Newfoundland. Shortly before the war started, Kercher received his naturalization papers and became a British subject. In 1914, Kercher was working as the chief engineer on the *Florizel* and was married to a Newfoundlander. When the public learned that there was a German working on the *Florizel*, they demanded that the Bowring Brothers fire him immediately. The Bowring Brothers caved to public pressure and dismissed Kercher solely on the basis that he was German. Writing in his diary, Governor Davidson noted that Kercher had "no hostile intent" but "had to lose his job all the same, through the force of public opinion."[37]

When the rest of the POWs at Donovan's left for Canada, authorities decided that Kercher was no threat to the British Empire. The guards at the camp described him as being of "most exemplary character" and pointed out that he had been a great help in preparing food and in the maintenance of discipline and order in the camp. The justice department agreed to release Kercher if he left Newfoundland for New York, paid a $4,000 bond, agreed not to return, and checked in every two weeks with the British Consular Agent in New York. It also seized Kercher's naturalization papers and refused to return them until the war was over.[38]

After the government exiled Kercher to New York, J.R. Bennett (a People's Party MHA for St John's West, and the minister of the newly formed militia department) decided to seize Kercher's Escasoni estate in St John's for use as a sanatorium for soldiers. There were discussions within the department of militia about paying Kercher for his property. Bennett advised against this because he was worried it could be considered "trading with the enemy." Nonetheless, Bennett seized Kercher's land for the sanatorium. It was not until 1921 that Newfoundland government agreed purchase the estate and paid Kercher's wife $280 for the use of Escasoni by militia department.[39]

Another German national who escaped the POW camps in Canada was Ernst Koch. Koch was born in Hamburg, immigrated to Newfoundland in 1893, and set up a tailor shop in St John's. When the war broke out, the HDC determine that he was not a risk to the dominion, and he was allowed to remain at large, under strict surveillance. Despite his "freedom," Koch found that being German in wartime Newfoundland was wearisome, and he faced constant harassment and threats of violence. By September of 1915, social ostracism, the loss of his friends, and the failure of his business caused Koch to become depressed, and he began drinking heavily. He believed that the only solution to his problem was to turn himself into the constabulary for voluntary internment. He wrote a letter to Inspector Sullivan of the Newfoundland constabulary that read:

> I have, with great patience, withstood many insults and often had to transverse long byways and lanes to escape the jeers of the ignorant of our community, and had also to travel on the street cars, then under normal circumstances, my pocket money would allow me to do.
>
> I also had to abandon the friendship of some of my earlier companions, who have tried to define my thoughts about the present conflict and have often miscontructed my honest expressions about the same and have twisted many of my sentences. Such friends? I have long discarded.
>
> At times when alone I feel that the strain on my mind cannot stand much longer, in fact, I have not been jolly for a long time either at home or abroad. Moreover, I have been taking more liquor than was my usual custom and at such times would have retaliated to my tormentors if they had been present.

> I shall not commit to paper all that transpired, but however, shall give you full explanation when sometime in the near future I shall request an audience from you and in all probability shall make arrangements for my internment.[40]

While life for Germans and Austro-Hungarians who remained in Newfoundland was difficult, many POWs found their experience to be much worse in the Canadian POW camps. The American Consul (who was looking after their welfare on behalf of the German government) received many complaints that the prisoners received much worse treatment than they had in St John's. After hearing about the conditions of her husband's internment in Canada, Richard Warschauer's wife, a British subject, described these camps as the "British atrocity in Amherst."[41]

After a short time in a Canadian POW camp, Richard Korner requested that the Canadian government release him and allow him to settle on a small farm in Québec. The Canadians could not process his request because Squires did not provide any information detailing why the constabulary arrested Korner in the first place. Without this information, Canada was unable to determine if Korner was a legitimate threat to Canada and felt they had no other choice but to intern Korner indefinitely. Major General W.D. Otter, the officer responsible for internment operations, pressed Squires for information about Korner's arrest. Squires replied that Korner was not arrested for any particular reason, other than a desire to rid the dominion of Austro-Hungarians. Unsatisfied with Squires's response, W.D. Otter refused Korner's request for release, and he remained in an internment camp.[42]

After the Canadian government denied Korner's request for release, he wrote several letters to Squires requesting that the justice department allow his wife to leave Newfoundland so she could travel to Nova Scotia to be with him. In one letter, Korner reminded Squires that the HDC promised to intern married POWs with their wives. Korner informed Squires that the Canadian government would allow his wife to live near the camp but would not provide support for her. He requested that the Newfoundland government pay for her transportation to Nova Scotia and her living expenses as it was doing in St John's. He told Squires, "I am sure it is not your intention to keep me interned apart from my wife over a thousand miles away in a different country." Squires agreed to pay for Mrs Korner's transportation but informed Korner that the remuneration for her cost of living would cease as soon as she left the island.[43]

After Squires denied Korner's request for support for his wife in Canada, Korner, growing desperately homesick, requested to return to Newfoundland. Squires informed him that if he returned to Newfoundland during the war, then the constabulary would arrest him and intern him in HMP with regular criminals. Korner was indignant that Squires would refuse to allow him to return home and that Newfoundland government would treat him as a criminal if he did so. He told Squires: "But why treat me like a criminal, not to be allowed to see my wife often as only once a month … I expect I could be treated as much as that German [Otto Rusch] who is still at large and even after 20 years residence didn't find it worthwhile to apply for his citizenship papers or the other German [Peter Kercher] he was allowed to go to New York. My main question which I beg to get an answer to is: why does your Hon. Government favour Germans and I as a Hungarian was even not given a chance to prove that I am not an enemy of your country. Sir even a murderer is given a trial and the right to defend himself."[44] In a letter to a friend, Korner explained how he missed Newfoundland: "I can't help it, but I am getting homesick. I guess it is no wonder if you are used to good and nice Nfld having there everything what is dear to me. I certainly get treated very well, but never mind how fair the treatment is there is nothing like the place like home." Despite Korner's petition to return home, Squires denied his request. The Canadian government released him in 1916, and he wrote for his wife to settle all business in Newfoundland and travel to meet him immediately.[45]

In addition to the POWs, the Newfoundland government had to decide what to do with the Moravian missionaries. Believing that they posed a dangerous threat, the HDC searched for a plan. Initially, the committee had decided to close all Moravian missions in Labrador and deport all missionaries to POW camps in Britain. Despite the HDC's desire to deport them, Governor Davidson was wary of closing down a mission that he believed benefitted the people of Labrador for nearly 150 years. Instead, Davidson suggested that all missionaries travel to St John's, where he would interview them and make them swear an oath of loyalty to the King. If the governor found them to be harmless and they agreed to swear an oath, then he would permit them to return to Labrador with several police officers to supervise their work. The Home Defence Committee believed that it was unnecessary for the missionaries to travel to St John's. Instead, it arranged for a justice of the peace travel to the Missions, take their oaths, arrest anyone who refused to sign and remain there to supervise the missionaries until the shipping season closed.[46]

The treatment of Germans in Newfoundland was the physical manifestation of wartime alterations to ethnicity and changes to the liberal order. A prime characteristic of classical liberalism is the equality of all individuals under the law. During the war, this was cast aside in favour of collectivist values, which prioritized the supposed safety of the community over the rights of the individual. In a highly misguided attempt at making the community safer, the government violated the rights of Newfoundlanders of German and Austro-Hungarian descent, some of whom were British subjects. They were arrested without warrant; some had their property seized, separated from their families and deported from their homes.

ALLIES AND NEUTRALS – GERMANS ALL

After Newfoundland dealt with the Germans and Austro-Hungarians living in Newfoundland, it turned its attention to others it believed might be spying for Germany. Throughout the war, there were dozens of newspaper articles claiming that thousands of Belgian, Swiss, Norwegian, and English-speaking spies had infiltrated every section of the British Empire.[47] Like other parts of the British Empire, Newfoundland was thrust into what Walter Davidson described as "spy mania." During this time, Newfoundlanders became suspicious of anyone who was not born on the island. Citizens across the dominion deluged the Home Defence Committee with letters about potential spies who came from neutral and allied nations. While Germans and Austro-Hungarians came from belligerent nations, residents who came from Allied or neutral countries were persecuted by those born in Newfoundland because many people believed their different language or culture made them "suspicious." This was a not-so-subtle way of telling those who were not born in Newfoundland that they did not belong in the dominion.[48]

Many of these reports stemmed from someone speaking a language other than English, which was often confused for German. During the war, a well-known Italian businessman named Antonio Nardini ran a sawmill and a dry goods store in Stephenville Crossing. His son had enlisted with the Newfoundland Regiment. In September of 1914, an overzealous Constable mistook Nardini's native Italian for German and arrested him for being a spy. It was only the insistence of a local customs officer, who knew Nardini well, that convinced the constable to release Mr Nardini. The incident amused the editor of the *Mail and Advocate* who noted that Nardini "neither looks nor speaks like a German."[49]

In 1915, two detectives with the constabulary began monitoring a soldier in the Newfoundland Regiment they believed was a German spy. Despite training with the regiment, the detectives were convinced the soldier was working for the German military. On the evening of 23 February 1915, Detectives Byrne and Tobin arrested Dominic Foley as an enemy spy. Under interrogation, Foley denied being German and explained to the detectives that he was born in Moscow. Not convinced by his story, the detectives held Foley for several more days. It is not clear what happened with their investigation, but the detectives eventually released Foley, who resumed serving with the Newfoundland Regiment. He died during the Battle of Langemarck in 1917.[50]

The Newfoundland constabulary did not limit its investigations to residents who spoke foreign languages. In 1915, James Hansen, a Scottish man, arrived from New York to purchase furs in Labrador. Shortly after arriving, he bought a motorboat and provisions at Battle Harbour and set out for Nain. Despite his honest intentions and British citizenship, someone made an anonymous report to the constabulary that Hansen was a German spy. The Newfoundland constabulary sent the steamer *Jennie Foote to* intercept Hansen on his way to Nain and force him to return to Battle Harbour. Upon his return, J.T. Croucher, justice of the peace, held Hansen until a constable arrived the next day, arrested him for being a German spy and took him back to St John's. After a lengthy interrogation, Hansen admitted that he had family living in Germany, and the constabulary deported him.[51]

Angered at the treatment he received in Newfoundland, James Hansen wrote a lengthy letter to the editor of the *Mail and Advocate* after he returned to New York. He explained the details of his trip and said that he was under the impression that British subjects were free to travel throughout the British Empire without carrying a passport. Furthermore, he pointed out that the family member of his living in Germany was his brother, who was interned in a German POW camp. In concluding his letter, Hansen expressed his outrage that the Newfoundland constabulary would accuse a British subject of espionage and deport him without a scrap of evidence.[52]

Another infamous instance of the harassment of a non-native resident of Newfoundland was the case of Rockwell Kent. Kent was a famous American painter who moved to Brigus in February of 1914. In the relatively short time after Kent arrived in Newfoundland, he found himself at odds with a pharmacist from Brigus. After the two men got into a heated argument over the local tennis club, Kent threatened to kill the pharmacist. The local magistrate held a trial and found Kent guilty of assault and issued him a fine.

In addition to his conviction for assault, Kent came under suspicion from other residents of Brigus who doubted the motives of an American painter, with a knowledge of German language and culture, who sang German songs, for taking up residence in Brigus. They were convinced he was a spy and reported their suspicions to the Newfoundland constabulary. As a result of these accusations, the constabulary launched an investigation of Kent and interviewed him on several occasions. During one of these interviews, Kent admitted to Sergeant Byrne that he was sympathetic towards the German cause. Byrne told Kent that the local authorities in Brigus would closely monitor him, and if he continued to express sympathies with Britain's enemies, then he would be arrested.[53]

Outraged at what he considered to be a violation of his right to free speech, Kent complained to the American Consul in Newfoundland, J.S. Benedict. He requested protection from unlawful arrest and unnecessary investigation. Benedict subsequently wrote to Prime Minister Morris, who guaranteed that the Newfoundland constabulary would no longer harass Kent. Despite these assurances, Kent was the subject of a second investigation, this time by Inspector Sullivan, after the constabulary received more reports that Kent was expressing sympathy for Germany. Kent again complained to Benedict that Morris had not kept his word. This time Benedict informed Kent that he should follow President Wilson's advice and abstain from making comments about the war. Furthermore, Benedict told Kent that, in his opinion, it was understandable that a foreigner praising their enemies would enrage the residents of any country.[54]

Following an encounter with a local magistrate in Brigus, the Newfoundland constabulary started the third investigation of Kent. In November of 1914, Kent was preparing to send one of his paintings back to the United States. Kent required a form with an officially witnessed signature to send it to the US. When Kent approached the magistrate to request his signature, the judge was suspicious of his parcel and demanded that Kent unwrap the painting and show it to him. When Kent refused, the magistrate declared that he was "almost beyond doubt in the service of Germany." Following this third round of questioning by the police, Kent again complained to Benedict that the Magistrate's unwarranted suspicion and the subsequent ham-fisted investigation had infringed on his privacy and had further convinced everyone in Brigus that he was a German spy.[55]

Frustrated at the constant accusation of spying, Kent endeavoured to make himself as offensive as possible to the people of Brigus. He hung a sign over the door of his workshop that read "CHART ROOM, WIRELESS STATION, BOMB SHOP" and had a painting of the German eagle. In another incident, Kent was travelling through Harbour Grace in a horse-drawn cart when he passed a group of POWs. Kent stood up in the wagon and shouted in German: "the Kaiser is winning, you will be out soon," to which the prisoners supposedly cheered.[56]

Kent's outlandish behaviour concerned the Newfoundland constabulary. In December 1914, Governor Davidson asked both the American consul in St John's and the justice minister to investigate Rockwell Kent. This investigation concluded that Kent's open disrespect and disdain for the people of Brigus, his flagrant displays of his sympathy for Germany, his love of German culture, and his attempts to anger the residents of Brigus proved that he was not a spy. They reasoned that no spy would draw such extreme attention to himself. Furthermore, Squires informed the colonial secretary that the government could not protect Kent from the ire of Brigus if he continued to antagonize them.[57]

The final straw in the case of Rockwell Kent came in the form of an article, written by Kent, titled "From a British Wilderness," and published in the American *New Republic* on 22 May 1915. In this article, Kent lamented being a lonely American in a "dismal little British colony." Kent expressed his distaste for Newfoundland, saying: "The thought of the land is stupefied by dogma – the dogma of British virtue, British heroism, sea power, loyalty – all that pile of trash that seems to be a part of the pretension of empire." He expressed his disgust for Governor Davidson's demonization of Germans. Perhaps the most inflammatory part of this article came in the conclusion when Kent wondered if *New Republic* readers in Germany were praying for their country to "come, capture, transform, [and] annihilate" Newfoundland.[58]

For Governor Davidson, this article was the last straw; he believed that there was "ample evidence officially on record that he is hostile in intention." The justice department ordered Kent to leave the colony immediately. In August 1915, Kent and his family boarded a steamer bound for New York. Inspector John Byrne, cigar in mouth, met Kent at the docks. Upon seeing Byrne, Kent asked, "So you have come down to see me off?" "Yes, [we had] to make sure you really left," replied Byrne. Kent's final words to Byrne expressed his extreme frustration with Newfoundland: "Fair enough ... I hope it was a lot of trouble. I hope your cigar is a bad one. I hope it burns your nose. I hope you slip on the gangplank and fall in the water. I hope the Germans blow up your damned country." With that, the alleged German spy left Newfoundland.[59]

While Rockwell Kent drew a great deal of attention from the police, there was another individual who attracted even more suspicion: the Norwegian millionaire Christoffer Hannevig. Before he arrived in Newfoundland, Hannevig had built a large shipping company with branches in Norway, England, the United States, and Argentina. Hannevig arrived in Newfoundland in June of 1917, after sailing his yacht, the *Adriane*, from Halifax. Following his arrival, Hannevig purchased a tract of land in Harbour Grace and told authorities that he was starting a shipbuilding operation to supply ships to the United States government.[60]

For reasons that are not entirely clear, the Newfoundland government became suspicious of Hannevig immediately after his arrival. After Hannevig established his business in Harbour Grace, he intended to leave the operations in the hands of his Norwegian employees and return to Trondheim. When the Captain of the *Adriane* requested to depart Newfoundland, G.H.F Abraham telegraphed the British Ambassador in Washington, asking him to verify that Hannevig was indeed building ships for the American government. He also told the Ambassador that the *Adriane* would not be allowed to leave Newfoundland until he received confirmation of Hannevig's story. The following day the Ambassador to Washington told Abraham that the United States did not grant Hannevig a contract to build ships for the government and the US government would never make such an arrangement with a foreign national who was building ships in another country.[61]

Governor Davidson also found Hannevig extremely suspicious. In a letter to the prime minister, he explained that if U-Boats were to operate in North American waters, they would need a base to keep supplies and several small and fast vessels to meet U-Boats for a clandestine resupply. Davidson told Morris that in his opinion, Hannevig's boat-building enterprise was a thinly veiled U-Boat supply operation. He recommended the government seize all of Hannevig's ships to prevent him from leaving the dominion until the police could conduct a thorough investigation.[62]

The first investigation into Hannevig consisted of a visit to Hannevig's operation by Inspector O'Reilly of the Newfoundland constabulary and the monitoring of Hannevig's postal and telegraph communications by Captain G.H.F. Abraham, the local intelligence officer. Following this investigation, Abraham was convinced that Hannevig's business interests were legitimate and recommended that the government allow him to conduct business, including the importation of a schooner, which the Canadian government held pending the outcome of the investigation.[63]

By 1918, Hannevig's shipbuilding enterprise was well established in Harbour Grace, and he began to diversify his business and set up whaling stations, pig farms, and fish stores. He also won construction contracts and brought in mineral surveyors to examine the potential for mining operations. Even though Hannevig proved to be a successful businessman, his activities came under renewed suspicion after Charles Alexander Harris replaced Walter Davidson as governor of the dominion in 1917. Shortly after he arrived in Newfoundland, Harris asked his secretary, Lt Col Knox-Niven, to write to Britain's intelligence service, MI5, and obtain any available intelligence on Hannevig.[64]

By the end of January, Knox-Niven received a response from V.G.W. Kell, the founder of MI5. Kell told Knox-Niven that Hannevig's company had come under investigation in 1915 when MI5 received information that Hannevig was selling coal to German ships. Scotland Yard had investigated the company on MI5's behalf, and Hannevig's brother admitted they were selling coal in Archangel, Russia. He insisted they issued strict instructions that coal could neither be sold to vessels suspected of travelling to any destination where Germans could obtain supplies, nor any ship from a neutral nation that could be in service of Germany. Kell also informed Knox-Niven that Hans Hannevig had been very forthcoming with the investigations, volunteering to turn over the company's books and his correspondence. Investigators from Scotland Yard examined these documents thoroughly and found no evidence of wrongdoing. Though Kell admitted that Christoffer Hannevig's operations in Newfoundland were suspicious, he disclosed there was no evidence that Hannevig was a spy.[65]

Undeterred by the lack of evidence, many government officials believed that Hannevig was working for the Germans. In May of 1918, C.H. Hutchings received several complaints that two of Hannevig's timber and mineral surveyors were travelling across the island, taking photos of sensitive areas of the coast. Hutchings recommended that newly appointed Prime Minister Lloyd prohibit these men from taking pictures as they could use them against the British Empire. Lloyd followed Hutchings' recommendations and ordered the Newfoundland constabulary to confiscate all of their photographs and cameras. Hannevig's brother Richard complained about having their pictures taken, protesting that he had previously travelled through England and France taking similar photos and had not run into trouble there. P.J. Summers, the deputy justice minister, informed Hannevig that the justice department would eventually return his photographs, which it did, over two years later.[66]

In addition to having his photographs seized, the justice department submitted all of Hannevig's operations to very close surveillance. It placed men onboard each of Hannevig's whaling vessels to monitor their activities. Governor Harris sent the commander of HMS *Briton*, Anthony MacDermott, to further investigate Hannevig's operations in June of 1918. In a report to Harris, MacDermott stated that he believed that "the operations of the Company are in no way suspicious and they are not engaged in anything but legitimate business."[67]

The justice department and the governor were not the only people in Newfoundland who believed Hannevig was a German spy. After the government allowed Hannevig to conduct business in Newfoundland, Dr Fraser, a surgeon from St John's, made many complaints to the Newfoundland constabulary that a spy was operating in Newfoundland. When the government refused to deport or detain Hannevig, Fraser took measures into his own hands. On 1 August 1918, Fraser wrote a letter to Prime Minister Lloyd George, expressing his concerns about Hannevig and the local government's inaction. Fraser informed Lloyd George that Hannevig's operations in Newfoundland were suspicious. Hannevig rejected land in areas rich with lumber and instead chose Harbour Grace, which Fraser described as "a little half-dead settlement in Conception Bay immediately opposite Bell Island. There is not a stick of wood for miles around, no water power or anything to commend this place, except its isolation and the innocence of its inhabitants."[68]

While Hannevig himself did not reside in Newfoundland for very long during the war, his Norwegian managers oversaw his business operations and the local employees. Hannevig's Norwegian employees faced constant harassment, surveillance, and the threat of deportation from the constabulary. During the two years that Hannevig operated businesses in Newfoundland, the justice department deported four of Hannevig's Norwegian staff and their wives after they deemed his employees to be "undesirable."[69]

Although the justice department was suspicious of Hannevig and his employees, the government permitted him to operate his business ventures in Newfoundland throughout the entire war. Interestingly, the government allowed Hannevig to run a business in Newfoundland when it had also deported other residents of neutral countries such as James Hansen or Rockwell Kent. This is likely due to the financial contributions that Hannevig and his company made to the dominion. Shortly after Hannevig arrived in Newfoundland, he made a large donation of $6,000 to the local Red Cross, which earned him a great deal of respect among Newfoundlanders. In addition to this, Hannevig's various businesses became a source of employment in Newfoundland, providing the government with enough of a financial incentive to allow him to continue to conduct business in Newfoundland.[70]

SYRIANS IN NEWFOUNDLAND

Though the Newfoundland constabulary and justice department focused most of their attention on Germans and Austro-Hungarians, there was a much larger group of residents who came from a belligerent nation. In 1914, the second-largest minority group in Newfoundland were Syrians who immigrated to Newfoundland from the Ottoman Empire.

Though Newfoundlanders referred to these people as Syrians, Assyrians, Maronites, or Turks, most of them were Maronite Christians from Mount Lebanon. Syrian immigration to Newfoundland began in the mid-nineteenth century amid brutal religious conflicts between Maronite Christians and the Druze during the Mount Lebanon Civil War. The majority of Syrians who came to Newfoundland were small business owners. They quickly set up many small businesses in population centres such as the St John's and Bay of Islands districts.

As part of the British Empire's initial monitoring of enemy aliens, Lewis Harcourt, secretary of state for the colonies, directed the Newfoundland government to treat any reservists from the Ottoman Empire as it would reservists from Germany or Austria-Hungary. Furthermore, on 7 November 1914, Harcourt suggested that the Newfoundland government detain any Ottoman citizens residing in Newfoundland.[71]

In many ways, the Syrian community would have made an easy target for suspicion and hostility for Newfoundlanders and the Newfoundland government. Like Germans subjects, Ottoman subjects in Newfoundland came from a nation with which the British Empire was at war. Like Germans, English was not their first language, and they would have spoken English with an accent. One would think that their nationality and language would have resulted in suspicion, accusations of spying, and hostility just as they did for Germans and Austro-Hungarians residing in Newfoundland. This was not the case. The constabulary neither detained, monitored, nor investigated any Syrians, and there is not a shred of evidence that any civilian or government official was suspicious of them. After Richard Squires received word from Harcourt that Newfoundland must detain Ottoman citizens, Squires wrote him demanding that Syrians be removed from the list of enemy aliens because they were law-abiding, loyal, quiet, hardworking, and had generously given to the NPA.[72]

One of the reasons that the Syrian community escaped persecution during the First World War was a concerted effort on behalf of Syrian residents to become ingrained in Newfoundland society. A primary example of this was their involvement in the religious life of Newfoundland. As Maronite Christians, the Catholic Church readily accepted the Syrians as part of the Catholic community. As such, Catholic churches across Newfoundland were eager to host Maronite priests, and for years before the war, Syrian priests came from Boston and New York to provide religious services to Syrians in their native language. These visitations occurred yearly and often began with a mass at the Catholic Cathedral in St John's, followed by mass in other communities across Newfoundland. Service given by Maronite priests was popular not only among the Syrian community but those who wanted to hear a service offered in the "language of the lord." In 1913, many residents of St John's attended a church service given by Father Soaib, a Syrian priest from New Glasgow. The service was held in the "Syrian Language." One newspaper described it as "strange but beautiful."[73]

In addition to their service to the Catholic Church, the Syrian community also made a strong commitment to philanthropic work in their new home. A group of Syrians living on Bell Island founded a major charitable organization in 1910 when they created the Syrian Charitable society of St Joseph (also known as the Syrian Benevolent Society). This society, formed by Father Sapp, called on Syrians in Newfoundland to "lend a helping hand to those of their country and others who were in distress." Father Sapp told Syrians that though they sought refuge under the shield of Britain, they should reach out their hand towards the less fortunate in their new communities. The editor of the *Evening Telegram* was so impressed by the Syrian Benevolent Society that he wrote: "to know [the Syrians] is to admire them, for removed from us Northernmen in custom, manner, and dialect, when once they come amongst us, they change into exemplary citizens."[74]

The Syrian Benevolent Society wasted no time in gathering donations and holding fundraisers for its charitable work. One of its first charitable donations was an expensive bell and altar for the Catholic Cathedral in St John's. To accept this donation, Archbishop Roche travelled to Bell Island and personally thanked the Syrian Benevolent Society: "To our worthy people of the Syrian race and Maronite rite who dwell among us I must this day address a special word of congratulation. You are to-day making two beautiful and costly [presentations] to the Church, an altar and a bell. These will, for generations to come, stand forth as monuments to your faith and generosity … I am sure here in Newfoundland you will hold sacred the traditions of your Faith and Country and keep your names unsullied as good and upright citizens of your adopted country."[75]

Another notable philanthropic contribution by the Syrian Benevolent Society was a night school the organization built on Bell Island. The project was the idea of the President of the Syrian Benevolent Society, Michael Carbage, who wanted to provide a way for young men to get an education in the evening while working in the mines during the day. In addition to the night school, the Benevolent Society constructed living quarters on the floor above the school. Carbage intended to use these living quarters to house men who came to Bell Island looking for work in the mines. The Benevolent Society would allow unemployed men to live in these quarters while they were looking for a job. After twenty-four hours, if the men did not find employment, the society would pay their fare back to St John's.[76]

In addition to their charitable work, another factor that contributed to Syrian acceptance into Newfoundland society was their public displays of patriotism after the war broke out. In 1914, in response to Newfoundland's war effort, the Syrian Benevolent Association formed a separate branch, the Syrian Patriotic Fund. Kaleem Noah, a manager of a dry goods business in St John's, managed this fund. Its sole mandate was to raise money for Newfoundland's war effort. Within four months of the start of the war, the Syrian Patriotic Fund had raised nearly $400. In addition to making contributions to the Syrian Patriotic Fund, many government officials in Newfoundland recognized the generous contributions Syrians were making to the Newfoundland Patriotic Association.[77]

The financial contributions made by the Syrian community in Newfoundland were not only charitable contributions but also expressions of patriotism, which they were eager to show. When the Syrian Patriotic Fund presented W.E. Davidson with its first $100 contribution, it told the governor that the Syrians of Newfoundland were "proud to find that [Newfoundland] is taking such an active part in contributing to the upkeep of the Union Jack, which brings equal rights and justice wherever it waves."[78]

The patriotic displays of the Syrian community earned them respect among many citizens and government officials. After receiving a deputation from the Syrian Committee, Governor Davidson wrote in his diary that the Syrians, despite their reputation for "turbulence and cruelty," made excellent citizens in Newfoundland. He remarked that the success of Syrians living in Newfoundland was proof that "you can turn the most unpromising material into good citizens if you treat them well." He qualified their success by noting that many Syrians had enlisted in the Newfoundland Regiment, liberally gave to the patriotic fund, and showed great enthusiasm for British institutions.[79]

In addition to the governor, other members of the Newfoundland government showed great respect for the Syrian community. On 13 April 1915, Walter Jennings, addressed the house during a discussion on the Naturalization of Aliens Bill. He expressed his belief that Syrians were undesirable, complained that they do not keep the Sabbath, and suggested that they provide no benefit to the dominion. In response to this statement, William Higgins told the house that Syrians were devout people who kept the Sabbath, were of great benefit to Newfoundland and declared that he would not allow Jennings to sully their name in the house of assembly.[80]

By January of 1915, many Syrians were concerned about the fate of their family members in the Ottoman Empire. In February, a group of Syrians visited Governor Davidson and expressed their concern over their families in Damascus. They heard that Turkish soldiers were executing church leaders and mistreating women and village elders. As a result of this meeting, Davidson wrote a letter to Lewis Harcourt. He explained that Newfoundland had a "considerable colony" of Syrians, and they were becoming desperate for news from their home. The governor told Harcourt that the Syrians in Newfoundland were an industrious, law-abiding community who had sent many young men to enlist in the regiment. Davidson requested that Harcourt send him information on the situation in Mount Lebanon so he could ease the minds of the Syrian community with news of their kinsfolk.[81]

In one particular case, Kaleem Noah requested that J.R. Bennet help him contact his sons Sakr and Wanis, who were attending university at the Syrian Protestant College in Beirut. Noah had not heard from his sons in three months and was concerned that they had been killed. Governor Davidson agreed to look into the case, as it was forbidden for British citizens to send correspondence to the Ottoman Empire. Davidson posted a telegram to Cecil Spring-Rice and requested that he send a telegraph, which the governor would pay for personally, to the American Consul General in Beirut to inquire about Noah's sons. Later in January, Davidson received a telegram from Spring-Rice that informed him that the American Consul in Beirut had sent word through the Embassy in Rome that Sakr and Wanis were alive and well. Governor Davidson's eagerness to help the Syrian community contact their loved ones in the Ottoman Empire show just how strongly that he felt about their place in Newfoundland. His gesture of paying for Kaleem Noah's telegraph is nothing short of remarkable. Not only was he willing to help Noah contact his sons, which was forbidden by law, but he was also willing to pay for the telegraph personally.[82]

The treatment of the Syrian community by the Newfoundland government is a fascinating case in the reconstruction of citizenship during the First World War. While Newfoundlanders treated Germans, Austro-Hungarians, Americans, Russians, Italians, and Norwegians with deep suspicion and often outright hostility, the Syrian community wholly escaped persecution.

It is important to note that although the Syrian community escaped persecution during the war and became respected citizens of the dominion, they did not escape racism while living in Newfoundland. Though Governor Davidson spoke highly of Newfoundland's Syrian community, he referred to them as "unpromising material" who were improved by life in the British Empire. Similarly, while Archbishop Roche praised the Syrian community for their charitable works, he cautioned them to "keep their names unsullied."

CONCLUSION

During the First World War, Newfoundland underwent a profound renegotiation of ethnic perceptions. The complex geopolitical realities of the war meant that Newfoundlanders found themselves fighting a war against Germany, the Austro-Hungarian Empire, and the Ottoman Empire. As a result, there was a restructuring of underlying assumptions of who deserved protection from the state and from whom the state should protect citizens. As ethnic categories shifted, so did the concept of the liberal individual. Before the war, Germans, Austro-Hungarians, Norwegians, and Americans were all granted the status of individuals by the liberal state and received its protection. However, as the war caused the Newfoundlanders to demand protection from alleged German spies, these people were denied the status as liberal individuals. They were not afforded equal treatment under the law. As a result of the war, conceptions of ethnicity were altered across the British Empire. Donald Avery has shown that between 1869 and 1914, the Canadian government encouraged thousands of immigrants to come to Canada to satisfy the needs of the labour market. By the start of the war, these workers were viewed as threats to Canada's security and faced "intense Anglo-Canadian hostility."[83]

While some ethnic groups were stripped of their status as liberal individuals, the Syrian community in Newfoundland found itself not persecuted but praised and protected by the government. While this community was a visible minority, who spoke a different language, and emigrated from a belligerent nation, they faced none of the suspicions that Germans, Austro-Hungarians, or even individuals from neutral countries faced. Their commitment to charity (particularly the Syrian Patriotic Fund) and their public expressions of support for the British war effort won the hearts of the Newfoundland government. Instead of being persecuted as potential spies, they were lauded as model citizens and defended by members of the Newfoundland government.

The difference in treatment between German, Austro-Hungarian, and Syrian Newfoundlanders proves just how powerful the reconfiguration of ethnic perceptions was to the liberal state. Equality under the law was a core element of classical liberalism, and while it was never evenly applied, it was still held as a societal ideal. During the war, however, the government abandoned liberal ideals of the equality of the individual as native-born citizens of Newfoundland demanded protection from the spies they thought were lurking around every corner. Conversely, as Syrians were held as ideal citizens during the war, they received higher praise and protection from the state. In many regards, the treatment of "enemy aliens" during the war shows that the Newfoundland government was much more concerned with doing what they believed was in the best interest of the community than they were in protecting foreign-born Newfoundlanders

5

Recruiting

Following the declaration of war against Germany in 1914, the British Empire needed to quickly recruit a substantial number of troops. Before the war, the British army acted primarily as a colonial police force, fighting poorly armed and insufficiently trained opponents in British colonies. In this period, Britain's armed presence in international conflicts consisted primarily of its powerful navy while the British government provided financial support to its allies. While most European nations had established compulsory military service, Britain relied on voluntary recruitment. As a result of their compulsory military service, Germany and Austria-Hungary had active and reserve forces of 4,500,000 and 3,000,000, respectively. Comparatively, Britain's active and reserve troops only amounted to approximately 100,000. Britain's shortage of troops meant that it had to recruit a tremendous number of soldiers to keep up with the Germany army. The resulting campaign of voluntary enlistment relied on reconfiguring concepts of ethnicity and gender to portray soldiering as the pinnacle of masculinity and a duty that every male citizen owed to the state.[1]

Newfoundland's recruitment campaign was in many ways similar to Britain's. On 4 August 1914, Governor Davidson notified the people of Newfoundland that they were at war with Germany and the Austro-Hungarian Empire. The residents of Newfoundland (St John's in particular) greeted this news with great enthusiasm as thousands took to the streets singing patriotic songs. On 12 August, hundreds of people flocked to the Church Lad's Brigade (CLB) Armoury in St John's to hear Davidson's announcement that the dominion would equip, train, and send five hundred men to fight with the British Expeditionary Force.

Sixteen days after the war began, the Newfoundland Patriotic Association began recruiting in earnest. It sent letters to the magistrates in each of Newfoundland's eighteen districts requesting that each of them form local branches of the NPA, hold public meetings, and forward any names of citizens who would like to enlist. Various branches of the government put up notices in public areas, and churches across the island gave sermons that encouraged recruiting. By the end of August, the recruiting efforts of the NPA had reached every settlement on the island.[2]

The NPA's initial recruiting blitz was highly successful. By the end of September, 880 men had come forward to enlist. The NPA deemed just over 500 of these men fit for duty. After some training in at a makeshift camp near Quidi Vidi in St John's, 538 men, popularly known as "the first five-hundred" departed on the *Florizel* on 3 October. They would receive several weeks of training in the United Kingdom before they proceeded to the frontlines.

Shortly after the first five hundred left Newfoundland, the British government informed the NPA that 538 soldiers were insufficient for Newfoundland to have a distinct regiment. A standard regiment in the British army comprised 1050 soldiers. For Newfoundland to have its own regiment in the British Expeditionary Force, the NPA would have to recruit another five hundred soldiers for a second contingent.[3]

Recruiting for the second contingent began on 30 November 1914, and enthusiasm for enlistment had not waned in St John's. 179 enlisted on the first day of the recruiting drive. Despite the excitement in St John's, the NPA and the general public were concerned about recruiting rates in rural Newfoundland as the vast majority of enlistments came from the city. The editor of the *Western Star* expressed his concern in an article titled "Second Contingent: What Will the Outports Do?" In this article, the editor asked if rural citizens were willing to let St John's men get all the honours. He called on the men of rural Newfoundland to do their duty, show their patriotism, and enlist to defend their country as the men of St John's had done.[4]

Several historians have examined why enlistment rates were lower in rural Newfoundland. Some have suggested that high fish prices, poor communication between St John's and rural communities, or the overconfidence of the primarily St John's based recruiters was to blame. Chris Martin argues that the nature of household labour in rural Newfoundland meant that all family members were vital to the prosecution of the fishery and could not easily be replaced. He contends that the Newfoundland Patriotic Association failed to take this into account and enact recruiting strategies explicitly aimed at rural Newfoundlanders. Regardless of the actual reasons for rural enlistment rates, the government largely believed that men who refused to enlist were unpatriotic, unmanly, or uninformed. As a result, recruiting efforts played on Newfoundlanders' concepts of both their ethnicity as "Britishers" and their masculinity in an effort to persuade men to fulfill their "duty." Throughout the war, the recruiting campaign would reconstruct concepts of gender and ethnicity and renegotiate the relationship between male citizens and the state.[5]

"MOTHERLAND TAKES PRECEDENCE TO MOTHERS"

In *Men of War: Masculinity and the First World War in Britain*, Jessica Meyer argues that British soldiers displayed two different constructions of themselves as men. One construction focused on their roles as providers, good husbands, and fathers. The other focused on themselves as protectors, soldiers, and defenders of the nation. Before the First World War, constructions of masculinity in Newfoundland more closely resembled the former. As the war progressed, however, ideas of masculinity much more closely resembled the latter. Since the mid-nineteenth century, Britain and other parts of the British Empire, such as Canada, had begun to portray military service as an additional, important aspect of men's masculine identity. Without a permanent military presence, Newfoundlanders put less emphasis men's roles as protectors. his changed as recruiters appealed to wartime conceptions of masculinity to fill the ranks of the regiment and naval reserve.[6]

The importance placed on men's roles as protectors and defenders began with recruiters who argued that by enlisting in the NRNR or the NR men were not only defending Britain but also defending Newfoundland. The *Evening Telegram* published an early example of this argument in a letter to the editor by "The Mark." The Mark said that if Britain lost the war, Germany would seek to annex British colonies and would use Newfoundland as a naval base. They argued that life would be tough for Newfoundlanders under German rule. They said that Germany would conscript every male citizen into the army or navy for three years, force them to pay heavy taxes and strip them of their political rights. The Mark concluded their letter by challenging the masculinity of Newfoundlanders. They said that if thousands of cowards stayed home, Newfoundland's masculinity would be irreversibly damaged.[7]

One month after this letter appeared in the *Evening Telegram*, William Temple, the editor of the *Twillingate Sun*, expressed a similar opinion. On 5 February 1915, Temple lamented that few men from Twillingate had enlisted. He reminded his readers that many of the young men who refused to serve would be fathers one day. He questioned whether these men's children would one day cheer their fathers for fighting to preserve freedom, or would they groan under the oppressive heel of German soldiers, cursing the day they were born. By encouraging men to think about their children's futures, Temple reminded his readers that it was not enough for men to provide for their children – they also had a responsibility to enlist and protect the young from German aggression.[8]

In an article published in 1915, W.F. Lloyd, then editor of the *Evening Telegram,* gave more credibility to the notion that Germany desired to seize British colonies. Lloyd provided a quotation, supposedly from the German colonial minister, which stated that following a German victory, the German government would seek to increase German overseas colonies to provide Germany with increased natural resources. The editor pointed out that the Krupp company had purchased iron ore from Newfoundland before the war, and the German government knew of the mine's value. He warned the readers that Germany wanted British colonial possessions and reminded young men that they must fight until Germany was no longer a threat to the dominion.[9]

The perceived threat of Germany grew stronger in July of 1916 when the merchant U-Cruiser, U-Deutschland crossed the Atlantic and arrived in Baltimore. Before this, the British Admiralty thought the possibility of U-Boats attacks in the Atlantic was remote. This remote possibility became a reality when the heavily armed German U53 docked in New Port, Rhode Island, on 7 October 1916. The following day U53 attacked and sunk the Dutch *Blommersdijk;* the Norwegian *Christian Knutsen*; the British *Strathdene* and *West Point*; and the Newfoundland *Stephano*, owned by the Bowring Brothers. The news that a German U-Boat sunk the *Stephano* sent shockwaves through the dominion.[10]

After the sinking of the *Stephano*, the editor of the *Western Star* played on the fear of U-boats to encourage men to join the NRNR.

Barrett said that the few U-boat voyages to the United States were only a small sample of what was coming. He believed it would not be long until German U-boats were attacking Newfoundland's fishing vessels on the Grand Banks. He told his readers that Britain was building as many ships as it possibly could to regain its dominance over the seas and to protect Newfoundland. He implored his readers to sign up for the NRNR because these British vessels desperately needed crews: "Now these ships must be crewed, Newfoundlanders are amongst the best sailors of the world, and they have proven themselves to be second to none for bravery and endurance, and we believe that they are without peers in loyalty."[11]

The threat of submarine warfare constantly played on the minds of Newfoundlanders. In a dominion where the majority of the population made their living by the sea, the risk of U-Boat attacks meant that while most Newfoundlanders lived on the home front, they fished on the frontlines. On 28 November, the *Mail and Advocate* published an article calling for a total war effort to defend Newfoundland against the "submarine menace." In this article, the editor stated that U-boat attacks in Newfoundland waters were inevitable, and the dominion had to do everything it could to defend against them, including the recruitment of 2,000 more men for the NRNR and the NR.[12]

In another article in the *Daily News*, a writer from Grand Falls painted a grim picture of what would happen to Newfoundland if Britain lost the war:

> Imagine, if you can, the imperial flag of Germany floating to our hitherto free Newfoundland breezes, and remember that, were that to happen, every mother's son, and the husbands of thousands of Newfoundland women, would be compelled to serve – not invited – in the armies of Germany, and at a daily wage of six or eight cents, be sent hither or thither, at the crack of their Hunnish task masters' whip, to slay and be slain – perchance to carry death and destruction to their cousins in Canada and the United States.

Here, the *Daily News* used the threat of German conscription to encourage men to enlist. In essence, the editor told men that they had two options: voluntarily enlist with the Newfoundland Regiment or be conscripted into the German Army.[13]

Once recruiters had established that the war with Germany was not only a threat to the British Empire but a direct threat to Newfoundland, they worked hard to emphasize men's traditional masculine roles of protectors. Initially, the recruiting campaign did not wholly prioritize men's function as protectors over their function as providers. They acknowledged that men had a primary duty to support their family and a secondary duty to defend the empire. The NPA insisted that early recruiting for the regiment and reserve exclusively focus on unmarried men. This shows that in the eyes of the NPA, men had greater responsibilities to their families than they did the state.

In November 1914, the *Daily News* published an article that demonstrated this principle. The editor outlined a list of reasons why young men should enlist. These reasons included: to defend the British Empire, the cradle of freedom and the fountain of justice; to defend the rights of small nations; to defend the sacredness of treaties, which Germany violated; to destroy German militarism; to save Newfoundland from becoming a German naval station that would conscript Newfoundland men; to prevent their children from speaking German; and to defend their mothers, sisters, homes, churches, and businesses. In creating this list, the editor articulated the importance of men as defenders of not just their home but the world. Despite this, the editor maintained that not all men have a duty to fight. He argued: "Any young man who is unmarried, and without responsibility for a family's support, the call is one of duty. To others, it becomes one of conscience." In this statement, the editor of the *Daily News* made it clear that a man's primary responsibility was to provide for his family. His duty to defend the nation came second.[14]

The editor of the *Twillingate Sun* also believed that the responsibility of defending the nation fell to the single men of Newfoundland. In an article titled "What Civilization Means," William Temple declared that making sacrifices separated civilized people from barbarians. According to Temple, married men already sacrificed most of their freedom, rights, time, and money for the greater good of the community. Temple described single men as barbarians who spent all of their money on themselves and did as they pleased. He argued that St John's was far more civilized than rural Newfoundland because the single men of St John's enlisted in much higher numbers and made more considerable sacrifices. By arguing that self-sacrifice was a prime characteristic of civilized masculinity, Temple insinuated that low recruiting rates in rural areas meant that rural citizens were both less civilized and less masculine.[15]

After recruiters established a narrative that all unmarried men had a duty to defend the empire, they challenged the notion that single men had a primary responsibility to help their parents provide for their families. In February of 1916, the *Daily News* published a message from the Grand Falls branch of the NPA. It said there were hundreds of men across Newfoundland who wanted to enlist but were discouraged by their parents: "In all matters that affect the individual only, a son's first responsibility is to his parents. But when the integrity of the nation is at issue; when the lives, the safety, and the honour of women, children, and the aged are threatened; when British freedom as at stake; and when all that our fathers fought and bled for is in the balance, there is even a great duty than that of son to parent, the duty of humanity.

In this statement, the writer admitted that under normal circumstances, young men had a gendered expectation to help their parents to provide for their families. Given the unprecedented events of the war, a man's responsibility shifted from his parents to the state, and his masculine duty to protect came before his duty to provide.[16]

In the house of assembly, W.F. Lloyd expressed concern that parents were standing in the way of unmarried men enlisting. He told the house that it was only natural for mothers and fathers to want to protect their sons, keep them out of harm's way, and encourage them not to enlist. Despite this natural inclination, Lloyd warned that recruiters must surmount parents' love for their children. He said that it was the duty of the government to overcome this hurdle by teaching parents that their love of their child came second to the love of their country: "But this is an influence with which it becomes us to deal. It is the natural affection that a parent has for a son. Just the love that cannot bear to think of the son killed, maimed, and disabled for life; but paramount above this love of son is love of country, and the need is great."[17]

R.J. Devereaux, a People's Party MHA for Placentia, further emphasized the duty of parents to send their unmarried sons to the frontlines. In a speech to the house of assembly, Devereaux exalted those who gave their lives for Britain and said that they were closer to god than anyone else. He explained that parents who lost sons in the war held a special place in society. In Devereaux's mind, Newfoundland society held bereaved parents in such an esteemed position, that he was envious of parents whose sons had died fighting for the empire. Devereaux's pleas for parents to encourage their sons to enlist and his suggestion that it was an honour to lose a son was disingenuous, as he had only daughters and he knew it was highly unlikely that they would die in the war.[18]

Recruiters' focus on the recruitment of single men changed in 1917 when enlistment rates plummeted, and the department of militia struggled to fill the ranks of the Newfoundland Regiment. On 12 October 1917, J.R. Bennett published an appeal in newspapers across Newfoundland imploring men to do their duty and enlist for military service. Bennett informed the public that the government would be offering separation allowances to married men and unmarried men with dependents. The policy of separation allowances would change the gendered language of recruiting efforts in the dominion. Before this, recruiters argued that single men had to enlist so married men could stay at home and provide for their families. Now, the government was telling married men that the government would provide for their families so men could fulfil their true masculine duties, military service.[19]

Before the adoption of an official separation allowance, the NPA provided soldiers with support for their dependents on a case-by-case basis. The goal of NPA was to bring soldier's pay up to their pre-war salaries (minus the food, clothing, and rent a soldier would typically pay) by augmenting their regimental pay. For instance, if a soldier earned $10 a month before the war, sent home $5 per month to his family, and the NPA approved his application for support, then it would provide his family with an additional $2.50. This would bring the total money paid to his family to $7.50. While this sounds generous, soldiers' families criticized the NPA for rejecting many soldiers who needed assistance and not providing sufficient support for those who were approved.[20]

In one article, H.M. Mosdell, editor of the St John's *Daily Star*, implored the government to follow Canada's lead in providing separation allowances and pensions. Mosdell argued that without the government stepping in to provide for soldier's families, married men would never enlist in large numbers. In addition to the men it rejected, the NPA did not consider that rural Newfoundland relied on household labour to prosecute the fishery. While the NPA could replace the wages that a soldier would have made fishing, it could not replace the knowledge and labour that was necessary for the remainder of a soldier's family to earn a living catching and curing fish.[21]

Bennett based his separation allowance on a similar policy in Canada, which helped many married men to enlist in the Canadian Expeditionary Force. The allowance defined dependents as wives and children; motherless children; widowed mothers; and mothers who required support because their husbands could not support them. Soldiers with dependents in any of these categories would receive a monthly allowance in addition to his pay. The amount each soldier received was based on his rank and ranged from $20 to $60 a month.[22]

Despite the increased amount of money soldiers received from the separation allowance, some citizens claimed that $20 a month was not sufficient for women to support a household and would not encourage married men to enlist. In December of 1914, a frequent columnist to the *Evening Telegram*, writing under the Pseudonym "Patriot," commented on Canada's recent increase to its separation allowance from $20 to $25. To supplement the separation allowance, every Canadian soldier had to send home $15 a month to their families for a total of $40 per month. "Patriot" argued that the government had a duty to provide for families whose dependants were fighting in France. He demanded that the government treat Newfoundland soldiers as well as Canada treated its soldiers.[23]

In another article from the *Evening Telegram*, the editor pondered the reasons for Newfoundland's low enlistment rates. He proposed that the regiment's meagre rate of pay might have discouraged single men, and the insufficient separation allowance might have discouraged married men from enlisting. The editor argued that no man with dependents would join the ranks of the regiment if he thought that his family would not be taken care of after he left for France. The editor claimed that instead of imposing conscription, the Australian government decided to raise their separation allowance by 30 per cent. While the *Evening Telegram* failed to mention Australia's two plebiscites on conscription, it is clear he believed that increasing pay and separation allowances would increase enlistment rates.[24]

The separation allowance provided recruiters with a strong argument for all men, even those with dependants, to join the regiment. Recruiting advertisements published in the *Evening Telegram* informed readers that the government was willing to do everything it could to make it easier for men to enlist. All men would receive a free doctor's exam from the nearest doctor to their community. The regiment would provide free transportation for men from rural Newfoundland to the recruiting centre in St Johns. If the recruiting centre rejected them, they would be given free passage home. Finally, and most importantly, the advertisements emphasized that any men with children or parents who were dependent on them would receive an additional $20 a month on top of their regimental pay so they could support their families while they were away.[25]

Once the government offered to pay a separation allowance to married men and single men with dependants, recruiters began to target married men in their speeches, articles, and letters. In October of 1917, for example, "The Sentinel," a regular columnist for the *Evening Telegram*, called on the government to enact conscription because men were not living up to their masculine duties. Speaking directly to those who had not yet enlisted, Sentinel wrote: "and to those of you who remain at home and selfishly leave these real men to fight for your parents, your wife, your children, when you could just as easily go as not, you are not men, you are merely male inhabitants of Newfoundland."[26]

The pressure on married men to enlist peaked in April of 1918, when the department of militia attempted, one final time, to maintain the numbers of the regiment through voluntary enlistment. Shortly after Governor Charles Alexander Harris announced the final recruiting drive, he appealed to the men of rural Newfoundland. Harris told the dominion that God had allowed a nation of criminals to wreak havoc on the civilized world. He said that the people of Newfoundland had a divine responsibility to save humanity from destruction. He then reminded married men that by fighting the Germans, they would be defending their families and communities. By connecting his message of a higher, divine purpose, with the gendered expectations of men to act as protectors for their families, Harris made it clear that he expected married men to enlist.[27]

The *Daily News* directly told men that their primary responsibility was no longer to their families but to the state. John Currie acknowledged that before the war, men had an obligation to provide for their families. Despite this, he admitted the war posed such a threat to civilization that a man's primary duty was not to care for their family but to defend the state:

> Young men from 19 to 25 are rarely the arbiters of their own destinies. Thousands of our lads have been long anxious to play a man's part in the great tragedy of the centuries, but circumstances have proved too strong for their resistance. Honour thy father and mother is a commandment hoary

> with antiquity, and many of the morrow's conscripts have long and thoughtfully weighed their parent's wishes against their own. They have been volunteers in intention, if not in act. The State remained silent and the claims of the home came first. Now the State is no longer silent. Motherland takes precedence to Mothers and the voice of the people speaks more insistently than the voice of the parent.

In this article, Currie made it abundantly clear that he believed the war had fundamentally changed the relationship between citizens and the state, requiring that men put the state before their families.[28]

Recruiters in Newfoundland actively worked to reconstruct gender ideals to fit the war effort. By repeating the message that young men had a greater duty to their country than they did to their families, recruiters prioritized men's roles as protectors over their roles as providers. To facilitate this, the government offered more assistance to dependents to ensure that men's families were taken care of so they could live up to wartime conceptions of masculinity.

"YOU'D LOOK BETTER CARRYING A GUN"

In addition to shifting societal importance from men's ability to provide for their families to their ability to defend the empire, many recruiters in Newfoundland portrayed military service as the defining element of masculinity. This portrayal was a radical shift in how society constructed gender in Newfoundland. Before the war, there was little opportunity for men to serve in anything other than a quasi-military cadet corp. By the end of the war, the notion that military service was a fundamental aspect of masculinity was ubiquitous.

At the beginning of the war, recruiters used the supposed militaristic culture of Germany to show the superiority of British liberal freedom over German autocratic militarism. At a patriotic meeting in Catalina, in 1914, A.B. Morine, M.H.A. for Bonavista Bay, gave a speech on the importance of defeating German militarism. He said that Germany threatened the freedoms that British people enjoyed. He claimed that the average German citizen had no representation in their government, no free speech, and heavy taxation. The slightest criticism of soldiers or the Kaiser could result in a prison sentence. He said that German soldiers believed themselves to be superior to civilians and would publicly beat or kill any civilians who refused to acknowledge their superiority. Morine's speech represents a common theme in early war discourse that warned that militarism had corrupted German freedom and was threatening to pollute the world.[29]

In the early stages of the war, some recruiters abhorred cultural militarism. Ironically, as the war raged on, they began to argue that military service was the essence of masculinity and that soldiers were superior to civilians. In January of 1915, the editor of the *Daily News* contended that studious, industrious, and family-oriented men were rushing forward to enlist while the degenerate and criminal remained at home. The *News* believed that all true men would join, and anyone who refused was not really a man: "Unfortunately, there is a class of creatures, who masquerade as men, in all countries. They exude patriotism and are tremendously bellicose at a safe distance from the enemy, but their bravery evaporates with their beer, their fearlessness with their fags, and their loyalty with their liquor. These men do not do their duty because they are ignorant of the meaning of the word. They shout lustily 'Britons never, never, shall be slaves' and abuse their liberty at the expense of those who are maintaining it." In this article, the *Daily News* sent two messages. Firstly, Currie told his readers that those who came forward to volunteer were the very best men in the country and were worthy of praise. Secondly, he attacked the "slackers" who refused to enlist by denying their masculinity and humanity.[30]

Soldiers also spread the idea that military service was the pinnacle of masculinity. In October 1915, Cpl Hayward Hussey of Bunyan's Cove wrote a letter home to his parents. Hussey updated his mother on his situation and expressed frustration that, as an eighteen-year-old, the regiment would not allow him to serve in the frontlines because he was eager to participate in a bayonet charge. He also told his mother that more men would be needed to replace the casualties from Gallipoli. He asked her to encourage his friend Louis to join because "a man is nothing [until] he is in soldier or sailor clothes." Hussey also expressed disappointment that more men did not enlist from his community. The *Mail and Advocate* published this letter in November. Hussey's age, his enthusiasm, and his call for all true men to enlist would have provided a powerful message to the readers of the *Advocate* that society defined men by their military service and those not in uniform were less than masculine.[31]

The link between masculinity and military service became so strong that some citizens argued the state should deny basic rights to men who were not willing to perform military service. In September 1917, the *Daily News* ran an article titled "Conscientious Objectors." In this article, Currie advocated that the government should strip the citizenship of men who refuse to serve in the military and transfer their voting rights to the mothers and wives of soldiers. Describing those who refused to enlist, the editor of the *Daily News* said:

> such are unworthy not only of the rights not only of citizenship, but of citizenship itself. Their word is as valueless as a Hunnish pledge, and what more hollow than that? For such as these to be entrusted with that most sacred treasure – a freeman's vote – would be sacrilege ... it is inconceivable to a virile mind that there are in the world men who are content to allow their loved ones to become a prey to the infamies and the lusts of an unspeakable foe, rather than strike a blow for their safety and for the liberties that their sires have won. But if there are, is it reasonable that he who is unwilling to defend his motherland, and those whom he has sworn to protect, should be accorded the rights of a real man?

In the eyes of the *Daily News*, a defining element of masculinity was the responsibility to defend your family and your country. By refusing to fight, the editor was arguing that these were not real men, and they did not deserve the status and rights of an individual in a liberal democracy.[32]

Some recruiters argued that men who refused to fight were more than unmanly, they were effeminate. In an anonymous article written for the *Western Star* in October 1917, the author implored the men of Bay St George to enlist following the close of a bountiful season. He said that fishers had amply provided for the women and children of Bay St George, and men no longer had any excuse for not enlisting. He further declared that anyone who refused to join was shirking their duty. In a scathing attack on civilian men, the author wrote: "If, however, you are afraid of being killed, or of getting lost, or getting your feet wet even, why then stay right 'behind the hills' but for goodness' sake do something. Why not buy some woolen yarn and knitting needles and get your mammies to show you how to knit socks and mitts for the MEN who are at the front fighting your battles?"[33]

In 1917, when news reached Newfoundland that the British army was considering removing the Newfoundland Regiment from frontline duties, recruiting efforts that focused on the gendered expectation of military service for male citizens accelerated. In a desperate plea to the people of Newfoundland, J.R. Bennett published an appeal in every major newspaper on the island. He implored all military-aged men to "do your duty now; play the man's part, and never let it be thrown in your faces or the faces of your children, that you failed in your duty to your Country in her hour of greatest trial." Not convinced that an appeal from the government would convince men to enlist, Bennett also appealed to the parents, siblings, and spouses of military-aged men to help them realize what society expected of their gender.[34]

In response to this appeal, a columnist for the *Evening Telegram*, writing under the pseudonym "Sentinel," attacked fishers for their failure to enlist. Sentinel said that rural fishers were not living up to their masculine duties and stated that every able-bodied man who remained at home and allowed real men to do his fighting was not a man but a "male inhabitant of Newfoundland." Because the men of rural Newfoundland were failing to live up to their masculine expectations, "Sentinel" argued that the government ought to enact conscription to force men to live up to the duties of their gender.[35]

Another example of gender shaming for men who did not enlist appeared in an article in the *Evening Advocate* on 10 November 1917. This article started with the statement: "Men! Men of Newfoundland! If you are not a man, don't read this! This is for the attention of men, real men!" In this article, columnist "Avalond" discussed what he believed it meant to be a man. He said: "What is a man? Is the person who goes on day by day, week by week, month by month, in this everyday drudgery – get up in the morning – go down to work – come home to dinner – bolt back to work again – tea – nickel – bed – a man? God forbid!" This description of an unmanly life is an excellent example of the impact the war had on masculinity. Before the war, the majority of Newfoundlanders would have lived a domestic life very similar to the one described by "Avalond." During the war, however, they argued that such domestic life was not fit for a true man.[36]

Avalond continued his lesson on masculinity by asking: "Is he who can listen unstirred, unmoved, indifferently to the calls, pleadings from the brave lads – MEN! – out in the trenches, cold, dismal, shot-wrecked trenches – who can read of the glorious, undying acts of valour, of bravery, unequaled in the whole history of the world without growing cold down the spine – is he – a MAN? God forbid!" Following his argument that domestic life was unmanly, Avalond followed with this statement, which argued that no real man would hear the call for military service and ignore it. Between these two statements, he makes it clear that, in his mind, nobody could claim to be a man if they had not performed military service during the war.[37]

Recruiters did not stop at denying the masculinity of those who refused to enlist, but they also shamed these men. Harold Mitchell, the leader of the Returned Soldier and Rejected Volunteer Association published an appeal for men to join the Newfoundland Regiment. He argued that the British Empire had done so much for every citizen that men owed their service, and potentially their lives, to defend the empire. He announced that he would rather die in France than live in a country whose manhood was so degraded that its men cared more about the price of fish than the fate of the British Empire.[38]

Several recruiting posters also attempted to humiliate men who refused to enlist. One poster, titled "Men More Men," depicted a well-dressed man removing his hat while speaking to a woman in the foreground. In the background was a group of men in uniform, marching and carrying rifles. In the caption of the poster, the man says to the woman, "May I carry your grip?" To which she responds, "You'd look better carrying a gun."[39] On one level, this poster is an overt attempt at shaming civilian men by suggesting that women will not be romantically interested in men who were not in uniform. However, if the reader looks closely at the man, they will notice that his posture matches the woman's, and he and the woman are wearing the same high heels. By dressing the young suitor in women's clothing, the author of the cartoon insinuated that women would see civilians as unattractive and effeminate.

The *Evening Telegram* published another prominent example of a poster intended to shame men into enlisting. The Newfoundland Regiment designed this advertisement, and the space was paid for by Bowring Brothers Ltd. The poster read, "Are Your Folks Ashamed of You for Not Enlisting?"[40] This poster was a simple but effective suggestion that by not enlisting, men were bringing dishonour to their entire families.

Recruiters also used poetry to convince men to enlist. On 13 April 1916, the *Mail and Advocate* published a poem titled "The Song of the Shirker" by W. Ferrans:

When the war broke out, my
chum, he would go,
And join the Army, but I said
"No!"

In the list of the slain when his
name I did see
I shivered, and said, it might have
been me,
If I had been as foolish as he
Another I knew has lost a limb,
Oh, horror, to be the same as him
The Germans may win and come
over for me
Its grand to live in this land of
the free

'Tis dinned in my ears night, noon
and morn
To go, but to do so I steadily
scorn,
You'll never see me in the Barrack
Square
There's not much ease or pleasure
there
To make more money I eagerly
try
"Business as usual" I loudly cry,
Why, why should I go from my
Father's farm
Where I am safe and quite free
from harm?
And prices are good, oh happy are
we
'Tis grand to live in the land of
the free

Recruiting meetings, I never
attend
Some other way my time I spend
From the march of the men and
the roll of the drum
I walk in byways or slink away
home

I've Father and Mother, and Brothers
three
And what would they do at home
without me?
Don't bring in compulsion with
that I agree,
'Tis grand to live in the land of
the free

Liberty's tree I love you from leaf
to root
Oh, why do you bear such rotten
fruit?
Cowards they are, and traitors
they be
To this land of the brave, our land
of the free.[41]

This poem shamed shirkers in several different ways. It described conscientious objectors as feckless cowards who did not care about soldiers suffering overseas and were ignorant of the threat posed by Germany. The poem also portrayed shirkers as greedy hedonists. However, perhaps the most scathing indictment of men who refused to enlist comes in the final stanza when Ferrans changes from the perspective of the shirker to speaking from his perspective. Not only does he refer to these men as "rotten fruit," but he also calls them traitors. By calling conscientious objectors "rotten fruit," Ferrans insinuated that conscientious objectors were somehow defective. This shows how powerful the wartime connection was between masculinity and military service.

While Ferran's *Song of the Shirker*, portrayed civilian men as cowardly, pathetic, weak, and dangerous, other poems warned that an everlasting shame would befall any man who refused to enlist. On 3 May 1918, the *Evening Advocate* published "A Picture of a Slacker in Twenty Years," by an author known only as "Newfoundlander:"

A man sits by a big log fire,
A fine looking man in evening attire
Dinner is over, 'twas quite a success –
His wife sits opposite in evening dress.
A voice from the stair-top reaches his ear,

"May I come in Daddy? I'm here."
Why, yes! My boy, come along right in,
would we keep you out? 'twould be a sin.
Son in runs a darling of seven, I'd say
A golden head laddie with eyes of grey.
He looks at his father and says, "Dad, say
Won't you tell me a story to finish the day?"
And of what shall I tell my little man?
A fairy tale from old friend Hann,
Or of Goblins or Orphan Ann;
Or again the Three Bears or Red Riding Hood,
Or of some little boy who was very good?
"No, Dad, no, no more of that,
I want the kind that Jimmie Mack
Told me to-day, his father told
Of when he was young and a soldier bold.
"Oh! Dad it was great, how he went away
To fight the foe and save the day.
He sailed away on the ocean blue.
And Jimmie says – 'tis every bit true.
So I want to hear all about you,
For you were brave and noble and true
I know you were one of the first to go
I told Jim Mack, he said t'aint so.
Your Dad said, HE WOULD NEVER GO
I said to Jimmie, "I'll fight you soon
For saying my Daddy didn't shoulder a gun."
And you did, said his father full of pride,
Well – no – said the boy I only cried
The boys always hurt me when they give me a blow
And I fear being hurt, Dad you know.
Mother, take the boy away
What can I say to him, what can I say?
I cannot answer my boy to-day
Take him away, Mother take him away
I stayed back at the bugle's call,
I stayed back for fear I would fall
I stayed back afraid to go with Jim Mack's Dad
To fight the foe.
And now my son must suffer instead

For the sons of his Father are on his head
Better, I'd gone and been found dead
Then stayed at home and have been wed
And give to the world a coward instead.

Which will it be, boys?
Which will it be, when the war is over and done,
Will you be Jim Mack's Dad, or will you be me?
When you talk to your little son.[42]

This poem was an attack on both non-enlisted men's masculinity and on their ability to raise children. Newfoundlander accused the father of being a coward, and implied that his cowardice would be a hereditary curse on his children. The father in this poem was proud that his son told him that he was going to fight Jimmie Mack. His son dashed his hopes when he admitted that he only cried and was afraid of being hurt. By suggesting that the non-enlisted men would not pass down traditionally masculine qualities of bravery, stoicism, and violence, Newfoundlander implied that these men would leave an eternal black mark on their families for their failure to do their manly duty.

Wartime employment was another pervasive aspect of gender shaming faced by non-enlisted men. By 1915, many in Newfoundland believed that soldiering was the only masculine work in wartime. In June, the editor of the *Mail and Advocate* lamented that there were thousands of young men in the British Empire who were staying at home and doing "women's work" in jobs that could be filled by older men or by women. Initially, those who were attacked for doing "women's work" held positions in the civil service, as telegraph operators, shopkeepers, etc. As the war progressed, recruiters attacked fisher, who made up the majority of men in Newfoundland.[43]

The *Evening Advocate* published a clear example of employment-based shaming on 30 November 1917 in a poem titled "The Man Who Won't" by Frederick H. Bailey:

Don't you feel a little lonesome when you talk the "city" street,
    And read the signs that's really meant for you;
Don't you feel a little shameful when at every step you meet
    A lad that's dressed in khaki eyeing you.
Have you chosen to ignore them?
    Have you stopped to count the cost?

In future years you'll figure up the toil,
You have earned the name of slacker, and the chance that you have lost
Will mark the desolation of your soul.

Don't you think 'twill be forgotten, no matter where you are,
The question to be answered first of all
Will be "what was the battalion that you served with at the war?"
Can you tell them that you never hear the call.
Why there's some men who are longing to take that trip to France.
But are hampered, age or sickness foil the plan,
I can bring them by the dozen, who'll go with you on chance
If 'tis only just to help you play the man

You're at work in store or office, there are girls to do your job,
Another pay-roll's waiting for you name.
There are comrades looking for you, there are medals for your fob,
There are honour that are waiting for your claim.
If it's dying that you are scared of, well you have to die some day.
You're bound to live through your allotted span.
And if old "Death" should claim you, could you find a better way
Than meeting him a "Soldier and a Man?"

You'll be first to do the shouting at the finish of the war
You'll be standing mid the women with a flag;
You'll be cheering for the Empire as you've never cheered before
And forget that days your knees were on the sag,
Then you'll go back to the office, the workshop or the store,
To find your paycheque waiting with the "can."
The smiling boss will tell you "You're not wanted anymore.
The job you held is handed to a man."[44]

Bailey's poem was typical of narratives that criticized men who stayed at home to work, instead of serving with the military. These narratives argued that jobs once held primarily by men were no longer masculine. By this logic, recruiters argued that men working in civilian jobs were effeminate. The final two lines of Bailey's poem highlighted the perceived effeminacy of civilian employment by suggesting that a civilian's employers would fire them at the end of the war and hire "real" men who served overseas.

Throughout the war, recruiters reconstructed conceptions of gender in Newfoundland so that fishing and providing for one's family was no longer an acceptable lifestyle for healthy young men. In wartime rhetoric, military service was the defining characteristic of masculinity. This change was so powerful that some called on the government to deny voting rights for the un-enlisted that it typically awarded to men in a Liberal democracy.

NO BERTHS FOR SLACKERS

During the war, many soldiers expressed anger at those who stayed at home making money while they fought overseas. As a result of this tension between soldiers and civilians, many men argued that businesses should not hire young able-bodied men who did not volunteer for service. On 9 December, W.B. Grieve, manager of Baine, Johnston & Co. and secretary of the NPA, requested that the government force all single, military-aged, male, government employees to offer themselves for enlistment or resign their positions. The colonial secretary was not pleased with the NPA's attempted interference in government matters and eventually forced Grieve to withdraw his request and apologize.[45]

While Grieve's scheme failed, other efforts to deny employment opportunities to the non-enlisted were more successful. In February 1916, the vast majority of sealing vessel owners refused to hire any single man under the age of thirty who had not offered himself up for service. These ship owners vowed to give preference to those who had not "shirked his responsibility or failed his duty to his country." The denial of a berth on sealing vessels would be a financial disaster for many young men in Newfoundland. In parts of the dominion, men relied on the spring seal fishery as a crucial element in their seasonal rotation of employment. For many, this income was vital as there were few ways to earn a living in the spring before the cod fishery began.

While this caused hardship for young men who relied on the seal fishery as a form of seasonal employment, the editor of the *Daily News* encouraged other businesses to follow the lead of the sealing fleet. Currie cautioned that "a young man who fails to measure up to the duties of citizenship and lends an unheeding ear to the call of his country, is not at all unlikely prove a shirker in other things. And the business world of to-day has no room for the slacker." By warning that the non-enlisted would make poor employees, the *Daily News* went beyond Grieve's call to get young men to enlist and suggested that there must be a character flaw for young men who refused to fight.[46]

Several recruiting posters attempted to discourage employers from hiring un-enlisted men. Some of these contained veiled threats that young men who refused to enlist would lose their jobs. One example, from the *Evening Telegram*, informed men that their "chums" had given up their lucrative employment to serve and asked, "Does your employer know why you haven't offered?" This was a threat that men would lose their jobs if their employers found out their reasons for not enlisting.[47]

Other advertisements were much more direct. One ad paid for by the Returned Soldiers and Rejected Volunteer Association warned employers to hire unmarried military-aged men "at their own risk."[48] This advertisement declared that the patriotic business owner would neither hire men who were eligible for military service nor do business with any other company that hired these men. These calls to patriotism were particularly successful as the language of patriotism pervaded Newfoundland society, and accusations of unpatriotic behaviour often carried severe consequences.

The campaign encouraging companies to refuse to hire non-enlisted men was effective, and some men had trouble finding work. In May of 1916, Alfred George, a resident of Trinity Bay, moved to Grand Falls to find work in the paper mill. Upon arriving there, a manager at the mill informed George that he would not offer him a job unless he could prove that he attempted to enlist in either the Newfoundland Regiment or the Newfoundland Royal Naval Reserve. George had offered his services to the Newfoundland Regiment, but he failed his medical examination because he was underweight. Despite this, when the regiment turned him away, it did not provide him with proof that he attempted to enlist. To obtain evidence of his rejected volunteer status, George wrote to the colonial secretary, who secured a letter from the adjutant of the regiment stating that George had volunteered his services but failed the medical examination.[49]

The issue of civilian employment was so controversial because many believed these men were shirking their duties to take advantage of the wartime economy. This was true for rural fishers who recruiters accused of refusing to enlist because they could make more money by staying at home. The *Evening Telegram* addressed this issue in a scathing editorial titled "To the Fishers of Newfoundland." In this article, the editor spoke directly to fishers, saying that the men of St John's had done their duty, but rural Newfoundlanders had not. The editor accused these men of profiteering off misery and suffering caused by the war:

> But you have not only caught the fish, you have sold it. Have you ever got such a price for it before? Have you ever made so much actual cold hard cash before? You know you have not. Has it occurred to you to ask why this has been? Perhaps it has; perhaps you know in a vague sort of way. We will try to tell you a little more exactly. Fish has cost more to those who buy it because there has been a great scarcity of it. That is the main reason, almost the whole reason ... there is a great scarcity of food in general the world over. What is the meaning of that? It is what we have stated above, that thousands of human being are dying for want of it, many of them helpless women and children, emaciated mothers and pitiful shrunken babes. Do you see the connection? It is this misery that has helped to make your calling so profitable, directly in some cases, indirectly in all the rest. Think of it, when you count over your money or reckon up your bank account. If you have more to count, a larger figure to reckon, than in years past, ponder a little the reason why.

Through his inflammatory language, the editor of the *Evening Telegram* accused Newfoundland fishers of profiteering off the misery caused by the war. The editor's argument was hypocritical. On the one hand, he admitted that the world had a critical shortage of food, and people were dying from starvation. However, in the same breath, the editor shamed fishers who worked to help alleviate the global food shortage.[50]

Following this section, the editor explained that the only true way for Newfoundlanders to help win the war was to enlist and fight. He said that the only way to win the war was for every young man to come forward and fight. Refusal to enlist was aiding Germany. In this statement, the editor of the *Evening Telegram* told fishers that they only had one responsibility during the war: to fight. Any other action, including fishing, was not only shirking their duty as men but was also aiding the enemy and made them complicit in the suffering of millions in Europe. Lieutenant Cyril Carter, a soldier who was injured in Gallipoli, expressed this same sentiment at a recruiting meeting in 1916 when he declared that fishers who did not enlist were "nothing less than accessories to murder."[51]

In the house of assembly, William Coaker expressed concern about the impact of non-enlisted employment on recruiting efforts. Speaking in the house assembly, Coaker expressed his belief that voluntary recruitment was unfair. He pointed out that some young men were fighting and living in the trenches, others keeping watch on ships defending the empire, while still others "stay behind, enjoying what our soldiers are sailors are preserving for us, and laughing at them for their pains." Coaker expressed a common concern among recruiters in Newfoundland: men who refused to enlist would stay at home, earn healthy profits from the fishery, and discourage other young men from enrolling. Recruiters believed by refusing to join non-enlisted men not only discouraged other men from enlisting, but they weakened the narrative that the only acceptable form of male labour was military service.[52]

"REGENERATE THE MOST USELESS ELEMENTS OF THE NATION"

The final theme in the gendered language of recruiting was that military service could have a redemptive, healing quality for the nation and individual men. In the early twentieth century, many British newspapers espoused the supposed purifying and cleansing nature of warfare and military service. This notion was rooted in contemporary social Darwinist ideas that warfare was the ultimate test for a nation and its people. Glenn Wilkinson's examination of Edwardian newspapers shows that many Britons believed not only that war could revitalize a decaying Britain but also that war could rejuvenate Britain's withering masculinity. Warfare was so crucial to Edwardian masculinity because it created the ideal separation between the gender identities as many British men believed that war was as natural for men as childbirth was for women. Many men believed that warfare alone could revitalize "a generation of 'degenerate' unmanly males who were either unable or worse, unwilling to defend the honour of their country, due to a loss of masculine martial spirit."[53]

Before the war, Newfoundlanders had very few opportunities to perform military service. Therefore, soldiering did not hold the same importance to male gender identity in the dominion of Newfoundland as it did in the British Isles. As the dominion's recruiting campaign began to falter, recruiters highlighted what they considered to be the benefits of military service on the individual and the nation. In an article from February 1915, John Robinson argued that soldiers were prime examples of masculinity and referred to the non-enlisted as "creatures who masquerade men." Robinson said military service could be a benefit to both the nation and to the effeminate men who refuse to enlist: "it would be a national benefit, and a blessing to the slackers themselves, if the old methods were temporarily revived, and they were compelled to serve. A few months' training would make men out of them; and regenerate the most useless elements of the nation. Military or Naval discipline would, in their cases, be permanently reformatory; and though the gin-palace graduate would be poor material to mix with our splendid volunteer soldiery, even the drunkard, the hooligan, and the wastrel may be changed by discipline into men." In this article, Robinson argued that Newfoundland's participation in the war could not only be beneficial for the dominion's citizen-soldiers, but it would also benefit the nation by turning effeminate men into archetypes of masculinity who would uphold the values of the nation.[54]

H.A. Winter also expressed similar sentiments in the *Evening Telegram*. Winter encouraged recruiters to do more than just remind men of the "abstract principles of duty and honour." While he admitted honour and duty were the first and primary consideration for recruiting, he also implored recruiters to emphasize the benefits and privileges that accompanied the fulfillment of a citizen's obligations. Winter stated that Newfoundlanders would get an education superior to that available in schools. He said that the knowledge that soldiers received would be invaluable to the progress of the dominion. While Winter was vague on what educational experiences he believed soldiers had, it is clear he was trying to convince potential recruits that military service could be a transformative experience.[55]

Some recruiters advocated that a righteous war not only had a transformative impact on men but also on the nation as a whole. Speaking before the house of assembly, W.F. Lloyd argued that war had shaped the most influential countries throughout European history. He explained that these countries were forged in battle and flourished not only in democracy but also in the arts, literature, commerce, and science. Lloyd said that the benefits of the war extended not only to soldiers but to every citizen in the nation. He believed that the positive impact of wars on societies was so profound that the Great War would lead to a revolution in arts and literature; science and technology in the Newfoundland, sending the dominion down the path of influential European powers.[56]

"OR PERHAPS WE SHOULD SAY COLONIALS"

In addition to rearranging conceptions of masculinity, Newfoundland's recruiting campaign also altered notions of ethnicity as many people re-evaluated their beliefs about what it meant to be a citizen in a British dominion. Throughout the nineteenth and twentieth centuries, many people believed that there were two groups of people living in the colonies: Britishers and Colonials. Britishers lived up to British ideals of class, ethnicity, and gender, while colonials did not. Although the people of Newfoundland had long considered the colony a loyal cornerstone that made the empire possible, Newfoundland's weak economic position and dependence on the fishery meant that many Newfoundlanders struggled to justify the place they believed they held within the British Empire.[57]

Kurt Korneski's work on Newfoundland's railway development in the nineteenth century demonstrates that support for the railway was spurred on by a belief that it would bring the dominion closer to British ideals of gender, ethnicity, and class. Railway promoters believed that a railway would help fishers break their dependence on merchants while supporting British masculine standards, emphasizing individualism and independence. Furthermore, railway promoters were also eager to point out that by 1880 every British dominion and colony had a railway except Newfoundland and China. By highlighting that Newfoundland and China lacked railways and the differences between Newfoundland and other British dominions, railway promoters capitalized on traditional British notions of race, class, and gender.[58]

Like the railway, recruiters often described Newfoundland's war effort as an opportunity for Newfoundlanders to live up to British expectations of gender, ethnicity, and class. This was a profound change in the way Newfoundlanders thought about their ethnic identity. Before the war, Newfoundlanders believed that the dominion was a loyal bastion of the British Empire, and they never considered military service to be a fundamental part of their place in the empire. During the war, however, there was a radical shift in Newfoundland's understanding of what it meant to be British and military service became the defining element of British ethnicity.

Shortly after the outbreak of the war, recruiters began to argue that Newfoundlanders had to enlist to show that they deserved the title of Britisher. A.B Morine espoused this belief at a speech given to the

Society of United Fishers in St John's. Morine said that as Britons, the empire charged Newfoundlanders with the responsibilities and privileges afforded to all Britishers. He told the audience that the free Briton would defend himself. To rely on others for their defence was the badge of serfdom. Furthermore, Morine argued that Newfoundland had not done enough in the past to defend the empire, having contributed neither a dollar nor a man to the Royal Navy. He accused the people of consenting to be protected by the tax payers of Britain while complaining when Britain did not offer the dominion a considerable role in governing the empire. In short, Morine believed Newfoundlanders were failing to live up to the title of Britisher because they were not willing to defend the British Empire.[59]

In an article from June 1915, the editor of the *Mail and Advocate* highlighted the difference between Britishers and Colonials. John St John said that, because of poor recruiting rates, the rest of the British Empire should call Newfoundlanders Colonials and not Britishers. He observed that many people were quick to discuss the prowess and patriotism of Englishmen while dismissing the supposedly "effete" Southern Europeans. Despite their outward patriotism, St John argued that thousands of men in Newfoundland refused to enlist and stayed at home and doing women's work. In comparison, the editor praised the Italians for taking decisive action raising 10,000 troops in one day, banning public meetings, instituting rigorous censorship, and suppressing the postal service. By referring to Newfoundlanders as "colonials," St John intimated that Newfoundlanders had to be willing to support the war effort through higher enlistment rates and sacrifices of personal freedoms if they were to deserve the title of "Britisher."[60]

Shortly after the announcement that the NPA would raise a second battalion of the Newfoundland Regiment, the editor of the *Evening Telegram* relied on tropes of Britishness to encourage men to enlist. W.F. Lloyd argued that the war against Germany was nothing short of a struggle for the survival of the British Empire. He said Newfoundland's British forefathers had fought for liberty, freedom, and Christianity, and the Kaiser would see all of that destroyed and replaced with "state force and frightfulness." Lloyd told Newfoundlanders that the British blood in their veins would draw them to enlist: "We have to win out as our forefathers have done in the past. They fought against great odds. We are fighting against greater forces. If we are to win out we must make even greater sacrifices of blood than they made. If we are worthy of them, we shall do it. If we are degenerates, we must be the Kaiser's slaves. Newfoundland is called upon to do her part. We are confident that Newfoundland will not fail. The sturdy blood of England, Ireland, Scotland is on our veins, which will be freely sacrificed that we remain free." By drawing on symbols from British history and by reminding people of their British heritage, the editor emphasized Newfoundland's connection to Britain.[61]

An author, writing under the pseudonym "Public Opinion," made a similar argument, in February 1916, when he wrote a letter to the editor of the *Mail and Advocate* praising the government's decision to raise and maintain a second battalion of the Newfoundland Regiment. "Public Opinion" told the editor that recruiters must remind men that they have the same rights and privileges as any citizen of the British Empire. They also addressed English, Irish, and Scottish Newfoundlanders, the various "races" that made up the British Empire, describing the proud heritage of each race. He concluded his article by highlighting the military prowess of the English, Irish, and Scottish saying: 'No better combination than English, Irish, and Scotch can be found. They are loyal, patriotic, and enthusiastic and are ready at all times to lay down their lives in defence of Freedom and Liberty. The iron rod of oppression never aided or never will appeal to a true Briton."[62]

Other editorials capitalized on shared British history to rally Newfoundlanders to the Union Jack. In a letter to the editor of the *Mail and Advocate*, J.W. Nichols tried to reassure Newfoundlanders that the superiority of the British Race meant that Britain could not lose the war. Nichols told the editor that in 1588, King Philip of Spain prepared to conquer Europe, and his "Invincible Armada" was destroyed when all classes of Britain worked together to raise a fleet, destroy the Spanish Armada, and usher in a hundred years of peace. Nichols compared the First World War to British campaigns against King Louis XIV and Napoleon. He argued that these three British victories, won in the face of great odds, showed that "the dogged determination of the British race is bound to win."[63]

Those who refused to enlist were treated in similar ways across the British Empire. In her work on conscientious objectors, Lois Bibbings has shown that many Britons reviled "shirkers" because they refused to live up to wartime expectations of British masculinity. As a result, men who refused to fight were often labelled as cowardly, unmanly, homosexual, and presented as a threat to Britain's war effort. Newfoundlanders who refused to enlist were treated in much the same way, with one exception. In wartime Newfoundland, Britishness was intricately tied to military service. Some Newfoundlanders felt insecure about their position in the empire, and recruiters capitalized on this by suggesting that those who refused to enlist were not true Britishers.[64]

"THE INITIATION OF OUR COLONY INTO THE BROTHERHOOD OF NATIONS"

While many recruiters saw the First World War as a chance for Newfoundlanders to prove their Britishness, they also believed the war was an opportunity to show that the dominion deserved a more prominent role in the empire. These recruiters thought that by contributing to the war effort, the British government would recognize Newfoundland's loyalty and give the dominion a greater role in the governance of the empire. William Coaker made this position clear when he claimed that the deaths of twenty-five naval reservists aboard the *Viknor* would mark Newfoundland's initiation into the "brotherhood of the nations" that made up the British Empire.[65]

Many people in the dominion believed that the First World War had finally allowed Newfoundland to show the British Empire its true loyalty. This belief stemmed from the nationalism of D.W. Prowse, a prominent historian of Newfoundland, who argued that the dominion was a long-serving, loyal, cornerstone of the empire that was the victim of constant stumbling blocks that prohibited growth. Newfoundland's participation in the war was an opportunity to show the rest of the empire how important it was. In May of 1915, M. Harnett of Marystown wrote a letter to the editor of the *Evening Telegram* that beamed with pride over the dominion's contributions to the war effort. He told the editor that "never before in the history of the world have Newfoundlanders been so intimately connected with – and played such a prominent part towards the Mother Country as they have since the starting of this war by the Kaiser whose idea it was to become supreme ruler of the land and sea."[66]

The NPA also harnessed this belief to stimulate recruiting numbers. In a recruiting drive in November 1916, it said that Newfoundland had earned an esteemed place in the British Empire. The dominion sent 4,500 soldiers and sailors to fight, many of those had been decorated for bravery, and all had acquitted themselves with courage and valour. According to the NPA, the performance of Newfoundland's sailors and soldiers had won undying fame for the dominion. Despite their success, the NPA argued that more men had to be sent to the front to finish the job and to cement Newfoundland's place in the empire for good. It claimed that the government had spent too much money and lost too many men for the war effort. Failure to commit every last resource to ensure that Germany was defeated, and Newfoundland secured its place in the British Empire, would be an insult to every man who died in France.[67]

In addition to an increased position in the British Empire, some concluded that Newfoundland's participation in the war had earned the dominion recognition on the world stage. On 22 April 1918, the Returned Soldiers and Rejected Volunteers published a recruiting advertisement in several local newspapers. This ad informed readers that before the war, very few people around the world knew what Newfoundland was. It said that the actions of the RNR and NRNR had the whole world speaking of Newfoundland's greatness.[68]

In December 1916, the government of Newfoundland received a cable from David Lloyd George that proved, in some people's eyes, that Newfoundland had earned a new place in the British Empire. This cable was an invitation from Lloyd George for Edward Morris to travel to London to participate in the Imperial War Cabinet. This cabinet comprised David Lloyd George, George Curzon, Bonar Law, and Walter Long from the United Kingdom; Robert Rogers, John Hazen, George Perley, and Robert Borden from Canada; Jan Smuts from South Africa; Billy Hughes from Australia; William Massey and Joseph Ward from New Zealand; Austen Chamberlain, James Meston, and Ganga Singh from India; and Edward Morris from Newfoundland. For many in the dominion it was a profound honour for Newfoundland to be represented at a meeting of the British Empire's leaders.[69]

Shortly after Morris returned from London, he addressed his participation in this conference in the house of assembly. Morris expressed the importance of the conference and asked that all the members of the house join him in "rejoicing at the fact that Newfoundland, the oldest Colony of the Crown, was privileged to participate in this great council." He then emphasized that Newfoundland's role in the war was important as a source of pride because it earned the respect of the British government and the British people. It showed that Newfoundland men were manly, and most importantly, it showed that Newfoundlanders were indeed made of the same cloth as their British counterparts.[70]

In response to Morris's speech, Richard Devereaux told the house that the Imperial Conference ushered in a new epoch in which Britain would rely on its colonies not only for the physical efforts of their soldiers but also the intellectual efforts of their politicians. Devereaux compared Lloyd George's call to the prime ministers of British dominions to the Emperor of Rome calling in his consuls from across the Roman Empire. He said that he was proud Morris was able to represent Newfoundland at such a historic occasion and was able to give "from his full knowledge and extensive experience in colonial and parliamentary life, much help to those who are the principal advisers in relation to this war."[71]

Despite the importance and pride placed upon Morris's trip to London by some members of the house, not everyone in Newfoundland supported his participation in the Imperial Conference. The Liberal-Union opposition felt that Morris had abandoned his responsibilities to the dominion by leaving for London. They attacked Morris, arguing that he should have remained at home to help solve the rising cost of living and coal shortages that threatened to leave Newfoundlanders starving in the cold. This came to a head in April when the opening of the legislature was delayed until Morris returned. In the house of assembly, W.F. Lloyd attacked the prime minister, demanding that the legislature open in his absence so the business of the dominion could continue as normally as possible.[72]

As the war progressed, the number of men required to keep the Newfoundland Regiment in the frontlines grew, and the Newfoundland government had difficulty in recruiting enough soldiers. As a result, recruiters not only used Newfoundland's British heritage to encourage men to enlist but increasingly used it to shame them into enlisting. Recruiting advertisements that denied the Britishness of the non-enlisted became more frequent. A typical example appeared in the *Daily News* on 30 October 1917: "Young able-bodied men, put this question to yourselves – Is your blood tingling in your veins? It must be if you are the true sons of British parentage. Breed must tell. The sons of sires who sprung from Dorset and from Devon, from Cork and Waterford, and along the Forth and Clyde cannot but be loyal to their heritage and give proof of the mettle of their sires' pasture and their own. The blood tingles as you see the Empire's bravest sons pass by in sailor's blue or soldier's khaki. It cannot be otherwise. But is it tingling with pride, the joy of duty recognized and accepted, or with the shame of self-contempt?" By suggesting that all those of British heritage would be eager to enlist, this advertisement suggested that any man who refused to join was a colonial, not a true Briton.[73]

In a similar article, Miranda, a frequent columnist for the *Evening Advocate*, informed their readers that Newfoundland soldiers were living up to the best of British ideals. They said that Newfoundland had long boasted of being "Britain's oldest and loyal colony" but was not living up to that reputation during the war. Instead, Miranda pointed out that Newfoundland had only sent one or two thousand soldiers when they should have sent 10,000 soldiers to set a good example for the other British dominions. Miranda then posited that any eligible man who did not enlist was cowardly, indifferent, and un-British. The editor of the *Evening Advocate* shared the notion that no British man could resist the call to duty, arguing that no man, through whose veins British blood flows, could resist their duty.[74]

The argument that no true British man would refuse to enlist is compelling evidence of a renegotiation of British ethnicity that placed great importance on military service. This argument reinforces the link between Britishness and military service by ascribing Britishness to soldiers and denying it to the non-enlisted. Due to the wartime connection between British ethnicity and military prowess, Newfoundland was very concerned about showing the other dominions just how British they were. Newfoundland recruiters consistently told the public that Newfoundland's war effort was an opportunity to show the empire that Newfoundland men were equal to men from any other dominion.

As a result of the desire for Newfoundland to prove itself, from the very start of the war, recruiters made nearly constant comparisons to recruiting rates in other British dominions. Four months into the war, people were proud of the contribution Newfoundland was making to the war effort. In January 1915, the editor of the *Evening Telegram* praised the various dominions for contributing such large amounts of sailors and soldiers to the war effort. In particular, he highlighted the eight hundred Newfoundlanders serving in the Royal Navy. The editor commended Newfoundland for supposedly keeping up with the recruiting rates of other dominions.[75]

By January of 1916, W.F. Lloyd grew disappointed with the level of recruiting in Newfoundland. By this point, Britain had recruited approximately 6,000,000 out of a population of 46,000,000. Among the other dominions, much to the Lloyd's dismay, Newfoundland had the lowest recruiting rate. According to him, Australia was leading the pack with a large contingent sent from the Australian Naval Squadron, 250,000 soldiers in the trenches, 50,000 more soldiers departing by June, and additional drafts of 9,500 soldiers each month. He praised New Zealand for sending forward 30,000 from a population of 1,000,000. Finally, Lloyd pointed out that Canada was lagging behind the other dominions and that Newfoundland had the lowest recruiting rate out of them all. In concluding his article, Lloyd called on the government to step up and take measures to ensure that Newfoundland could keep pace with the other British dominions.[76]

A few days later, the Lloyd followed up with another article in the *Evening Telegram* on recruiting rates. He noted that a year ago, Newfoundland had the "pride of place in the friendly rivalry in regards to recruiting here and in Canada." The editor informed his readers that this rivalry was now over, and Canada was outpacing Newfoundland. He credited Canada for setting a recruiting goal and encouraged the government to do the same. He recommended that Canada's current enlistment of 220,000 (roughly 2.75 per cent of the total population) would make an appropriate goal for the dominion and would double the number of soldiers in the Newfoundland Regiment.[77]

In February of 1916, the *Evening Telegram* was pleased that the government announced that Newfoundland would raise a second battalion of the Newfoundland Regiment with ample troops in reserve. Despite this good news, the editor warned that the increases in the size of the Newfoundland Regiment were only moderate. If Newfoundland wanted to keep up with recruiting rates in Britain, then the government would have to raise seven times as many troops as they currently had. The *Evening Telegram* admitted it would take a lot of work to live up to the moderate increases the government proposed but stated that it was "a task which must be faced and carried out if Newfoundland is to hold up her head and carry herself with proper pride and patriotism among our kin across the seas." It seems clear that from these series of editorials that Lloyd was concerned about keeping up with the other dominions and how Newfoundland's recruiting rates were viewed in the British Empire.[78]

While the announcement of the formation of the Second Battalion of the Newfoundland Regiment, temporarily placated some Newfoundlanders, they did not remain satisfied. Two weeks after the tragic loss of life at Beaumont Hamel, the newly appointed editor of the *Evening Telegram*, H.A. Winter, suggested that Newfoundland was not doing enough for the war effort. He said that Newfoundland was thinking too parochially and selfishly, and the causalities at Beaumont Hamel should serve as a lesson. He warned the people of Newfoundland that the ranks of the regiment were depleted and advocated that they should be filled immediately. Winter told the readers of the *Evening Telegram* that Canada set a goal of 500,000; Australia 350,000; and New Zealand 80,000; each representing approximately 7 per cent of their total population. Comparatively, Newfoundland had only sent just over 5,500. For Newfoundland to reach the standard set by the other dominions, it would have to raise a total of 16,000 soldiers. Winter concluded this article by praising the majority of the island for their exceptional performance in enlisting. Despite his praise, Winter said that they still needed to increase their recruiting rates, and while St Johns was doing admirably, other districts were not. He recommended that every time a name appeared on a casualty list, another young man should rush to the recruiting centre to take his place.[79]

Despite the pressure to increase recruiting, the recruiting situation became worse as the war dragged on. In September of 1917, many became worried that the high casualty and low recruitment rates would result in the depletion of the Newfoundland Regiment and its removal from active service or incorporation into another regiment. As a result, the Recruiting Committee of the NPA and the editors of all major newspapers in Newfoundland coordinated their efforts to recruiting enough volunteers to maintain the regiment.[80]

In October, John Currie, the editor for the *Daily News*, made a desperate plea for Newfoundland to raise the 500–600 soldiers that the British army required to keep the regiment in the frontlines. He provided a grave warning to the men of Newfoundland that if this final voluntary recruiting drive failed, then the government would likely have to resort to selective conscription, this was their last opportunity to come forward voluntarily. In addition to his threat of conscription, Currie sought to encourage men to enlist by highlighting what he believed would be the national shame that would follow the removal of the regiment from the field. He wrote:

> It is unthinkable now that the Regiment will be withdrawn or cease to exist as a separate unit. For more than two years it has gallantly held its place in the line, winning undying glory and bringing great imperishable honour to the country. It would be to our eternal shame, if at this stage, when the end is near and

> victory in sight, we should fall in our duty at home, be disloyal to the great cause, to the men who are to-day so nobly upholding our name and fame, and to the memory of our honoured dead, who, having given their all, peacefully rest beneath the shell-torn fields of Gallipoli, of France and Flanders. The Regiment cannot be disbanded, it must be maintained.

Currie suggested that it would be a great national disgrace for the Newfoundland Regiment to be removed from the field, and the failure to maintain the regiment would be an insult to every soldier who died.[81]

By April 1918, the threat to the RNR was still present and recruiters across the island desperately attempted to recruit enough soldiers to keep the regiment in the field. Andrew Bartlett, the editor of the *Western Star*, told his readers that the RNR needed three hundred recruits immediately, or the British Expeditionary Force would withdraw them from active service. Bartlett suggested that if every community in rural Newfoundland sent one man to enlist in the RNR, the recruiting deadline would be met immediately. The RSRVA also called on rural Newfoundland to maintain the regiment. In an advertisement published in the *Evening Advocate*, the RSRVA informed rural men that the regiment was suffering badly and needed their help to stay in the trenches. The author told rural Newfoundlanders that refusing to enlist was just the same as seeing a friend falling overboard and watching them drown. The editor of the *Evening Telegram* made the same analogy, arguing that a refusal to enlist would be akin to watching a friend drown while saying, "Let him drown, I'm quite comfortable where I am, in my boat ... If I get out after him, I may get wet," or "I am too busy catching fish to attend to him."[82]

Despite the many attempts of recruiters to encourage enough men to enlist to keep the regiment in the field, on 3 May 1918, J.R. Bennett announced that the RNR had been removed from active duty with the 29th division and stationed as guards at Haig's headquarters in Montreuil. C.T. James described the withdrawal of the regiment as a national shame and blamed the government for failing to recruit more men. James imagined that the soldiers, who earned their glory, who were removed from the field, must by enraged at the national government for not doing more to fill the ranks. To make matters worse, James declared that the removal of the regiment from the field was a disgrace that would haunt Newfoundland for eternity. Not only did James place the blame for the withdrawal of the regiment squarely on the shoulders of the Newfoundland government, but he also demonstrated just how important the Newfoundland Regiment had become for Newfoundlanders.[83]

In the pages of the *Western Star*, Andrew Barrett also expressed anguish over the removal of the RNR. In an editorial, Barrett summarized the performance of the RNR, reminding the readers of the pride that Newfoundlanders shared as they followed the regiment from its formation, training, and departure. He said that the hearts of the dominion had rejoiced when the British Expeditionary Force raised the Newfoundland Contingent to an independent regiment that would bear the dominion's name for the empire to see. He recounted with pride the regiment's accomplishments from Alexandria to the Dardanelles and to its glory on the fields of Flanders, which earned them the title "Royal." Unlike the *Evening Telegram*, the *Western Star* did not blame the government for the failure of the regiment. Instead, Barrett suggested the people of Newfoundland failed the RNR by raising insufficient numbers of troops to preserve them. Barrett said that Newfoundland's failure to maintain the regiment and live up to the expectations of a British dominion was "one of the saddest incidents in the history of Newfoundland."[84]

The association between military service and British identity was a substantial shift in conceptions of ethnicity in Newfoundland. While many Newfoundlanders had traditionally viewed themselves as proud Britishers, their identity as British subjects was not previously based on military service. Given wartime conceptions of British masculinity, the First World War allowed Newfoundland to show how British they were. When the Newfoundland Regiment was removed from frontline duty, many citizens believed the dominion failed to live up to British standards.

CONCLUSION

Newfoundland's involvement in the First World War caused a profound renegotiation of conceptions of gender and ethnicity. Before the war, concepts of masculinity focussed on men's abilities to provide for their families. During the war, recruiters in the dominion argued that the pinnacle of masculinity was military service, and they emphasized men's roles as protectors of the state over their roles as providers for their families. In addition to changing concepts of masculinity, recruiters in Newfoundland attempted to alter what it meant to be

British, by suggesting that all true British men would rally around the flag and offer their lives for the empire.

The renegotiation of gender and ethnicity by recruiters in Newfoundland seems to have been effective. Once recruiters had established that manly, British citizens would offer themselves up for service, the public reacted with incredible disdain towards the "slackers" who refused to enlist. Recruiters designed a host of letters to the editor, recruiting ads, poems, and public speeches to shame men into enlisting by suggesting that that the un-enlisted were unmanly, un-British, and even potentially a threat to the dominion. Some businesses also refused to hire able-bodied, military-aged men if they had not offered their services to the naval reserve or the Newfoundland Regiment.

Public and government expectations that all young men enlist in either the naval reserve or Newfoundland Regiment indicate a significant change in the liberal order. McKay's definition of liberalism suggests that in a liberal democracy, the individual was not responsible to anyone but themselves and the voluntary commitments they made to others. During the war, recruiters made it clear that the men of Newfoundland were not accountable to themselves alone. They were responsible for the dominion and the British Empire. The liberal state expected all young British men to be ready to lay down their lives for the greater good.

6

Conscription

In 1904, Canada passed the Militia Act, which stipulated that the governor-general could require all male inhabitants between the ages of eighteen and sixty to take up arms in a "*levée en masse.*" This meant that Canada did not strictly have to pass the *Military Service Act* of 1917 to enforce conscription. Newfoundland, on the other hand, had no such legislation before the war. At the outbreak of the war, the government passed the *Volunteer Force Act*, which allowed the dominion to raise a force of volunteers to serve at home and abroad for the duration of the war or one year. This legislation only gave the government the authority to raise a volunteer regiment, not to require service from any citizens. The first conversations of conscription in Newfoundland did not occur until several years into the war.[1]

The conscription debate in Newfoundland highlights wartime changes to conceptions of gender and ethnicity. The voluntary recruitment campaign successfully altered perceptions of gender and ethnicity to include military service as the prime criteria for British masculinity. By 1917, voluntary recruitment was no longer able to attract enough recruits to fill the ranks of the Newfoundland Regiment. As a result, some citizens demanded that the government ensure men lived up to the wartime expectations of British citizens and that the sacrifice was spread equally over all families and communities across the dominion.

"A WORSE REPTILE NEVER ENCUMBERED GOD'S EARTH THAN A MAN THAT IS SUCH A COWARD TO HANG BACK AND WILLINGLY ALLOW HIS COUNTRYMEN TO BE SLAUGHTERED."

The imposition of conscription by Britain, New Zealand, and Canada started a public conversation in Newfoundland about whether or not the dominion needed compulsory service. One persuasive argument for conscription was that many "slackers" were refusing to do their duty as British citizens. An early promoter of this argument was John Robinson. In December of 1916, Robinson believed that if conscription were to become necessary, it would be a bitter pill for any Briton to swallow as it would take away personal liberty, the centre of British freedom. Despite this, he concluded that the freedoms enjoyed by British citizens came with a responsibility to defend the flag, and anyone who refused to do so was worthless. He said that, because "slackers" in Newfoundland were not living up to the expectations of British men, the government should force them to serve. He set up a dichotomy between volunteers and conscripts that held the volunteer soldiers of the British Empire as "the most glorious achievement of the ages." In contrast, he considered conscripts to be "the refuse of Britain's manhood."[2]

In the *Western Star*, Andrew Barrett also argued that the Newfoundland government should pass conscription if the NPA could not recruit enough volunteers for the regiment. Like Robinson, Barrett also recognized the inherent contradiction in stripping the liberty of citizens and forcing them to fight for freedom: "That individual liberty is a precious boon, all will agree. Everybody likes to be allowed to choose for himself. There is always a certain amount of repugnance against being ordered or compelled. But when the very existence of a nation and the ideals for which it stands are threatened, the collective good becomes paramont [*sic*] to the individual pleasure. That each should shoulder his share of the burden, and that the sacrifice involved should be equal is an axiomatic principle." In this article, Barrett highlighted the core argument of the conscription debate. He admitted that citizens should be free to choose the direction of their lives. However, he thought the dire circumstances of the war required a decisive response. Therefore, Barrett reasoned that the rights of the nation outweighed the rights of the individual, and as a result, the government should coerce all eligible men into military service.[3]

In November of 1916, a fisher from St Mary's, writing under the pseudonym "Coal Pits," wrote a letter to the editor of the *Evening Telegram* advocating for conscription. "Coal Pits" said that the state should compel any man to enlist who was cowardly enough to stay at home while other men did his fighting for him. They thought that if Newfoundland allowed only the volunteers to fight and die in the trenches, the best men in the dominion would die, leaving behind only the slackers. "Coal Pits" said that a worse "reptile" had never encumbered God's earth than the slacker and argued that they should be "shunned like a mad dog." "Coal Pits" not only believed that non-enlisted men were undeserving of their status as male citizens, but he also denied their humanity by comparing them to reptiles and encouraging the community to treat them like dogs. For him, conscription was a way of ensuring that Newfoundland's best men did not die in Europe while inferior men survived by remaining at home.[4]

Another article published in the *Evening Telegram*, surmised that voluntary recruiting was harming the dominion. In this article, an author writing under the pseudonym "Bull" told the editor that intelligent men had always been scarce in Newfoundland. The few smart men were enlisting and leaving the ignorant and vicious to damage Newfoundland society permanently. They thought that a selective draft would allow the government to pick and choose who should serve, allowing them to select men whose absence would least damage the dominion's culture and economy.[5]

Eugenicist concerns over the biological impacts of the war were common throughout the British Empire. Paul Crook has shown that prior to the war many people in the British Empire believed that a system of voluntary recruitment would result in an army that consisted of primarily working-class soldiers. This meant that more upper- and middle-class citizens (those who were traditionally viewed as biologically superior) would remain at home. After the outbreak of the war, however, many citizens argued that those who rushed to enlist were the best and brightest of the British Empire. They argued that conscription would spread out the sacrifice so that those who were considered "biologically superior" did not make up the brunt of casualties. While the class-based nature of the conscription debate differed in Newfoundland, this same school of thought was present and crystallized in many supporting conscription to prevent the destruction of Newfoundland's bravest and brightest while allowing the cowards and shirkers to remain safely at home.[6]

The idea that only Newfoundland's best and brightest were dying in the trenches feeds into reconfigured conceptions of ethnicity and gender that existed in wartime Newfoundland. As shown in the previous chapter, recruiters in Newfoundland argued that those who refused to enlist were either uneducated, unmanly, or unpatriotic. The idea that voluntary recruitment damaged the dominion had a lasting impact on public discourse and eventually became part of Newfoundland's collective memory. Robert Harding has shown that authors, journalists, and reporters suggested that Newfoundland's problems in the post-war period, which ultimately led to the end of self-government, could have been avoided if Newfoundland's best and brightest were not killed in the war.[7]

In November 1917, H.A. Winter got into a debate over the responsibility of the lack of recruits with P.T. McGrath, editor of the *Evening Herald*. According to McGrath, the people of Newfoundland were mostly to blame for the lack of recruits for the regiment. He complained that many young men raged against the Russian withdrawal, yet they risked the withdrawal of the Newfoundland Regiment by refusing to enlist.[8]

Conversely, Winter argued that the government had a responsibility to the empire to ensure that citizens of the dominion were encouraged, and if necessary, forced to do their patriotic duty. He said that from among the slackers in Newfoundland, over a thousand could be found who were of military age, physically fit, without dependents, or a valid excuse for not signing up. He believed that forcing these men to enlist would not be a hardship or injustice but would be righting a wrong. In a vicious attack on the unenlisted, Winter denied the human value of shirkers, saying that the dominion would not suffer if they died in France.[9]

In February of 1918, the *Evening Telegram*, and its newly appointed editor C.T. James, found itself at odds again with P.T. McGrath over the reasons for Newfoundland's slow recruiting rates. This argument began on 15 February when P.T. McGrath published an article on recruiting for the forestry corps and the Newfoundland Regiment. McGrath argued that the lack of recruits was so low because of cowardice, indifference, and high fish prices.[10]

James took umbrage with McGrath's assertion. He agreed that some communities were indifferent to the war effort and seduced by the lure of high fish prices, but he adamantly denied that Newfoundland men were cowards. Despite denying their cowardice, admitting that men were encouraged to stay home by fish prices was a scathing indictment. Throughout the war recruiters declared that fishers who refused to enlist due to high fish prices were at best greedy war profiteers and, at worst, accessories to murder.[11]

In response to James's defence of fishers, P.T. McGrath redoubled his accusations that recruiting was slow because of cowardice. McGrath explained to James that Canada, Britain, and the United States had its share of cowards and Newfoundland was no different. He suggested that James spend some time in clubs, theatres, hockey games, and professional societies to see all the slackers who refused to enlist.[12]

James replied that labelling men as slackers would not help recruiting. He said that if the calls to patriotism and duty had not motivated men to enlist, they would need to be conscripted and attempts to shame them by calling them cowards and slackers would not work. Despite their disagreement over the reasons for men not enlisting, both the *Evening Herald* and the *Evening Telegram* agreed that conscription was required to ensure that men performed the patriotic duty that Britain expected of male citizens.[13]

Three years of voluntary recruitment resulted in a drastic renegotiation of gender and ethnicity in Newfoundland. Recruiter's speeches, articles, and letters to the editor reconfigured conceptions of masculinity and Britishness to include service to the state as the primary responsibility for all British men. When enlistment rates declined, many recruiters resorted to a campaign of gendered and ethnic shaming, suggesting that those who refused to enlist were un-British, unmanly and of little value to the dominion. When this campaign of shaming failed, many recruiters argued that the government needed to enact selective conscription to ensure that the government forced every man in Newfoundland to live up to the expectations of male citizens in a British dominion at war.

"A MORE UNJUST SELECTION IT WOULD BE IMPOSSIBLE TO DEVISE"

During the voluntary recruitment campaign, many citizens and government officials believed it was the primary duty of every man in Newfoundland to provide military service for the state, giving their life if need be. By 1916, the Newfoundland Patriotic Association was having difficulty getting enough recruits to fill the ranks of the

Newfoundland Regiment. Many supporters of conscription argued it was unfair to allow men to choose if they would enlist or not because every eligible man was required to provide service to the empire. Those who made this argument believed that it was only fair for the government to decide who served and who did not.

An early proponent of this argument was William Coaker, who initially opposed conscription. On 27 March 1916, Coaker gave a speech in the house of assembly that addressed the voluntary recruiting campaign and conscription. He told the house that he believed in voluntary recruitment. He described those who enlisted and risked their lives for their country as the "noblest creature that God ever made."[14] Despite this, Coaker also said that if men stopped coming forward to support the regiment that he would support conscription:

> In connection with this subject I may state that I am a firm believer in the principle of conscription at such times as those we are now passing through … I say that should the day ever come when every young man is required to do his very best to safeguard our Empire to uphold its flag, and to further the cause which it has espoused, and the volunteer system should fail, then every available man should compulsorily be called upon, and it should not be left to any man to refuse to go, and remain idly home and allow a few splendid, brave young men to go forth and fight for them. It ought to be the duty of every young man of a certain age, who is physically fit, to come forward and respond. Why should a certain number of men come forward voluntarily and go forth prepared to meet hardships and privations, to live the life of the trenches or to ceaselessly watch on one of the ships that helps to guard our Empire, to chance death itself, whilst others stay behind and live on the fat of the land, enjoying what our soldiers and sailors are preserving for us, and laughing at them for their pains? If ever conscription becomes necessary … I, for one, will have no hesitation in supporting a conscription act in this House.

Coaker's statement makes it clear that even those who initially opposed the formation of the regiment now believed that every Newfoundlander had an obligation to enlist. For Coaker, conscription was not about forcing "cowards" to join but making sure the duty placed on all British men was spread out equally.[15]

Some opponents of conscription worried that it would damage the fishery, while supporters of conscription argued the opposite. In July of 1917, in the *Evening Herald*, P.T. McGrath warned that enacting conscription would destroy the economy. McGrath admitted that conscription had worked in other jurisdictions, but he argued that conditions were different in Newfoundland. He claimed that the nature the fishery prevented women from taking over men's work if they were conscripted. Therefore, McGrath contended that mass conscription would strip Newfoundland of the male labour required for a successful fishery.[16]

In response to this, H.A. Winter responded in the *Evening Telegram*, informing his readers that selective conscription would not be a press-gang that would ham-fistedly conscript every single military-aged man in Newfoundland. Winter believed that Newfoundland's system of voluntary recruitment was unfair to everyone involved. He said that under voluntary enlistment, only the best men enlisted, leaving the worst remaining at home. Winter also argued that the optional recruiting system was unfair to communities across Newfoundland because some had sent more recruits than others. For example, Winter showed that Portugal Cove had sent nearly every eligible man, while barely a single man enlisted from their neighbouring communities. Selective conscription could rectify this, according to Winter, by having the Recruiting Committee select who it would draft from each town so that the least damage was done to the fishery in any one area.[17]

In July of 1917, the Methodist Conference of Newfoundland passed a resolution calling on the government to pass selective conscription. C.A. Whitemarsh, secretary of the conference, wrote a letter to Governor Davidson informing him that conference opinion was that it was imperative to maintain the regiment as an act of loyalty for those who had given their lives and those who were currently fighting. Whitemarsh emphasized that the conference believed every citizen had a responsibility to provide military service to the state. He made this clear in their resolution when said that the rights of a citizen came with the responsibility to sacrifice all their possessions and even their lives in the defence of their country. Whitemarsh concluded his resolution by calling on the government to enact a law that required all male citizens to enroll so that it could draft a sufficient number to fill vacancies in the Newfoundland Regiment.[18]

Another argument used in favour of selective conscription was that the injustice of voluntary recruiting was discouraging men from enlisting. In April of 1918, "Imperialist" wrote a letter to the editor of the *Evening Telegram* explaining why he believed that the voluntary recruiting system was a waste of time. Imperialist claimed he had travelled through many rural communities, and everywhere he went, men told him that they were neither disloyal nor unpatriotic. Instead, they said that they would not enlist while there were slackers in their community who refused to go and lived comfortably at home. They said that if the government passed a bill making it mandatory for everyone to do their duty, then they would gladly come forward to enlist. Imperialist urged the government to pass a selective conscription bill because he believed it to be the best way to raise men for the regiment while ensuring that some able-bodied men did not stay home and get rich from the war.[19]

"Orlick," a frequent columnist for the *Evening Advocate*, also extolled the judiciousness and equitability of selective conscription. In May of 1918, Orlick argued that under voluntary enlistment, some patriotic families had sent all of their sons to fight in the war, while less patriotic families had sent none. Orlick thought it was unfair for some men to have served for three or more years without a furlough home, while other men lived comfortably at home. He attacked men who remained while soldiers were wounded multiple times and forced to return to the front because there were not enough new recruits. For Orlick, selective conscription was not just a method of obtaining soldiers for the regiment but a way to ensure that all families equally shared the burden of the war.[20]

The belief that conscription was fair represents a clear deviation from classical liberal principles. Proponents of conscription turned away from the classical liberal prioritization of individual liberty and towards collectivist values that ensured every family, community, and citizen sacrificed equally for the collective security of the dominion.

"NEWFOUNDLAND MUST AND WILL DO HER FULL DUTY"

When the house of assembly met in 1918, the most significant matter of discussion was selective conscription. In his Speech from the Throne, Governor Harris warned that Russia's withdrawal from the war left allied lines vulnerable to German attack. In order to defeat Germany, Harris said that the British Empire needed men now, more than ever. He reminded the house that the Newfoundland Regiment had brought glory to the dominion, earning itself the prefix "Royal."

He said that conscription was needed to replenish the ranks of the regiment and fulfill the dominion's duty to the British Empire. Harris's speech emphasized the importance of conscription by drawing on the patriotic sentiment of the house of assembly; reminded them that the British Empire desperately needed more men, and exploited the pride that many citizens had for the Newfoundland Regiment.[21]

In response to the Throne Speech, George Grimes stated that before the Spring Offensive, he believed the only proper way to enact conscription would be to hold a referendum. However, the unprecedented advances by the German army convinced Grimes that the state had to take decisive action. He warned the house that while Newfoundland was waiting for a referendum, Germany was quickly striking a deathblow against Allied armies. Given the urgent nature of recruiting in the British Empire, Grimes argued that it was now necessary for the dominion to pass conscription to protect its honour, to save the Royal Newfoundland Regiment, and to prove that Newfoundland was the most loyal dominion in the British Empire.[22]

On 24 April 1918, Prime Minister Lloyd introduced a bill in the house of assembly titled "An Act Respecting Military Service." The bill would allow the conscription of unmarried men between the ages of nineteen and forty. If passed, it would split single men into four classes. The first class included single men between the ages of nineteen and twenty-four, the second comprised men between the ages of twenty-five and twenty-nine, the third class consisted of men between the ages of thirty and thirty-four, and the fourth class included men between the ages of thirty-five and thirty-nine. The Governor in Council could call up each of these classes, and the men in each category would automatically become "soldiers of the King" at a date specified in a proclamation. Lloyd told the house that he introduced this bill because it was right and just, because the returned soldiers demanded it, and because it was essential to maintain the regiment.[23]

The bill also provided a process for men to seek exemption from the draft. The government could exempt them for one of four distinct reasons: if their work served the national interest, if they already had brothers serving, or if single men were primarily responsible for supporting their parents, brothers, or sisters. The final reason for exemption was for men whose health was so poor that their service would be of "no military value." Unlike Britain and Canada, conscientious objection was not a valid ground for an exemption in Newfoundland.[24]

There was minimal opposition to the first reading of the conscription bill. John Currie declared that he had supported conscription from the beginning of the war because it was the best way to support the regiment. Currie also advised the house that he did not care if his support for conscription cost him his seat in the next election. He declared that if young men were willing to sacrifice their lives for the war effort, he was more than happy to sacrifice his political career.[25]

Similarly, J.R. Bennett also said that he was a supporter of conscription since the war began. While Bennett admitted that patriotism and loyalty fuelled the voluntary recruiting campaign at the beginning of the war, he advocated that the government pass new legislation to ensure the conscription of 1000 soldiers needed to maintain the regiment. Bennett concluded his speech by saying that the bill was not only the most efficient way to attract enough recruits but also that selective conscription was the most judicial way of preserving the regiment because it would put the least burden on families.[26]

The only instance of opposition to the conscription bill occurred on 25 April, when the house of assembly resolved itself to a Committee of the Whole on the bill. The first to address this bill in the committee was William Walsh, a People's Party member for Placentia and St Mary's. Walsh acknowledged that conscription was necessary, but he was adamant that the government had no business enacting conscription without consulting the people. He told the house:

> The point I wish to emphasize, Mr Speaker, in connection with [the conscription bill], is that, if it had been introduced by an assembly representative of the people, who had been sent here by the people, and would have to go back to the people, it would be a different matter. This measure is being introduced by men who have not the slightest intention of ever offering themselves for re-election, men who have come here with their commissions in their pockets, men who have been taken out of one office, because there was not sufficient work there and put into another office, so that they might be retained to give the appearance of a representative assembly to pass this measure or any other measure. I say, sir, it is unconstitutional, un-British, unfair, and the country will not have it. When the people of this country are aroused and find out the tactics of this administration there is going to be trouble. It is not for love of the British Empire that this bill is being put through, and it is not for the good of the country that these gentlemen are roused to this pitch of patriotism.[27]

Following a second reading of the bill, Walsh requested that it be deferred for two days to allow all members to give it some serious thought. Lloyd told Walsh that it would be impossible to delay the bill because it was urgent and of the utmost national importance. Walsh was outraged that the prime minister denied his request. He told Lloyd that to deny a deferral on one of the most serious bills to have ever been introduced in a British house of assembly was un-British and unfair. He told the house: "We are asked here to-day to conscript blood, and I do not think in view of the nature of the Bill that it is reasonable to have this request refused." Despite his protest, the bill was read a second time the next day, passed, and sent to the legislative council.[28]

Michael Gibbs, a former Conservative MHA and mayor of St John's, was the only voice of dissent on the conscription issue in the legislative council. With a little debate on some amendments, the legislative council passed the Military Service Act, and the governor gave it royal assent. It is clear from the speeches given by the various members of the council that while all members lamented the failure of voluntary recruitment, there was some debate over who was responsible. Augustus Goodridge, a former Tory premier of Newfoundland, and Robert Bishop, a partner in Bishop Brothers Ltd, believed that citizens had been given ample opportunity to enlist and that it was a failure of the people. Richard Squires, on the other hand, laid the blame on members of the opposition for a failure to fully support the formation of the Newfoundland Regiment at the beginning of the war. Still others, like Mr Gibbs, argued that it was the government that failed in its duty to set concrete goals and make detailed plans to achieve those goals. Despite the debate over who was to blame, it is clear that the vast majority of members of the legislative council believed that Newfoundland had a duty to maintain the Newfoundland Regiment and was failing to do so.

OPPOSITION TO RECRUITING AND CONSCRIPTION

Throughout the war, recruiters told the people of Newfoundland that military service was the pinnacle of both masculinity and Britishness. They argued that all men had a duty to provide military service to the state, and those who refused were cowards, slackers, un-British, and unmanly. Despite the powerful influence of recruiters, who sought to redefine masculinity and Britishness, not everyone in Newfoundland bought into this wartime renegotiation of British manhood.

Gauging the level of opposition to Newfoundland's war effort, recruiting and conscription is difficult. There is no evidence that there was any organized opposition to the war or pacifist movement in Newfoundland. Despite this, it seems clear that some parts of Newfoundland society were less than receptive to the war effort, recruiting campaigns, and particularly conscription. The lack of source material hinders any analysis of the prevalence of opposition, conscientious objection, or pacifism. Given the importance placed on patriotism during the war, it is likely that newspapers would have been unwilling to publish anything that could be considered "unpatriotic." Therefore, it was very reasonable that newspapers would not publish editorials or letters to the editor that could potentially damage Newfoundland's war effort. To make matters worse, in 1917, the colonial secretary appointed a press censor who had the power to ban any newspapers publishing "unpatriotic" material. Despite this, there is some evidence of varying levels of opposition to the war effort.[29]

Some of the first criticism of Newfoundland's participation in the war came from William Coaker. Shortly after the war began, the *Mail and Advocate* published an article that criticized both the *Evening Telegram* and the *Daily News* for advocating for the formation of a Newfoundland regiment. Coaker thought that forming a regiment was an unnecessary expense that the dominion could not afford. Instead of wasting money on its own regiment, Coaker argued that the dominion should focus on recruiting men to enlist with the Newfoundland Royal Naval Reserve and encouraging those who wanted to serve with the army to join the Canadian Expeditionary Force.[30]

Coaker's opposition to the Newfoundland Regiment drew the ire of many people. The *Daily News* published an angry letter from a naval reservist stationed on the *Calypso*. The reservist warned Coaker that if he lived in the United Kingdom, his printing press would have been destroyed by angry mobs an hour after the paper was printed. William Temple said Coaker had disgraced the dominion by giving anything less than his full support to the formation of a regiment. Temple also accused Coaker of being a hypocrite for taking advantage of the freedoms the British government offered its citizens that allowed him to publish such treasonous material. Instead of hindering recruiting efforts, Temple recommended that Coaker support the defence of the British law that allowed him to print his "obnoxious sheet."[31]

In response to the *Daily News*' letter, the editor of the *Mail and Advocate* criticized the publication of a threat against Coaker. H.M. Mosdell, editor of the *Mail and Advocate* in 1914, highlighted the hypocrisy of a British newspaper editor publishing an article that called for mobs of angry men to destroy the *Advocate*'s printing press while describing Britain as the defender of freedom and tolerance. Mosdell asked the fishers of Newfoundland to carefully consider what respect the *Daily News* had for the rule of law and concluded that "it is time the fishers kept their powder dry and their guns well primed. Those who play with fire must not complain if by so doing they burn their fingers."[32]

The *Mail and Advocate* also published several letters to the editor that opposed the war effort. One note, written by an author named "Determined" from Elliston, expressed the author's desire to take up arms, not against the Germans, but against "Surtax Morris" and his party that were ruling the dominion with an iron rod. "Determined" argued that Morris's policy of taxation was unfair to producers and was starving their families. Before going to fight the Germans in Europe, Determined declared that the fishers of Newfoundland should unite and defeat the Germans who were ruling the country. In another letter to the editor, an author by the name of "Common Sense" defended his belief that fishers were the lifeblood of the country and that the war effort should not deplete them.[33]

Despite Coaker's initial opinions regarding the formation of a Newfoundland regiment, the hostile reaction he received from the general public meant that his vocal opposition was very short-lived. By early 1916, John St John, the new editor of the *Mail and Advocate*, admitted that Coaker initially opposed the regiment and still felt the same way. However, St John noted that Coaker would not publicly oppose recruiting efforts to avoid dividing the public during such a national crisis. In the same article, seemingly to prove that Coaker was not unpatriotic, St John highlighted Coaker's efforts to obtain recruits for the Newfoundland Royal Naval Reserve on behalf of the Newfoundland Patriotic Association.[34]

Coaker's opposition to the formation of a Newfoundland regiment was very well documented but lasted only a brief period. The aversion to conscription is much harder to discern. In early 1918, some newspapers published editorials that did not outright oppose conscription but warned about the repercussions of it. On 6 April 1918, P.T. McGrath published an article in the *Herald*, which argued that compulsion would not work in Newfoundland because women and children could replace men neither in the fishery nor the lumber camp. McGrath's concern, which seems to be shared by many fishers, was that selective conscription would strip rural Newfoundland of its male labour and result in economic decline.[35]

Shortly after McGrath published this article, Miranda, a frequent columnist for the *Evening Advocate*, also expressed concern about the number of fishers taken from rural Newfoundland. Miranda told their readers that the country was entirely dependent on the fishery and that women could not fish because the work was too strenuous. Similarly, Miranda also stated that women could not perform the work of lumbermen. They argued that the removal of large amounts of men would be detrimental to the economy of Newfoundland and would result in the dominion requiring financial assistance from Britain. Miranda concluded their article by placing the blame for the recruiting situation directly on the shoulders of men who were eligible but refused to enlist.[36]

As the support for conscription increased, those who opposed conscription also became more vocal. On 27 April 1918, W.J. O'Neill, editor of the *Plaindealer*, published a scathing article, attacking the government's attempts to pass a conscription bill without consulting the people. The editor, W.J. O'Neill, had two primary issues with the government's handling of the Military Service Act. The first was that the government refused to hold a referendum on the conscription issue. O'Neill was outraged that the government would attempt to force men to enlist in the military without consulting them on the debate. He reminded his readers that Canada and Australia had elections or referendums where the people had an opportunity to vote on conscription and said that the government believed its citizens were too stupid or unpatriotic to be trusted to vote on the matter. O'Neill did not necessarily disagree with conscription in principle, but he firmly believed the government should consult the people on the issue before it was passed into law.[37]

W.J. O'Neill's other issue with conscription was W.F. Lloyd's coupling of the Military Service Act with another act titled "An Act to Further Extend the Term of the Present Legislature." Lloyd explained that this bill would allow the current government to serve for another year without an election, and it was vital to the successful implementation of the Military Service Act because it would prevent a general election, which would potentially derail conscription.[38] O'Neill, on the other hand, did not believe that the national government sincerely thought that an extension of parliament was necessary for the implementation of compulsory service. Instead, he accused Lloyd and Coaker of making a pact with the governor, whereby they would support conscription in return for an extension of their mandate. O'Neill strongly believed that the combination of these two acts was wholly unconstitutional and a gross violation of the rights of the people:

> we can promise that any attempt to override and ignore the sovereign rights of the people will meet with strong opposition on the part of the entire electorate. It would be an outrage and a gross violation of our constitutional rights if the present "Rump" Parliament were to be firmly installed to power as a result of this corrupt and dishonest bargaining. We can assure that parties involved that the question will not be allowed to rest, and to be decided within the four walls of the House of Assembly … Throughout the length and breadth of the land the people are demanding an election, in order that they may be enabled to express their opinions upon many momentous questions that have lately arisen. They are entitled as of right to the exercise of franchise at least once in every four years. By their dishonorable and corrupt compact, the Governor has made himself a consenting party to this violent assault upon the liberties of the people, he has consented to become a tool in the hands of Coaker and his satellites in order that the passage of conscription may be assured.

O'Neill's attacks on the prime minister, the governor, and the Military Service Act quickly earned him the ire of the prime minister.[39]

On the morning of 27 April, after reading the *Plaindealer*, Prime Minister Lloyd took his copy of the newspaper and requested an urgent meeting with Governor Harris. In this meeting, Lloyd told Harris the *Plaindealer* had accused them of making a pact with Coaker to pass conscription and called for an uprising against the Military Service Act. Lloyd requested that Harris sign a minute of council that would allow him to suppress this issue of the paper and to seize the office of the *Plaindealer* to prevent any additional anti-conscription material from being printed. The governor told Lloyd he believed in giving people like O'Neill "enough rope to hang themselves," and suggested that very little would come of one edition of a disreputable newspaper. The prime minister maintained that this issue could cause a "violent outburst" against the conscription bill. Lloyd insisted that this newspaper was so inflammatory that he might as well withdraw the bill, as it would have no hopes of passing if the *Plaindealer* published this edition.[40]

The governor eventually acquiesced to Lloyd's request. He believed that his personal feelings on the censorship of the *Plaindealer* should not influence the matter, and he signed a minute of council that allowed the constabulary to take control of the *Plaindealer*'s office and equipment and destroy any copies of the 27 April edition of the newspaper. This order also allowed the postmaster general to destroy any copies of the paper circulating in the mail.

Within the hour, the Newfoundland constabulary had seized the office of the *Plaindealer.* Shortly after the police had entered the premises, C.H. Hutchings called Lloyd, while he was still in Harris's office, to determine how much he should interfere with the operations of the *Plaindealer.* Lloyd informed Hutchings and the governor that they would allow the *Plaindealer* to operate, but the police would ensure the newspaper did not publish anything that would interfere with the passing of the Military Service Act.[41]

On the same day that the Newfoundland constabulary seized the premises of the *Plaindealer*, the prime minister addressed the house of assembly on the issue. He confirmed that the government would not hesitate to shut down any opposition to voluntary recruiting or conscription. Lloyd informed the house that the police had taken charge of the *Plaindealer* and were preventing the anti-conscription issue from circulating. He also promised the house that the constabulary would not interfere with the daily operations of the *Plaindealer*, other than ensuring that O'Neill published no more anti-conscription material.[42]

Despite giving his word to both the governor and the house of assembly that he would allow the *Plaindealer* to operate under police supervision, Lloyd ordered the constabulary to shut the *Plaindealer* down for two weeks and prevent any publication whatsoever. On 6 May, P.J. Summers drafted a bond that would finally allow the *Plaindealer* to resume printing. The following day, W.J. O'Neill signed a bond that allowed him to continue publication if he agreed not to publish any material that was not pre-approved by the inspector general of the Newfoundland constabulary. The penalty for breaking this bond was an exorbitant fine of $5,000.[43]

The day after Governor Harris gave the Military Service Act royal assent, he wrote to the secretary of state for the colonies to inform him that conscription had passed in Newfoundland. He told Long that St John's undoubtedly supported conscription. Despite the support in St John's, Harris stated he believed rural Newfoundland opposed conscription.[44]

Harris was right about the anger over conscription in rural Newfoundland. Two days after the conscription became law, there was a riot in Wesleyville, a small community in Bonavista Bay. While the details of this incident were scarce, the *Evening Telegram* reported that a group of men in Wesleyville were upset with the passing of the Military Service Act and rioted through the community, interrupting a patriotic parade. The riots came to a crescendo when a local priest gave a pro-conscription sermon, resulting in many parishioners storming out of the church.[45]

Two days after the *Evening Telegram* reported on the rioting in Wesleyville, W.W. Halfyard (an FPU MHA for Fogo who replaced J.R. Bennett as colonial secretary) sent a letter to the editors of every major newspaper. Halfyard informed the editors they could not publish any material that could potentially encourage opposition to conscription. He used the "trouble at Wesleyville" as an example of precisely the kind of content that newspapers were not to be allowed to publish. Halfyard warned that if any newspaper published articles that could damage conscription, the government would shut the paper down and suppress any offending issues.[46]

Despite this stern warning from the colonial secretary, H.M. Mosdell published several articles in the *Daily Star* that criticized how the government was enforcing conscription. On 23 May, Mosdell complained that it was unfair for the government to require men, who would undoubtedly receive a medical exemption, to travel to St John's for a medical exam. Mosdell said that this process was slow and resulted in fishers waiting in St John's instead of fishing. He complained that regulations prohibiting men of military age from going to sea unless they possessed a rejected volunteer badge inconvenienced fishing crews. He pointed out that many boats had rejected volunteers who offered their service before the government began issuing badges. In instances like this, customs officers held up entire fishing crews while they verified a single man's status. On 28 May, Mosdell also reported that he had received many angry letters from fishers who were unable to obtain exemption papers, resulting in the fishery coming to a standstill in some areas.[47]

The following day, W.W. Halfyard, asked Harris for approval for a minute of council that would allow the constabulary to seize the *Daily Star*'s premises and remain for two or three days to ensure they did not publish more material that interfered with the enforcement of conscription. Harris gave his approval, and a minute of council was issued that allowed the constabulary to seize the premises and equipment of the *Daily Star* and to destroy any copies of the newspaper from 23 or 28 May. When the police entered the premises of the *Daily Star*, they not only destroyed the issues included in the minute of council, but they also shut down the presses and refused to allow the printing of any material.[48]

By 5 June, the Newfoundland constabulary had yet to leave the office of the *Daily Star* and had utterly shut the newspaper down for six days. When news reached Governor Harris that the police were still prohibiting the *Daily Star* from publication, he was outraged. Harris sent a telegraph to W.W. Halfyard chastising him for interfering with the business of the *Daily Star* for so long. The governor reminded Halfyard that when he approached him to approve the minute of council, he promised that the constabulary would only be in the *Star*'s office for two or three days, and they would not impede publication. Once Harris learned that Halfyard had broken his promise, the governor phoned the deputy minister of justice. Harris told him to lift the embargo immediately and declared that he was committed to avoiding all tyrannical use of the War Measures Act.[49]

The governor was not the only person who thought the closure of the *Daily Star* was overzealous. Richard Squires, the majority shareholder of the *Daily Star*, argued that the ham-fisted censorship of his newspaper was a violation of fundamental British principles: freedom of thought, speech, and conscience. He said that the suppression was a vengeful attack on his newspaper for political reasons. Squires defended the articles, arguing that they were legitimate criticisms of the way the government was implementing conscription and did not attack the Military Service Act itself. On 2 June, Squires applied for an injunction from the Supreme Court of Newfoundland for the removal of the constabulary from the premises.[50]

When the colonial secretary replied to Harris's letter. He told the governor that there must have been a misunderstanding because he had made no promises to be out of the *Daily Star*'s office within two or three days. In a separate letter, Michael Cashin informed Harris that the government intended to close the *Daily Star* for approximately one week, and they would lift the embargo by 6 June. Despite this, Cashin admitted that Richard Squires's application to the Supreme Court would delay the reopening of the newspaper because opening it before the court issued a decision would give the appearance that the government believed its actions were not legal. Cashin also criticized the governor for becoming involved in an issue that was wholly the responsibility of the government: "I would respectfully point out that it would be an unwise policy for Your Excellency, as a constituent factor in the administration of this dominion, to proceed with the policy which your letter suggests and insist upon a raising of the embargo in the meantime. I would suggest that our proper course is to await the decision of the Supreme Court, and if this should be against the Government, of course the lifting of the embargo will follow automatically; but if it should be in favour of the government, then we would be in a position ourselves to at once allow the 'Star' to republish."[51] Cashin further expressed displeasure that the governor would directly interfere with the government by ordering the deputy justice minister to life the embargo: "I hope I may be pardoned if I express my surprise that Your Excellency should have thought it proper to communicate directly with the Deputy Minister of Justice to tell him that the embargo must be withdrawn at once. I write this at the close of the Committee of the Council, to which I submitted your letter, and this embodies the views of both my colleagues and myself."[52] Upon receiving Cashin's response, Governor Harris drastically changed his tone. He admitted that it was inappropriate from him to call the deputy justice minister as it may have seemed that the governor was ordering the end of the embargo, which was not his prerogative to do. Despite his change of tone, Harris did not back down on his recommendation that the government end the shutdown of the *Daily Star.* He reminded Cashin that the people would likely blame him for the excessive use of the War Measures Act to censor the *Star*.[53]

Harris's recommendation that the government end the embargo on the *Daily Star* meant little as the Supreme Court had reached a decision on 6 June. Chief Justice William Horwood ruled that the government had every right to suppress, seize, and destroy issues of the *Daily Star* that it deemed were a threat to Newfoundland's war effort. However, Horwood also stated that the constabulary carried out the objectives of the Order in Council, to suppress, seize, and destroy the offending issues by 30 May. He ruled that while the War Measures Act did allow the government to censor certain material, the government had to interfere as little as possible with the rights of citizens when imposing censorship. Given that the *Daily Star* had not attempted to publish any more material that could compromise the Military Service Act, Chief Justice Horwood agreed that the government was overzealous, and granted an injunction that ordered the constabulary to vacate the office of the Daily Star immediately.[54]

Lloyd's crackdown on the *Plaindealer*'s and *Daily Star*'s anti-conscription articles suggests that there was significant opposition to conscription in rural Newfoundland. This opposition common enough that the prime minister feared a single article could whip rural fishers into a frenzy that would crush attempts at imposing conscription. By using such authoritarian measures to stop civil discourse, the government showed how determined it was to enact conscription despite the opposition.

These incidents also represented tension in the wartime renegotiations of the relationship between citizens and the state. In this case, the government not only believed that male citizens owed their lives to the state but also that private citizens had no right to interfere in how the state obtained military service from citizens. The *Plaindealer* and *Daily Star* pushed back against the government, arguing that they were not interfering with conscription but legitimately criticizing the way the government was enacting it. By reacting swiftly to the protests of these newspapers, the government showed that it cared little for the liberal right to free speech and that it would ensure conscription passed regardless of the opposition.

Another vital source of information about opposition to conscription in Newfoundland came from correspondence between William Coaker and the various FPU councils across the dominion. On 26 April, Coaker sent a circular to all FPU councils in Newfoundland. Coaker told FPU members that if enough recruits came forward, the government would not need to enforce the Military Service Act until the fall, if at all, and men would be free to prosecute the Labrador fishery without interference. While encouraging men to enlist might seem benign, many recruiters viewed Coaker's circular to be a wilful call for men to oppose the Military Service Act. The *Evening Telegram* was one of many papers that accused Coaker of attempting to encourage men to resist the Military Service Act.[55]

Speaking in the house of assembly, William Coaker defended this circular, maintaining that he intended to ease the vehement opposition to conscription in Northern Newfoundland. His statements to the house show just how much aversion existed to the Military Service Act: "I want this House and the Country to understand, that the people did not want conscription. I tell you that if it had gone to the vote, it would have been defeated two to one ... Why did I send that circular? Because the people were aflame. I know that the slightest friction would be as a match to powder, and the whole North would have been aroused in opposition." Coaker told the house that he had received hundreds of messages from FPU members and FPU councils calling on him to oppose the Military Service Act. Despite this, he was determined to do his duty and support conscription.[56]

Unlike Britain and Canada, Newfoundland did not make any allowance for conscientious objection in the Military Service Act. Without any religious groups that opposed the war effort, such as the Mennonites, Doukhobors, Brethren in Christ, Hutterites, and Quakers in Canada, it is likely that the Government of Newfoundland saw no need for legislation allowing for conscientious objection.[57] Despite this, there is still some evidence of individuals who ethically objected to military service.

In July of 1918, Job and Jabez Taylor of Kelligrews received draft papers but refused to report to the Newfoundland Regiment in St John's. On two occasions, the local Magistrate allowed Job and Jabez to present themselves for enlistment, but the brothers refused twice. On 11 July 1918, the constabulary arrested the pair for breaching the Military Service Act, and a magistrate sentenced them to two years in prison. After seven days of imprisonment, the Taylor brothers requested that the justice department release them so they could join the Newfoundland Regiment. Initially, both P.J. Summers, the deputy justice minister, and Governor Harris agreed to pardon them and release them on the condition that they join the regiment. However, before Summers released the men, he found out that they had applied for exemption, which Jabez had received. Summers was now convinced that neither brother had the intention of enlisting. He withdrew his request for clemency for the two men and asked the governor to allow them to remain in prison. On 1 September, following a ruling by the Military Service Tribunal, Governor Harris requested that Jabez be released because he had received an exemption and that Job be released on the condition that he immediately join the Newfoundland Regiment. Job never reported for enlistment.[58]

In October of 1918, the constabulary arrested Berkley Davis of Pinchard's Island for defaulting on the Military Service Act. Magistrate

Mifflin of Greenspond sentenced Berkley to three years in prison. Upon arrival, P.J. Summers recommended that Governor Harris release Davis on the condition that he enlist in the regiment. Davis refused Summer's offer to join and claimed that he had conscientious objections to military service and chose to remain in prison. Berkley remained in HMP until the governor released him after the war ended.[59]

Poor record-keeping by the justice department makes it impossible to tell how many men the constabulary arrested for refusing to report after receiving draft papers. Government records indicate that constabulary arrested John Peddle and Matthew Ryder for defaulting. After spending some time in prison, both men agreed that they would prefer to enlist than spend several years in Her Majesty's Penitentiary. It is impossible to tell how many men refused to buy into the rhetoric that masculinity was determined by ability to perform military service. The cases of the Taylor brothers, Peddle, Ryder, and Berkley show that at least some men refused to accept wartime conceptions of masculinity and were willing to face jail time to stand up for their principles.[60]

CONCLUSION

Despite the efforts of Newfoundland's recruiters, by 1918, the voluntary recruiting system did not provide enough soldiers to fill the ranks of the Newfoundland Regiment. Many people viewed the withdrawal of the regiment from the field as a profound national shame as Newfoundlanders believed the regiment was proved to the world Newfoundlanders were ideal specimens of British masculinity. To rectify this situation, the government of Newfoundland introduced the Military Service Act, which allowed them to force young men into service. The supporters of this bill argued that it was necessary to ensure that Newfoundland men lived up to the gendered expectations of British citizens during the war. This shows how powerful wartime renegotiations of gender were.

Another argument in favour of conscription arose from wartime alterations to the liberal order that prioritized the rights of the community over the rights of the individual. Supporters of conscription argued that all young men had a duty to the state and allowing them to decide whether or not they would serve was unfair. In their eyes, the fairest method of supporting the Newfoundland Regiment was for the government to ensure that the service was spread equally among all families. This would ensure that the sacrifice did the least damage to the community as a whole.

Despite the power of wartime conceptions of British masculinity, there were those in Newfoundland who resisted them. William Coaker maintained that a Newfoundland Regiment was a costly endeavour that the dominion could not afford. Low recruiting rates in rural Newfoundland may have indicated resistance to recruiting propaganda. It is unclear whether rural were apathetic to the war effort or simply could not afford to enlist. During the debates over conscription, several newspaper editors attempted to speak out against conscription, but the government used the War Measures Act to silence them. Similarly, there was some rioting in opposition to the Conscription Act in Northern Newfoundland, but the War Measures Act ensured that little evidence of this was left for historians.

During the First World War, citizens and the liberal state negotiated a new wartime social covenant. The prime characteristic of this new covenant was a renegotiated conception of masculinity that resulted in the loss of men's liberty through conscription. The imposition of conscription was perhaps the most significant wartime alteration to the philosophy of the liberal state. Before the war, the liberal order praised the liberty of the individual above all else. During the war, however, the Newfoundland government decided that the freedom of the individual took a backseat to the needs of the war effort. In response to the sacrifices of lives and liberty, the citizens of Newfoundland expected the government to take a more significant role in the lives of everyday citizens to ensure the people could cope with the conditions created by the war effort.

7

Women's War Work

On 31 August 1914, Lady Margaret Davidson announced the formation of the Women's Patriotic Association (WPA), whose mandate was to "arrange for the providing of necessary articles for the sick and wounded, and also for those who are going to the front to uphold the honour of Newfoundland in defence of the Empire." Davidson held the inaugural meeting of the WPA at the British Hall in St John's. Over seven hundred women who wished to support the war effort, showed up to hear Lady Davidson speak. She addressed her audience:

> Let me first say how very glad I am to welcome you all here to-day and to see how many have responded to my appeal – an appeal, which I verily believe was not necessary – for I am convinced that it was only a call that was required – and you were all waiting ready to respond. I felt sure that there were many wishing to work to do something for our brave soldiers and sailors, who are risking their very lives for us, and who yet did not know the best ways of helping or what the needs of those at the front might be. That this is a unique time, when we are required to make personal sacrifices, such as we have never thought or dreamt of before, there can be no doubt. It is the best we can do for those who are enduring daily hardships, and giving their health and their strength for our beloved Empire … All of the best kind of men either volunteered, or if they only realized how desperate the situation was would volunteer and I feel sure will still do

> so – and it is the duty of us women to cheer them on and encourage them to go. I do feel so very strongly … I do feel the call to arms very strongly – and the call comes to us women just as much to do our duty, and there are many ways in which we can and should answer it.[1]

While the Women's Patriotic Association started with seven hundred women in St John's, it quickly exploded across the dominion. By the end of the war, the WPA sent thousands of articles of clothing, medical supplies, and comfort items worth over $6,500,000 in modern Canadian dollars.[2]

WOMEN'S WORK AND WOMEN'S SUFFRAGE AT THE BEGINNING OF THE WAR

At the outset of the war, coverage of women's suffrage was overwhelmingly negative. Newspapers bombarded the people of Newfoundland with articles and news cables covering the suffrage movement in Britain and the activities of Emmeline Pankhurst (founder of the Women's Franchise League) and other "militant suffragettes." Editorials vilified British suffragettes daily, publishing sensationalized accounts of suffragist assaults, arson, and bombings. These articles continuously sought to delegitimize suffrage by portraying suffragettes as irrational extremists.[3]

In April of 1914, for example, the *Twillingate Sun* published an article arguing against women's voting rights. William Temple opined their right to vote would be of little value to women because they would naturally vote the same as their husbands did, merely doubling the number of total votes. Temple also argued that being able to vote would not give women any more power. He said that while men boasted about their superiority as the "stronger sex," women gave birth, nursed, taught, married, cared for, and managed men's homes. In Temple's mind, women's power derived from the labour in the private sphere, therefore giving them rights in the public sphere would lend them no additional power.[4]

While some articles attacked suffrage directly, others undermined women's suffrage by portraying women as incapable of making an informed decision. In May of 1914, the *Mail and Advocate* published a poem titled "Just Like a Woman":

She had been through school and
  college
And could write herself A.B.;
She had studied a profession,
  Which had added an MD.
She had dwelt in college settlement
  And had clear decided view

On political developments,
  And she read the daily news.
But still she remained all feminine
  Despite acquired lore –
She could never meet a woman
  Without noting all she wore.

This poem attacks suffrage by suggesting that although women could gain an education and become experts in politics and current affairs, they could never truly escape their femininity and obsession with aesthetics.[5]

To further cement the attack on the suffrage movement, the *Mail and Advocate* also published a cartoon on the same page titled "Helpful." This cartoon depicted two upper-class women, one of which was reading a magazine. The woman reading declares, "These magazines are so helpful." "What's the latest?" asked the other woman. The first woman responded: "Here are the home hints they tell you how to make a lovely suffragette bomb out of an old tomato can." This cartoon makes a negative association between women's literacy, voting rights, and extremist violence.[6]

The *Evening Telegram* also published poems that attacked the suffrage movement. On 22 June, for instance, the *Evening Telegram* published a poem that ridiculed women who wanted to vote:

> The suffrage dames who play their games just like the whiskered fellers, who bravely stand and make demand for votes are the city dwellers. The squawky ones behind the guns have homes that need attention; they run outdoors, neglecting chores too numerous to mention. The city wife an idle life of ease and sloth is leading no more she makes the ginger cakes, no more the dough she's kneading; she pulls with vim her husband's limb for rhino for her spending, and spends her days in useless ways,

> in foolish schemes unending. The farmer's Fraus have hens and cows to keep them sane and busy; they fix the coops no give three whoops for movements vain and dizzy. They sell their ducks and earn some bucks to buy ten yards of gingham; they hen fruit sell and husband well the money it will bring 'em. The farmers wives lead useful lives, and not an hour is wasted; the city ways, the slothful days, they have not learned or tasted. They drive to town in modest gown behind old Prince and Polly, with cash to spare, and do not care for votes or other folly.

The author of this poem associated the suffrage movement with several unrelated phenomena. First, the author argued that only urban women wanted to vote, while rural women were content with their traditional roles. By associating suffrage with urban life, he was drawing on an idea that was present in Britain since the beginning of industrialization, namely that urban life was causing a decline in both morality and health. Secondly, the author implied that women who campaigned for voting rights were doing so at the expense of their families. The author claimed that women's suffrage would be a threat to the family and the entire patriarchal structure of western society.[7]

Criticism of the suffrage movement was not limited to the activities of British suffragists. In 1908, there was a resurgence of suffrage activity that coincided with the activities of Emmeline Pankhurst in Britain. As a result, anti-suffragists in Newfoundland turned their attention to suffrage advocates in the dominion. In 1909, for instance, two women were kicked out of a predominately male reading club after they advocated for women's suffrage. As a result, a group of ten women decided to form the Ladies Reading Room. The Ladies Reading Room provided its members with a wide variety of newspapers and other reading material, lectures, and weekly debates. The Ladies Reading Room would be vital to the development of the suffrage movement in Newfoundland as it politicized many middle-class women in St John's.[8]

In December of 1913, Myra Campbell, another prominent suffragist, gave a speech at the Current Events Club of the Ladies Reading Room that highlighted just how hostile Newfoundland society was to suffragists. In a lecture titled "Women's Wrongs," referred to marriage as "slavery at home" and highlighted the fact that women's work at home and in the community was not valued or appreciated. At the conclusions of its lectures, the Current Events Club would usually provide local papers with a written copy for publication. In this case, however, the officers of the Current Events Club feared the political fallout from Campbell's speech and suppressed its publication. It was not until 1920, and she was living in Canada, that Campbell felt comfortable enough to ask that the *Daily News* publish her speech. When it was finally published, the *Daily News* warned its readers that the article was "subversive of the sanctity of the home."[9]

In particular, Armine Nutting Gosling, a prominent suffragist and future secretary of the Women's Patriotic Association, was the target of incredible vitriol. Displeased with the coverage of suffrage in Newfoundland newspapers, Gosling wrote many letters to the editor in the hopes of putting the acts of militant suffragists in context. While Gosling condemned the violence, she pointed out that the actions of suffragists in Britain were the result of a long history of the British government ignoring women's grievances. Gosling attacked the argument that militant suffragists proved that women were unfit to vote. She reminded her readers that men committed the vast majority of violent crime, yet nobody argued that men should not have the right to vote.[10]

Many newspapers attacked Gosling's pro-suffrage articles. The *Daily News*, for example, suggested that Gosling was proof that even the most educated women were not able to escape their narrow point of view. The editor reminded his readers that voting required manly consideration and reason. He argued that women lacked these skills. The editor did not stop with attacking suffrage and also censured Gosling personally, stating that she was a Newfoundland manifestation of the evil suffragists in Britain.[11]

Despite the profoundly negative press coverage of the suffrage movement before the war, anti-suffrage articles ended when the war began. The absence of wartime coverage of the suffrage movement was due to the cessation of political activities by many suffrage organizations. The largest suffrage organization in the United Kingdom, the National Union of Women's Suffrage Societies, led by Millicent Fawcett, agreed to a cessation of political activities for the duration of the war. The most militant organization, the Women's Social and Political Union, led by Emmeline Pankhurst, also agreed to end all militant activity. In the absence of political and military suffrage activity, newspapers instead focused on covering the patriotic activities of the Women's Patriotic Association.

THE WOMEN'S PATRIOTIC ASSOCIATION

Once Margaret Davidson had established the Women's Patriotic Association (WPA), the organization spread rapidly across Newfoundland. Two weeks after Davidson's announcement, twenty-six branches had been set up across the island. Wasting little time, the WPA set to work on making comfort items to send to soldiers on the front lines and in hospital. Desiring a standardized production, the WPA sent patterns and instructions to each branch. When items arrived at the central office in St John's, the St John's Branch inspected them for quality.[12]

Initially, the WPA focused on items of clothing that would complement soldiers' issued uniforms. This clothing would make life easier and more comfortable for soldiers on the front lines and in hospitals. By October of 1914, the WPA had sent two shipments for the war effort. These shipments were destined for the front lines, British hospitals, and the Newfoundland Regiment. While there were many branches outside St John's, the centre for the WPA was at Government House in St John's. Here the WPA converted two bedrooms that Mary Brehm and her cutting committee used four days a week as cutting rooms. Once volunteers cut the pieces, they would be assembled in the ballroom, which was used as a sewing room on Mondays, Tuesdays, Thursdays, and Fridays. The WPA also had a stock room at Government House where it kept wool and other fabrics that would be sent to various branches across the island.[13]

The WPA's efficient system allowed them to send a tremendous amount of material to the front lines. In October of 1914, it sent its second shipment, which comprised thirty-four cases: twenty-six went to the front lines, four went to British hospitals, and four went directly to the Newfoundland Regiment. This shipment contained 5,276 pairs of socks, 726 day shirts, 473 pairs of mittens, 454 handkerchiefs, 440 pillow slips, 272 nightshirts, 164 pillows, 120 pairs of cuffs, 110 sets of pyjamas, 100 body belts, 76 helmets, 30 bed jackets, 24 pairs of bed socks, 9 scarfs, 7 pairs of underwear, and 6 pairs of surgical socks.[14]

The WPA also formed a Red Cross branch to produce medical supplies for the war effort. Over fifty women met twice a week at the house of Adelaide Browning to make bandages, sterilized swabs, dressings, and other various medical supplies. Trained nurses supervised the workers of the WPA who also worked with Newfoundland's St John Ambulance brigade. One incredibly valuable contribution made by the WPA was the production of sterile dressings. During a visit to England, Margaret Davidson toured several hospitals. During one of these tours, a hospital administrator told Davidson that there was a desperate shortage of sphagnum moss that was crucial for making dressings. Upon her return to Newfoundland, Davidson requested that women across Newfoundland collect the moss and send it to St John's. The WPA received so much sphagnum moss that it took ten women two days to sort and store it all.[15]

Due to their extreme dedication and their efficient system and distribution of work, the WPA produced tremendous amounts of goods for the war effort. In May of 1916, John Anderson (owner of Anderson and Lumsden, a dry goods business) gave a report to the legislative council, tallying the total amount of material that the WPA produced for the war effort in the first two years of the war. This included: 28,602 dressings; 23,284 pairs of socks; 9,090 bandages; 3,104 pairs of mitts; 2,833 flannel shirts; 1,991 pillowcases; 1,614 handkerchiefs; 1,130 mufflers; 1,020 swabs; 970 night shirts; 791 sewing kits; 727 cholera belts; 683 pillows; 428 binders; 357 pyjamas; 143 balaclava helmets; 197 surgical socks; 200 rifle covers; 200 scarves; 199 pneumonia jackets; 63 bed jackets; 24 bed socks; 491 flannel shirts; and 8 sheets.[16]

Anderson told the legislative council that it was difficult to calculate just how immense the WPA's contribution was to the Allied war effort, but he estimated that the financial cost of all this material would be well over $250,000. Despite the occasional difficulty in obtaining funds to carry out its work, the Women's Patriotic Association maintained this level of production until the end of the war. While the WPA became famous for the socks it sent to Allied soldiers, it is clear that its contributions to the war effort amounted to more than just making soldiers comfortable. By sending large quantities of medical equipment such as bandages and dressings, it was taking an active role in saving the lives of soldiers fighting for the British Empire.[17]

In addition to the production of clothing and medical equipment, the WPA also raised funds to send the Newfoundland Regiment comfort items that would make its time in the trenches a little less awful. In December 1915, for example, the WPA raised enough funds to send a Christmas parcel to each soldier of the Newfoundland Regiment. Each box contained Christmas pudding, a pound of chocolate, a pound of gingerbread, a pound of raisins, one pipe, a plug of tobacco, warm underwear, and a pair of socks. The WPA sent these parcels to the Newfoundland War Contingent Association (an organization, based in London, that cared for sick, wounded, and captured soldiers from Newfoundland), who forwarded them on to Newfoundlanders on the beaches of Gallipoli.[18]

PUBLIC PERCEPTIONS OF THE WOMEN'S PATRIOTIC ASSOCIATION

Immediately following Davidson's announcement that she would be forming a Women's Patriotic Association; the *Daily News* published an article titled "Women Workers" that praised the patriotism of the WPA:

> The work of the Women's Patriotic Association is a work for Empire that is being shared wherever the grand old flag is flying; amongst the workers being British women of all classes, including the Queen and the Queen mother. We rejoice to see that the local association is taking the broader view and that its efforts are not to be confined to our own brave volunteers alone. What is needed for our lads will be gladly done; but the aim is to help other lads as well. The Empire to-day is one large family, her sons and daughters are working in a common cause; there are no parties now; no conflicting interests, no sections, no classes. Men are standing shoulder to shoulder as brothers; women know nothing of the limitations of rank or fortunes but are working together as sisters for the beloved family, whose peace and progress has been rudely disturbed by the insensate ambition and bloodlust of a vanity-crazed tyrant. Lady Davidson in her address has given wise counsel. The sons of Newfoundland are responding nobly to the call; and her daughters are doing the same. It may be true enough that "men must work and must weep," but the antidote to sorrow is work, and to sadness, service. At the close of the meeting the roll was signed by 500 women, recruits in the Army of Service, ready to devote time and skill and patience and means for home and throne and Empire; and for the comfort and assistance of their husbands, brothers and sons at the Front.

It seems that the *Daily News'* praise for the WPA was rooted in the organization's public display of patriotism. The WPA's patriotism reinforced the social underpinnings of the war effort by fostering imperial unity, class unity, and solidarity with the rest of the empire. In a time of great anxiety and uncertainty, the WPA suggested that no matter how dangerous the war was, all elements of the British Empire would stand together.[19]

In a speech at a meeting of the Current Events Club in St John's, Margaret Davidson affirmed the WPA's solidarity with the men fighting in the trenches. She stated that the war had the world holding its collective breath in anxiety and that every man and woman had a duty to provide whatever service the empire asked of them. She said that it was understandable that women wanted to go to the front so they could be close to the action. Despite this desire, Davidson said that a woman's duty was at home supporting enlisted men. She informed her audience that if Germany were to win the war, they would annex Newfoundland, strip away all British freedoms, conscript men into the German army, and ship them out to defend other German colonies.[20]

In another meeting, Davidson urged the women of the Ladies Reading Room to do everything it could to help win the war. She told them that there were several ways for women to help end the war: working with the WPA to send valuable material to the war effort; ensuring that rural Newfoundland was made aware of the grave threat that Germany posed to the dominion; and educating children about how wonderful it was to be a British citizen and how terrible it would be if Germany won the war. This speech highlighted a critical aspect of the WPA's work during the war. The women of the WPA understood that their work was not merely providing "comforts" to soldiers. They understood that socks, clothing, and medical supplies were more than just comforts and knew that their work could help to win the war.[21]

War work was an effective way for women to make public displays of patriotism, sacrifice, and service. Newspapers often publicized stories of women's sacrifice and service, applauding them for their patriotism. For instance, the *Daily News* ran an article highlighting a widow's contribution to the war effort. The article described the situation of an anonymous widow living in northern Newfoundland, who lost her husband and dedicated her life to raising her two daughters. By the time the war had broken out, one of the woman's daughters had gotten married, and the other was a "partial invalid," and relied on her mother for support. With the financial burden of a physically disabled daughter, the woman was unable to donate to the WPA.

Despite this, the woman had two sheep that she sheared, spun the wool into yarn, knit the yarn into socks, and donated those to the WPA. The editor of the *Daily News* applauded her sacrifice: "'She hath done what she could,' and unconsciously, has taught a lesson to thousands. Newfoundland has reason to be proud of her manly volunteers; and she has equal reason to rejoice in the devotion displayed by her daughters, foremost amongst whom must rank this noble woman, who out of her poverty, has enriched the service and patriotism of the land." By comparing women's war work to the service of soldiers, who society held as ideal British citizens, and intimating that people should be equally proud of the WPA, the editor showed just how valued the WPA was in Newfoundland.[22]

W.F. Lloyd, the editor of the *Evening Telegram*, also praised the WPA. In an article from 1914, Lloyd stated that "there is nothing which has occurred since the outbreak of the war more inspiring and gratifying than the whole-hearted way in which the Daughters of Newfoundland have risen in their strength to do 'their bit' to help along those fighting for King and Country." Lloyd demonstrated particular pride in the recognition that the WPA received from Major-General J.C. Dalton, Chief Commissioner of the Brigade Overseas, who oversaw branches of St John Ambulance across the British Empire. Referring to the WPA, Dalton said: "I am amazed to find such a noble list, though not surprised, because I know that there is practically no limit to the loyalty and patriotism of the dominions; and that you will certainly do more than your share to help the Old Country in her difficulties." This acknowledgement from the British leadership of St John Ambulance was incredibly powerful. Like the activities of the Newfoundland Regiment, the work of the WPA proved that Newfoundland was a loyal dominion, doing everything it could to help the British Empire.[23]

Letters to newspaper editors made it clear that many people in the dominion were proud of the WPA's work. While some believed the WPA focused its efforts on providing comfort to soldiers overseas, many in the dominion acknowledged that the contributions of the WPA were critical to the success of the Newfoundland Regiment. In January of 1915, an uncredited woman from the WPA published an article, which refuted the claim that the WPA solely focused on sending comforts to soldiers, the sick, and the wounded. Instead, the author argued that the WPA was providing lifesaving equipment to many allied soldiers. In this article, the author included a letter from Ethel

Perrot from St John Ambulance in Britain, thanking the Women's Patriotic Association for the clothing it sent:

> I write on behalf of the committee to thank the Women of the Patriotic Association of Newfoundland for the perfectly splendid consignment of clothing and comforts received. It came just in time to enable me to have the pleasure of announcing this most generous gift to the Queen's Committee of ladies, and I am desired to express their thanks to the ladies of Newfoundland for their generosity, which will add very largely to the grand total. Their gift has come just at the moment when we were badly needing garments to send off to the wounded at the Front. I cannot tell you how grateful we are for this most generous gift, and I hope you will convey to the ladies of our association, and to Lady Davidson our most grateful thanks.
>
> I might say that only a few days ago, a most urgent telegram came from the British Consul at Dunkirk, asking that warm clothing should be immediately dispatched. These were got off in two hours, and two days later a telegram was received saying "Most grateful thanks for the generous gift of warm clothing received, which was the means of saving valuable lives." Such telegrams as this encourage us to go on giving and donating our utmost, and indeed Newfoundland has come forward at the very moment to enable us to keep up our stock and supply the tremendous need. The first consignment will be sent to the troops in the fighting line near Boulogne.

Perrot's letter, stating that clothing donated by patriotic associations was a crucial tool for saving the lives of soldiers on the frontlines, is compelling evidence that the contributions of the WPA were an essential part of the allied war effort, and not merely comforts.[24]

In the *Daily News*, John Robinson also championed the importance of the WPA, particularly for the socks it sent to the front. Robinson asked his readers to think about the soldiers in the trenches, hurriedly darning socks, washing them in stagnant pools of water, and putting them back on wet. He stated that an ample supply of socks would not only prevent soldiers from the needless suffering, but having dry, comfortable socks would make the soldiers more efficient and better able to fight the Germans. Robinson declared that homemade socks were far superior to factory-made socks, and the Newfoundland Regiment immediately needed 1200 pairs and a reserve of 1200 to replace them as need be.[25]

The *Twillingate Sun* also stressed the importance of socks to the war effort. William Temple dispelled rumours that socks donated by the WPA were sold to allied soldiers, instead of given to them freely. To show how grateful soldiers were for these socks, Temple published a letter received by the WPA from a French soldier named Honore Hamel, who received a pair of its socks. The soldier wrote: "I am the man who received the socks, for which I heartily thank you, for I was in great need of them, and was very happy to have received them." Temple praised the work of the WPA for so promptly getting much-needed clothing to soldiers who needed it.[26]

Many Newfoundlanders recognized the vital work the WPA was doing for the Newfoundland Regiment. Despite this, the crucial role that the WPA played in the performance of the Newfoundland Regiment left it vulnerable to criticisms from those who thought it was not doing enough to support the soldiers.

In January 1915, a persistent rumour began to surface that the British Expeditionary Force were not issuing the soldiers of the Newfoundland Regiment enough clothing. John St John claimed to have received word from soldiers in Scotland that they only received two pairs of socks and one pair of boots that quickly wore out, leaving them improperly equipped to carry out their training. He argued that the WPA and NPA needed to ensure the men were issued socks and boots immediately. St John attacked the WPA and NPA, saying that it was the least they could do for the soldiers, who were risking their lives for their country, to ensure that they did not have to wear socks with holes in them and boots with worn-out soles.[27]

Rumours that the WPA neglected the Newfoundland Regiment reached a pinnacle in November of 1915 when the *Mail and Advocate* published a letter from an anonymous soldier at Gallipoli. The soldier accused the WPA of not sending any clothing or comforts to soldiers there. He complained that the clothing they were issued was insufficient for the weather in Gallipoli: "What we suffered from cold this past week nobody knows, only those men who went through it. It was not only cold by night but also by day. We have no drawers or shirts as we were told we did not need them." He further griped that the 5th Battalion of the Royal Scots had received ample supplies of cigarettes, tobacco, oatmeal, and chocolate, while the Newfoundland

Regiment received nothing. This soldier accused them of being generous to British and French soldiers while their "own flesh and blood go bare." He was so outraged that he claimed the alleged lack of support from the WPA was "enough to make one disgusted with everything Newfoundland and ashamed of his own country."[28]

The accusations of neglect by this anonymous soldier sent shockwaves through Newfoundland. John St John was one of the first newspaper editors to speak out against the Women's Patriotic Association. He demanded to know why the WPA had sent $250,000 worth of goods, which the WPA raised through public donations, to London while Newfoundlanders were suffering on Turkish shores. St John insisted that the WPA explain why it was sending clothing to British and French soldiers while Newfoundlanders had nothing and further requested that the government conduct a formal investigation into the matter. He insisted that the "WPA attend to the requirements of our Newfoundland Regiment before helping others who are likely well looked after by English ladies," and the establishment of a new committee to rectify the WPA's "blundering and negligence."[29]

In response to the *Mail and Advocate*'s attack on the WPA, the editor of the *Daily News* responded by pointing out that all necessary clothing was issued to the soldiers by the British army and that the WPA had sent a recent resupply of additional clothing. St John was not convinced. He replied to the *Daily News*, asserting that while the WPA may have sent clothing, it was clear that it had not sent any comfort items and, in failing to do so, brought shame to the dominion. St John compared the comforts of those at home with the suffering of the trenches. He said that those who remained at home were living comfortable lives while those at sea and in the trenches were enduring unimaginable suffering and hardships. If the WPA did not endeavour to make sailors and soldiers more comfortable, St John argued that every citizen should be ashamed. "The *Mail and Advocate's* outrage at the WPA's alleged neglect shows that many in Newfoundland viewed the WPA's work as an essential element of the war effort and more than simple comforts. The criticism of the WPA was similar to the criticism levelled against men who refused to enlist."[30]

Following the publication of the *Mail and Advocate*'s attacks against the WPA, readers inundated the newspaper with letters to the editor condemning the Women's Patriotic Association. "Teacher" praised St John for having the conviction to point out the deficiencies of the WPA. He demanded to know where the thousands of items of clothing had gone and if the WPA sent them to Canadian and French soldiers. Another letter by "Parent" argued that when parents sent their sons to fight, they assumed that they would be looked after by clothing and comforts sent by the WPA, however, now they were learning that it had sent none. "Parent" demanded an investigation to determine why the WPA sent clothing and comforts to Canadians, Belgians, French, and the British, while Newfoundland soldiers had none. Another concerned citizen demanded to know what happened to all the funds that the WPA raised and demanded a public meeting to prevent this "injustice" from happened again.[31]

In the face of the severe criticism by the *Mail and Advocate*, the Women's Patriotic Association responded with a letter to the editor. Adelaide Browning told St John that the *Advocate*'s attack on the WPA was an attack on all women in Newfoundland. Browning pointed out that the Newfoundland Regiment received the essential clothing it needed from the war office, and the WPA ensured that the Newfoundland Regiment had replacements for any clothes that were worn out by the tremendous wear and tear and loss on the battlefield. She reminded the *Mail and Advocate* that it was in the best interest of the war office and the staff of the Newfoundland Regiment to ensure that all soldiers were properly equipment to fight.[32]

In addition to tearing down the argument that the WPA was the reason that Newfoundland soldiers were supposedly poorly equipped, Browning also attacked the soldier who wrote the letter: "Reading the letter closely this boy seems to want tobacco and chocolate. It has been mentioned that those in command preferred that no chocolate be sent to the Dardanelles, as there is such difficulty in providing a sufficient supply of water, and it makes the soldiers suffer so much more from thirst. It is unfortunate that this peevish, jealous, unmanly letter should have been printed, for it gives people a very different impression from what we would wish them to have of the Newfoundland Contingents. And that anyone could pen such comments on the WPA as written in last night's paper is beyond belief." Browning concluded her letter by expressing gratitude that the majority of soldiers were intelligent and conscientious enough to realize everything the WPA was doing for them.[33]

Despite her attempts to win favour for the WPA, Adelaide Browning's letter did more harm than good. The day after the *Mail and Advocate* published Browning's letter, it published a reply written by "An Indignant Mother." She said that it was not a matter of how much clothing or comforts the WPA made, but if these things reached their intended recipients: the Newfoundland Regiment. She also chided Browning for suggesting this brave soldier was peevish, jealous, and unmanly and accused her of being uncharitable and unladylike.[34]

An anonymous member of the Women's Patriotic Association also criticized Browning's response. This WPA member, from Port Blandford, expressed outrage that she would blame clothing shortages on an individual soldier. She attacked Browning's argument that the War Office fully provided for each soldier, asking, "if this is so, why is it that our WPA are always making so much preparations for the comforts of our boys at the front?" She also defended the soldier, saying that he dared to speak out about the shortcomings in the work of the WPA so that the people could make things right.[35]

Despite the *Mail and Advocate*'s harsh attacks on the WPA, not all were convinced that WPA was failing to provide for the Newfoundland Regiment. At the height of this controversy, the *Western Star* called on its readers to increase donations to the WPA. The editor said that the soldiers needed warm clothing to get them through the winter. He reminded his readers that while they were relaxing in their warm homes, soldiers were freezing in the trenches or at sea. The editor then defended the WPA, saying that it had done excellent work but required additional funds if it was going to keep supplying Newfoundland soldiers with warm clothing.[36]

The *Daily News*, a zealous advocate of the WPA, also defended the group. Robinson argued that if the WPA was not able to send enough clothing and comforts for the regiment, it was not a failing on the organization's part but a failure of the people of Newfoundland to make sufficient donations. The *Daily News* rebuked those who would criticize the WPA and argued that they should praise them instead. Robinson further declared that no organization in the world was doing better or more useful work than the Women's Patriotic Association. He urged every person in the dominion to generously support the WPA as it ceaselessly worked for the soldiers, the sick, and the wounded at the front.[37]

The governor and the prime minister also came to the defence of the WPA. On 2 December 1915, Governor Davidson wrote a letter on behalf of himself and Prime Minster Morris to Arthur Steel-Maitland, chairman of the Newfoundland War Contingent Association, an organization based in London that was responsible for providing support to the Newfoundland Regiment, particularly wounded soldier who were convalescing in London. Davidson told him that both he and the prime minister agreed that the complaints about that WPA were without merit. Davidson dismissed these complaints as exaggerated accounts that young soldiers wrote to impress their mothers. He told Steel-Maitland that he could actively refute the accusations made against the WPA, but animosity toward them had already taken root in northern Newfoundland. Despite this, Davidson reassured Steel-Maitland that "most sensible people in the Regiment and at home realize that fighting involves hardship. Still, there is residuum (a thickish deposit at the bottom) in Newfoundland, which is prone to believe ill of those who shoulder responsibility."[38]

To quell fears that the British army was not caring for the Newfoundland Regiment, J.R. Bennett, the colonial secretary, wrote a letter to the editor of the *Mail and Advocate*. Bennett's letter included a statement from Bonar Law, about the Newfoundland Regiment's clothing. Law assured Davidson that despite the war office supplying the regiment with sufficient clothing for the winter, the NWCA had recently sent two shipments of shirts, socks, scarves, mittens, and thermal underwear made by the WPA. Law assured Davidson that the British army, the WPA, and the NWCA together had ensured that the regiment was more than adequately supplied with clothing for the winter.[39]

Henry Reeve, the secretary of the NWCA, wrote a letter to Margaret Davidson expressing frustration over accusations that Newfoundland soldiers were not getting clothing and comforts donated by the WPA. He assured Davidson that the NWCA was preparing to send the regiment a shipment of socks, mittens, scarves, chocolate, stationery, chewing gum, cigarettes, and playing cards. Reeve told Davidson that the Newfoundland Regiment was the envy of the entire division because the WPA had sent them such lavish gifts. He ended his letter by telling Davidson that he hoped his letter could convince the people of Newfoundland that the WPA was doing an excellent job looking after the soldiers.[40]

The controversy surrounding the Women's Patriotic Association sheds light on how important Newfoundlanders believed the work of the WPA was. On one level, this controversy is an example of a group of men (the *Mail and Advocate* and its readers) attacking a women's organization for failing to do, in their eyes, enough for the war effort. On another level, the outrage over the WPA's alleged neglect shows that many in Newfoundland recognized that women's work was important, if not vital, the war effort and were outraged at the allegation that it was not completing its essential work. Whether people portrayed the WPA as an organization that sent comfort items to make soldier's time in the trenches easier or as an organization that sent lifesaving medical supplies and clothing, everyone seemed to agree that the WPA played a vital role in the war effort.

The anger directed towards the WPA stemmed from a belief that every element of Newfoundland society had a role to play in the war effort. Eligible men had a duty to enlist with the Newfoundland Regiment or the Newfoundland Royal Naval Reserve. Men who could not enlist had an obligation to donate to the NPA. Many citizens believed that women had a duty to support Newfoundland's soldiers by encouraging men to enlist and by providing them with clothing, comforts, and medical supplies through the Women's Patriotic Association. Many citizens were outraged when the *Mail and Advocate* alleged that the women of the WPA were shirking their duties.

THE WHITE FEATHER

In addition to the WPA's work in providing clothing, comforts, and medical equipment, many people believed that women played an integral part in the recruiting process by encouraging their sons, husbands, fathers, brothers, and potential suitors to enlist. The overwhelmingly male recruiters wanted women to apply social pressure on potential recruits, sought to enlist women to help recruit men into the regiment and reserve. The *Mail and Advocate* published an early example of this in September of 1914. In an article titled "The Selfish Woman," the author argued that any woman who claimed they needed their husbands at home and discouraged them from enlisting was selfish for putting herself before the empire. Not only did this article suggest that women must put the needs of the empire before their own, but it also told women they had a patriotic duty to encourage men to enlist.[41]

A writer by the name of "Chaplain" also argued women had a patriotic duty to encourage their sons and husbands to enlist. In a letter to the editor in the *Daily News*, Chaplain told the story a mother and father whose son died when the *Viknor* sank. When the Chaplain told them of the tragic news, the mother told her husband, "Don't cry William … let us thank god that we have another [son] to take his place in such a noble cause." The woman's other son was currently training on the HMS Calypso and was due to leave shortly for service on a Royal Navy vessel. Chaplain argued that the mother's reaction was an accurate representation of the spirit of the empire and filled his heart with pride and gratitude. Whether or not the mother or her interaction with Chaplain was real, it is evident that Chaplain wanted mothers to believe it was an honour to lose a son for the empire.[42]

In response to Chaplain's letter, the editor of the *Daily News* extolled the virtues of this mother. Robinson stated that story was proof that Newfoundland had some of the most virtuous women in the empire and that their patriotism and devotion to the state matched ancient Roman and Spartan women. Later in this article, he told the story of a mother whose five sons were fighting in the war. Three had enlisted in the Newfoundland Royal Naval Reserve, and two were serving with the Canadian Expeditionary Force. He declared that as long as there were mothers like these, the British Empire would always be safe.[43]

These stories drew on the theme of the mother's martyrdom that was common throughout the British Empire in the First World War. Suzanne Evans explains that these stories were powerful propaganda tools because they emphasized how important the war was. If mothers were willing to sacrifice the powerful bond between mother and son, the cause must be worthy. Furthermore, Evans argues these stories suggest that if mothers were willing to sacrifice their sons, it would be shameful for citizens to reject any lesser of a sacrifice.[44]

In the previous articles, the authors covertly worked to break down the natural desire for parents to protect their children. In April 1915, a resident of Bonaventure argued in the *Mail and Advocate*, that a mother's desire to protect her son was a threat to the war effort. The author was disappointed that several young men from his community tried to enlist, but their mothers prevented them from doing so. He wrote: "We all know a mother's love for her children, but in a time of war, all mothers should share alike because for sure someone must fight, and fight hard to conquer our present enemy, the Germans, Austrians, and Turks." Unlike the editor of the *Daily News*, King did not glorify soldier's mothers. Instead, he portrayed mothers as a potential stumbling block to the British war effort. Despite their differing tactics, their message was the same: mothers must encourage their sons to fight for the sake of the empire.[45]

Governor Davidson also believed women had an important role to play in the recruiting effort. In December 1914, Davidson detailed the successes of the Women's Patriotic Association in his diary. He praised the WPA for spreading across the dominion and creating a host of goods for the war effort. He also congratulated the St John's branch of the WPA for doing their "duty manfully" by encouraging ample amounts of men to enlist with the regiment. In comparison, Davidson noted that in branches outside St Johns, "the women perform prodigies in the way of work but are not so far successful recruiting agents." By saying that women had a "duty" to recruit men into the regiment and by expressing disappointment with the ability of rural women to recruit men, Davidson made it clear that he believed women had an essential role in Newfoundland's recruiting efforts.[46]

Davidson publicly addressed women's roles in recruiting when he announced the formation of the Newfoundland Forestry Corps. In this announcement, he declared that men in the dominion no longer had an excuse for not enlisting. He explained that the Forestry Corps was a way to serve for men who were medically rejected from the regiment, fathers, and conscientious objectors. Davidson urged "the Women of Newfoundland – Mothers and Wives – to let their men go – nay, to urge them to go as becomes their manhood. Do not let your men have to endure the reproach of having been tried as True Men and found wanting."[47]

Some recruiters highlighted women's recruiting efforts. In April 1918, K.M. Blair wrote an article for the *Evening Advocate* that encouraged rejected volunteers to do their duty and encourage other men to enlist. Blair highlighted the success of the WPA and other women's organizations:

> Are the W.P.A., the Daughters of Empire, the Khaki Guild, and the many associations of the various churches, etc., in St John's and throughout the dominion working for the soldiers? Are they with the soldiers? Ask them! Are they going to see the Boys crying in vain for help? Are they going to see all their men's sacrifices, all their sacrifices go for nought? Are they not interested in the honour of Newfoundland and their own honor, or why did they bid their men go? The war bears harder upon mothers and wives who send their men forward to the battle than upon us mere men. We have more pursuits, more business duties to take up our minds, for them in their daily round of duties, are the long silences and quiet. But they brave it all! It has always been Woman who has been called up on more than man to make Supreme Sacrifices. Have the women of the world

> failed us in this great struggle? No! If anybody will fail in their duty, as we believe that the women's influence on behalf of the Regiment will be as strong as any we have in the community.

Blair believed women were making impressive contributions to the war effort by encouraging men to enlist. According to Blair, Newfoundland women convinced the men in their lives to go, even though they knew it might lead to their death because they had the best interests of Newfoundland in their minds.[48]

In conjunction with the efforts of male recruiters to get women's help in encouraging men to enlist, recruiters also called on women to shame men into enlisting. Precisely how women received this campaign was unclear as men's voices dominated historical sources such as newspaper articles, letters to the editor, and government correspondence. This meant that there is little evidence to suggest the extent that women shamed men into enlisting. What evidence does exist suggests that there was a limited "white feather" campaign designed to encourage men to sign up.

On 29 November 1916, the H.A. Winter, editor of the *Evening Telegram* published an article encouraging women to exercise caution when sending white feathers through the mail: "The young ladies or others who sent through the mails white feathers to young men who they believed to be 'slackers' should be very careful that the young men in question were justly entitled to receive them, as we know a number of cases where quite an injustice has been done." While this article is certainly not evidence of a widespread white feather campaign, it does suggest that a small group of women felt strongly enough about encouraging recruiting to send feathers that shamed men for not enlisting.[49]

The *Evening Telegram* also received a letter from a concerned citizen writing under the pseudonym "OU Slacker." In his letter, Slacker recounted an incident that occurred the previous night when he and three of his friends were insulted by two women as they were travelling along LeMarchant Road in St John's. "OU Slacker" told the editor that he and his friends were walking down the road when they were passed a group of women at the same time as the women were passing a returned soldier in uniform. The women greeted the soldier politely and one said, "Oh, there's some big slackers" while pointing at Slacker and his friends. The author took particular offence to these comments as he was a returned soldier with a permanent disability. His three friends had volunteered, but the regiment rejected them. Instead of insulting men, "OU Slacker" encouraged women to be constructive instead of belittling anyone not in uniform: "Before closing I should like to remind them that if they are so eager in forwarding the cause of recruiting by denouncing everyone not in khaki or blue, why not get them on a public platform and let us hear what they have to say about it. If they are not gifted with the power of eloquence, why then should they waste their energy in that direction? Why not spend an hour or so making comforts for our boys in order to relieve their suffering a wee bit, or in some other way which would be of some use to someone and not going around holding themselves up to ridicule and trying to be funny at the expense of others." "OU Slacker" was upset by having his masculinity challenged by the women who crossed his path. His criticism went beyond the women mistaking his friends for un-enlisted men and attacked women for attempting to stimulate recruiting by shaming men. Instead, Slacker recommended these women take on traditionally feminine roles of making clothing and comforts.[50]

Perhaps the strongest piece of evidence of the profound effect that shaming had on men in Newfoundland was the issuing of rejected volunteer badges. E. Parsons, a People's Party MHA for Harbour Grace, first brought up the idea to issue badges to men who had tried to enlist but had been rejected by the Newfoundland Regiment. He told the house that he attended a recruiting meeting in Harbour Grace and witnessed five or six men come forward to offer their service. Despite their intentions, the regiment found them medically unfit and turned them down. Parsons suggested that the government should issue badges to rejected volunteers to prevent men from being shamed as slackers.[51]

On 7 April 1916, in the house of assembly, Edward Morris proposed an amendment to the Volunteer Force Bill that would allow the government to issue rejected volunteer badges. The regiment would give these badges to military aged men who volunteered but were dismissed because they failed the medical examination or who were exempt from service because their work was vital to the war effort. Morris explained that offering rejected volunteer badges would be a symbol of governmental recognition that young men were willing to sacrifice themselves. It would allow their peers to recognize that they were not slackers.[52]

The house of assembly received Morris's amendment well, except some concerns expressed by William Coaker. He asked Morris if every single person who offered his service would get a badge, even if the person knew he would fail the medical examination. Coaker gave the example of a man with tuberculosis who attempted to enlist, knowing the regiment will not accept him but turned up to a recruiting station just to get a badge. He worried that there would be hundreds of men receiving badges who did not make an honest attempt at enlisting. In response, Morris told Coaker that there would be "rules and regulations" to prevent the abuse of the badges. This satisfied Coaker.[53]

The house of assembly unanimously passed the amendment to the Volunteer Force Bill on 11 April 1916, and the government began issuing rejected volunteer badges in October. The badge was made of bronze, had a map of Newfoundland in the centre, the words "I have offered for King and Country" appeared on top of the map, and "Newfoundland" was written underneath. The regiment issued these badges to any man of military age who tried to enlist and failed the regular medical examination. The regiment would deny anyone a badge who it deemed "obviously unfit" when they turned up for enlistment. The government expected recipients to treat these badges with the utmost respect. Anyone who lost or damaged their badge was subject to a fine of $10–25. Anyone caught wearing a badge, who was not issued one, was subject to a penalty of $50.[54]

Although this legislation pleased many citizens, it angered others because it did not provide badges for those who attempted to enlist in the Newfoundland Royal Naval Reserve. The omission of sailors from the legislation exacerbated existing tensions between the Newfoundland Regiment and the Newfoundland Royal Naval Reserve, who often felt that the government was overlooking them. The men of the NRNR often complained that soldiers in the regiment received higher pay rates and frequently petitioned the government to augment the pay they received from the Royal Navy. In addition to this, many naval reservists felt that the public held soldiers in greater esteem. This issue became prominent in shortly after the passing of the Volunteer Force Act when two men accosted a group of naval reservists, calling them cowards for not enlisting with the Newfoundland Regiment.[55]

With these tensions in mind, the recruiting committee of the Newfoundland Patriotic Association met and passed a unanimous resolution calling on the government to issue rejected volunteer badges to those who the naval reserve rejected. Following this resolution, Joseph Outerbridge wrote a letter to the justice minister to request that the government offer the same badges to rejected volunteers for the naval reserve as they provided to rejected volunteers for the regiment.[56]

In response, Squires informed Outerbridge that badges could not be issued to naval reservists because the legislation passed in the house of assembly only pertained to those who tried to enlist in the regiment. He recommended that the legislature re-examine this issue in a year when the house of assembly reopened. Following an intervention from the colonial secretary, Squires changed his mind and recommended that the legislative council pass a minute of council, allowing the government to issue badges to those who the naval reserve rejected. Squires believed it was of vital importance that the government make no distinction between the regiment and the naval reserve.[57]

IMPACT OF WOMEN'S WAR WORK

Throughout history, women's work has been vital to life in Newfoundland. In addition to their backbreaking domestic work, feeding, clothing, and caring for their families, women played a crucial role in Newfoundland's economy. Marilyn Porter has shown that in many parts of the island, women were responsible for turning raw cod into a marketable product by overseeing the process of curing, salting, and drying it. In a book chapter titled "Women in the Newfoundland Fishery" Miriam Wright has shown that in 1911, 38 per cent of the people catching and curing fish were women. David Alexander has estimated that women's labour amounted to approximately half a household's income. Despite this, their labour in the fishery, was seldom publicly credited to them.[58] Conversely, during the First World War, women's war work was widely publicized, lauded, and publicly praised. The women of Newfoundland displayed great patriotism, sacrifice, and service during the war, and this resulted in a great deal of pride in Newfoundland society. The question that remains is: what, if any, impact did women's war work have on the suffrage movement?

As previously discussed, before the war, the suffrage movement was a near-constant source of ridicule and sensationalism as the press focused on suffragists both at home and in Britain. When these groups abandoned their political and militant activities to support the war effort, the press coverage of the suffrage movement drastically changed.

By 1915, women's participation in Newfoundland's war effort had convinced the majority of newspaper editors that women deserved the right to vote.

On 26 March 1915, for instance, the editor of the *Daily News* anticipated that there would be profound changes coming to the British Empire. He believed women's franchise would be one of these changes. Robinson cited women's war work as the reason they will likely be given voting rights:

> The World War will bring with it many changes, and probably amongst them will be the franchise for women. What no amount of militancy, so called, could ever do, patriotism may accomplish. Women have played a noble part during these terrible times, a womanly part and the part of heroines as well. They have risen to heights of sacrifice and service that have never been excelled. Freely they have given husbands and sons to the cause of Liberty and done it with a pride and courage that is in itself an inspiration. In works of mercy, the highest and humblest in the land have been untiring ... Britain has always held woman in chivalrous devotion; but to-day they stand upon an even higher plane, and by their exalted patriotism have demonstrated that citizenship means to them all that it means to the most loyal and devoted sons of Empire.

In his high praise of women's wartime endeavours, Robinson emphasized that their devotion to the cause and their work towards improving the British Empire should and likely would earn them the right to vote.[59]

In 1916, there were some positive developments in women's suffrage as the municipal government in St John's granted voting rights to any female ratepayer in municipal elections. A motion was made to enlarge the list of voters to include any woman over the age of twenty-one, but the citizen's committee voted it down. Theobald, a columnist for the *Evening Telegram*, argued that the municipal government should give women the right to vote. He points out that since the war began, women had proven that they could take the place of a man who had gone to fight and, in many cases, were more effective than the men they were replacing. Theobald reminded his readers that women were working in engineering shops, running streetcars, serving as nurses in the trenches, and doing the urgent work of caring for the sick and wounded soldiers and sailors. Given their stellar record of work in the war, Theobald argued that it was unconscionable to deny them the right to vote: "How can it be possible to refuse their entry into full citizenship after such a record I cannot imagine, nor can conservation supply an adequate reason. After the war, if not during the war, women will be as a matter of course, not by courtesy, but by right, receive the full privileges and rights of citizenship."[60]

Wartime victories for the suffrage movement in Canada, Britain, and the United States increased supporters of suffrage in Newfoundland. A.W. Mews, the editor of the *Mail and Advocate*, highlighted the fact that soldiers in British Columbia had overwhelmingly voted for women's suffrage in light of the work they were performing in the war. Mews described women's suffrage as "one of the disputed rights which will come as a natural right after the war is over, if not before. There remains no doubt whatever about that." He said that by preventing women from voting, the government was denying the virtue and morality that women would bring to politics. By granting women the right to vote, Mews believed that the male-dominated political system would become a little less corrupt and a little more virtuous.[61]

One particular victory for women's suffrage that had an impact on conversations in Newfoundland was the passing of the *Franchise Act* in Canada. This act gave voting rights to the wives and mothers of men who were fighting with the Canadian Expeditionary Force. The *Daily News* contended that all loyal citizens of the British Empire must be proud that the wives and mothers of Canadian soldiers were being rewarded for their service with voting rights. Robinson said that women who had enough patriotism to sacrifice their husbands or sons were uniquely qualified to vote: "If these [women] are ready to immolate their dearest on the altar of their country, is it too much to demand for them a man's share in the country of their country's destiny? Surely not!"[62]

In November of 1917, the editor of the *Evening Advocate* reported on suffrage victories in the United States and Canada. The article praised the decision of the State of New York to give women full voting rights in state elections unequivocally. Winter told his readers that calls for suffrage in New York were based on women's contributions to the American war effort. He surmised that these arguments were undebatable, and the state government was forced to give women the right to vote. Similarly, Mews pointed out that Canada's *Franchise Act* gave the right to vote to 1,200,000 female relatives of soldiers who were serving in Europe. While he admitted he was unsure if the people of Newfoundland were ready for this change, he acknowledged that the women of Newfoundland were just as fit to receive the vote as the women in the United States and Canada.[63]

Some suffrage supporters argued that women's franchise was a solution to the conditions that brought about the war and, in some ways, were just as important as the soldiers to securing world peace. In 1917, the editor of the *Evening Telegram* praised the recommendations of the British Speakers' Conference on Electoral Reform, which unanimously recommended limited voting rights for women. Winter credited women's participation in the war effort with the Conference's recommendations saying, "it is not the war that has wrought this change, but woman's noble part in it." Mews believed that the British Empire would have to be rebuilt after the war. He argued women would play a vital role in rebuilding the empire in an era of world peace.[64]

CONCLUSION

In *Making Peace: The Reconstruction of Gender in Interwar Britain*, Susan Kent shows that, in Britain, the traditional notion of "separate spheres" for men and women were redrawn during the war and were no longer strictly defined as public and private. The renegotiation of gender in Newfoundland occurred similarly. During the First World War, women in Newfoundland worked tirelessly to support the war effort by donating and volunteering with the Women's Patriotic Association, working as nurses, VADs, and by endeavouring to stimulate Newfoundland's recruiting campaign. Shortly after the war began, women's war work became an element of national pride and women's wartime labour was seen as a patriotic duty, a gendered equivalent for men's military service.[65]

Before the war, the suffrage movement received widespread negative press in newspapers across the dominion. Newfoundland newspaper editors attacked Newfoundland suffragists and the militant activities of suffragettes in Britain, publishing sensationalized accounts of assaults, arson, and bombings. Despite this, during the war, nearly every major newspaper in the dominion began to actively support women receiving voting rights both in Newfoundland and the rest of the British Empire. Those who supported suffrage in Newfoundland argued women's war work had shown that women were every bit as deserving as men in determining the future of the dominion.

The effectiveness of women's war work in convincing men that women deserved the right to vote stems from the power of wartime conceptions of citizenship. Nicoletta Gullace has shown that British women renegotiated the belief that citizenship was tied to gender, shifting the criteria for citizenship from masculinity, majority and property to patriotism, service, and British heritage. Through their extreme expressions of patriotism, sacrifices of their time and money, and through providing vital services to the war effort, Newfoundland women convinced many citizens that they were every bit as deserving of voting rights as men.[66]

The editor of the *Daily News* clearly expressed the belief that patriotism, sacrifice, and service were more important to wartime conceptions of citizenship. In September of 1917, Robinson wrote an article calling on the government to strip voting rights from men who had conscientious objections to military service. He suggested that "[if men are] using conscience as a cloak for cowardice, disloyalty, or treachery, such are unworthy not only of the rights of citizenship but of citizenship itself."[67] Robinson advocated that these men have their voting rights stripped and given to patriotic women:

> it is inconceivable to a virile mind that there are in the world men who are content to allow their loved ones to become a prey to the infamies and lusts of an unspeakable foe, rather than strike a blow for their safety and for their liberties that their sires have won. But if there are, it is reasonable that he who is unwilling to defend his motherland, and those whom he has sworn to protect, should be accord the rights of a real man? … It is a matter for gratitude that there are those in Canada who stand ready to take from the spineless and disloyal the freeman's vote and transfer it to the brave and self-sacrificing women who have proved their worth by the part they have played in the greatest tragedy of time.

By advocating for voting rights to be stripped away from men who were unwilling to sacrifice themselves and giving them to women who sacrificed their sons and husbands, the *Daily News* made it incredibly clear that in wartime Newfoundland patriotism, sacrifice, and service were far more important determinants for who was and was not a liberal "individual" and deserved representation and the right to vote.

In addition to shifting conceptions of gender, the WPA also paved the way for a flurry of women's activism in the post-war period. Margot Duley has shown that women's experiences managing an island wide organization were crucial to future women's organizations in Newfoundland. After the war, WPA members took on leadership roles in many organizations such as Playground Association, Child Welfare Association, Girl Guides, Society for the Prevention of Cruelty to Animals, and the Newfoundland Outport Nursing Industrial Association. The most prominent of all of these organizations was the Women's Franchise League, which led the movement for women's suffrage in the 1920s. The leadership for the league largely came from prominent WPA members like Armine Gosling, Fannie McNeil, Adeline Browning, Mary Kennedy Goodridge, Margaret Burke, and Mary Southcott.[68]

Women's war work was so important to the suffrage movement that the Women's Franchise League listed it as one of the reasons why Newfoundland women deserved the right to vote on a petition to the Legislative Assembly: "The women of Newfoundland rose to every call made upon them during the Great War, and showed energy and executive ability in the organization of relief and other work, and many of them served as nurses, VADs, and ambulance drivers." It is clear that women's war work not only changed conceptions of gender in wartime Newfoundland, but also shaped the future of the women's suffrage movement.[69]

NOTE

Despite the outpouring of support for women's suffrage during the war, women in Newfoundland were denied voting rights until 1925. This was primarily due to the election of Richard Squires as prime minister in 1919. Squires was a fierce opponent of suffrage, going so far as to threaten to take government appointments from any men whose wives were active in the suffrage movement. A suffrage bill was brought before the house of assembly in 1921, and despite great public support for the bill, it was defeated with thirteen of Squires' Liberals voting against the bill and nine Conservatives voting for it.

In 1925, Prime Minister Walter Stanley Monroe introduced a suffrage bill to the house of assembly. In a speech to the assembly supporting the bill, Monroe told the house that women across the British Empire had earned the right to vote through their sacrifice and patriotic service during the war. He said: "I want to ask you to-day why we are in this position and why have we not given the vote to women? Surely our women did as much during the as the women of any other country." Monroe's words highlight the importance of wartime changes to public discourse. Even though women were denied the right to vote during the war, the public acknowledgement of the importance of women's labour continued to influence Newfoundland politics years after the war ended.[70]

Conclusion

The requirements of a total war effort caused the reordering of liberal governance. Whereas before the war, upper class, white men primarily received the status of "individual," the First World War required people of all ethnicities, genders, and classes to work together to prosecute Newfoundland's war effort and cope with the conditions of the home front. As a result, the government renegotiated a social covenant with the citizens of Newfoundland, redefining who was awarded the status of an individual based on wartime prescriptions of gender, ethnicity, and class. This social covenant changed not only what the liberal state expected of its citizens but what citizens came to expect from the liberal state.

In addition to the conception of the individual, a key element of liberalism is the concept of liberty, which maintained that the individual had an *inviolable* right to freedom of labour, speech, conscience, and the press. The individual was responsible only to themselves, and the state's primary goal was to safeguard the freedom of the individual, only restricting their liberty when the actions of one individual infringed on the freedom of another. The First World War caused a dramatic renegotiation of the perceived rights of the individual. As part of the wartime social covenant, the government coerced and conscripted citizens into the military and stripped their right to freedom of speech, press, and conscience. In return for the loss of these freedoms, citizens demanded that the government protect them from the conditions of the home front through market regulations, the prohibition of alcohol, and the imposition of taxation to support the war effort.

Ian McKay defined liberalism as a political philosophy containing three major categories: the concept of the "individual," a focus on the rights of individuals, and the right of all individuals to own property. In Newfoundland, during the First World War, changing conceptions of gender, ethnicity, and class altered two of these three pillars. Wartime conceptions of ethnicity, gender, and class vastly widened the concept of the individual to focus on people of all socio-economic classes and genders to support the war effort. At the same time, changing conceptions of ethnicity resulted in the government stripping the rights from ethnic groups it believed posed a risk to the dominion. The requirements of a total war effort caused the liberal state and the citizens to abandon the liberal focus on individual rights and to focus on the rights of the community, the empire, and the world.

During the war, temperance advocates used the language of sacrifice and service to suggest that alcohol was damaging the soldiers' ability to fight. As a result, pre-existing prohibition movements were given new life. Temperance advocates urged that Newfoundland needed prohibition not only to help the war effort but to protect the people, particularly producers, from the scourge of alcohol. They insisted that every patriotic Newfoundland should be willing to give up liquor for the greater good of the war effort and to make their country a better place. Strict prohibition, which criminalized the sale, possession, and consumption, indicates that the war caused many people to believe that the right of the community to be protected from alcohol far outweighed the rights of the individual to drink.

The rationing of food and controlling of prices was another example of the renegotiations of class that impacted the working of the liberal state. As the war caused the costs of living to increase, Newfoundland society debated what the government's role should be fixing this issue. Progressives in Newfoundland, who represented the producers, argued that the government should regulate prices to ensure that everyone would be able to afford to heat their houses and feed their families. Furthermore, they argued that the business class had a duty to provide the people of Newfoundland with the necessities of life at an affordable price. On the other hand, liberals argued that the government should not and could not interfere with prices, as these were a result of wartime conditions. Instead, they argued that the government should focus on ensuring that Newfoundland had adequate supplies of the necessities of life, whatever the prices would be.

Ultimately, both sides of this debate had successes during the war. The progressives were able to convince the government to regulate the price of coal, seize privately held stocks and sell that coal. On the issue of flour, the government agreed to form a Food Control Board to control prices, but its actions were focused on more liberal ideas: reducing flour consumption through rationing and substitutes. While both sides disagreed on what the government should or should not do, it is important to note that both liberals and progressives demanded government interference in free markets, a betrayal of traditional liberal values.

The implementation of a business profits tax and later an income tax was a drastic alteration in the liberal order that resulted from the renegotiation of conceptions of class in the dominion. Before the war, the government collected taxes evenly from all citizens through import duties. During the war, many producers felt that it was unfair for the business community to pay only slightly more than Newfoundland's poorest citizens. Instead, they advocated for a business profits tax and an income tax that ensured those who were best able to support the war effort did so financially.

The business profits tax was perhaps the most controversial issue throughout the war and caused a constitutional crisis between the House of Commons and the legislative council. This proves that the "passive revolution" in the liberal order was hotly debated as members of the business class refused to be shouldered with what they considered to be an unfair amount of responsibility for Newfoundland's war effort. Despite the hard negotiations of the business community, they ultimately lost. The government enacted the business profits tax and the income tax. This proves that under Newfoundland's wartime social covenant that patriotism and sacrifice came before profits. This becomes particularly clear with public outrage amongst producers as they viewed the business community as unpatriotic war profiteers who cared little about the soldiers who were sacrificing their lives.

The treatment of enemy aliens was a profound renegotiation of ethnic categories in the Dominion of Newfoundland. Before the war, many Newfoundlanders held Germans and Germany in high regard. Newspapers often described Germans as intelligent, clean, cultured, and efficient. Shortly after the war began, Newfoundland newspapers began to demonize Germans, like newspapers were doing across the British Empire. The justice department created a list of enemy aliens in 1915, and the Newfoundland constabulary began arresting Germans and Austro-Hungarians across the island.

While the majority of those arrested were German and Austro-Hungarian sailors who had the misfortune of docking in Newfoundland ports, several of the POWs detained in the dominion were long-time residents of Newfoundland or British Subjects. These people, though the state would have previously considered them "individuals" under the liberal order, were denied this status during the war. The government denied these people the right to a trial (a right that was offered to criminals), refused to treat them as POWs under international law, and denied them the fundamental rights of British citizens. The renegotiation of ethnic categories did not only extend to Germans and Austro-Hungarians but also Allied and neutral nations as well. Across the dominion, those born in Newfoundland treated Britons, Americans, Italians, Norwegians, and Russians with extreme suspicion and hostility and accused many of being German spies.

Perhaps the most critical element of this new social covenant between citizens and the state was the recruitment of soldiers for the Newfoundland Regiment and Newfoundland Royal Naval Reserve. During the war, ideals of masculinity were renegotiated to emphasize military service over providing for their families. The government, in essence, created this new social covenant by telling young men that their primary duty was to the state and not to their families. Both government and civilian recruiters told young men across the dominion that their place was in the trenches of the Western front and not with their families. In return for their service, citizens argued that the government should look after their families and dependants. This was the basis for the renegotiation of the relationship between the citizens and the state. Citizens began to expect the government to provide for families while their husbands were fighting the war.

At the beginning of the war, the Newfoundland government decided to rely on a campaign of voluntary recruitment. By 1917, the government believed that men were failing to live up to wartime conceptions of masculinity. As a result, the house of assembly debated and passed the Military Service Act, forcing men to enlist with the military. The passing of conscription in Newfoundland is evidence of the enforcement of the new social covenant. Under this unwritten agreement, young men were expected to be patriotic enough to offer their service to the state. When the government believed they broke this covenant, it passed conscription, coercing young men to abide by it.

The imposition of conscription is clear proof of a drastic change in the liberal order. The government breached the rights of individual when it passed conscription without a vote. By passing conscription without public consultation, the government violated the core tenant of liberalism, the liberty of its citizens. Furthermore, the state also rescinded the freedom of the press and speech when it refused to allow any public dissent to the conscription bill before it became law.

Women's work in support of Newfoundland's war effort reconfigured conceptions of gender and the relationship between citizens and the state. Throughout Newfoundland's history, women have played crucial roles in the formation of their families and of the dominion. Despite this hard work, women's contributions to the public sphere had often been overlooked or attributed to their husbands. During the First World War, women's war work was acknowledged by Newfoundland society, and it was recognized as crucial to the functioning of the war effort.

The impact on women's war work on perceptions of suffrage was astounding. Before the war, the majority of Newfoundland newspapers derided the suffrage movement, choosing to focus on the radical suffrage movement in Britain. Despite this, as the war dragged on, many newspapers praised the Women's Patriotic Association for its patriotism, sacrifice, and service. As a result, by the end of the war, nearly every major newspaper in the dominion believed that women had earned the right to vote through their war work and should be granted full voting rights.

Women's war work in Newfoundland shows that the liberal concept of the individual had begun to expand to include women, a group that had been excluded since its foundation. Women's war work showed many men women's valuable contributions to society. The drive to include women as "individuals" was so powerful that every major newspaper in the dominion argued women should have full voting rights.

Ian McKay argues that during the First and Second World Wars, liberalism made compromises, during a period he refers to as the "passive revolution," to maintain hegemony. In the dominion of Newfoundland, changing wartime conceptions of gender, ethnicity, and class caused drastic changes to who fit into the liberal concept of the "individual." With a broader inclusion of the "individual," the government in Newfoundland became much more concerned with the rights and protections of the community instead of the individual. Many residents of Newfoundland argued that protecting the rights of the community was the best way to protect the rights of the individual.

In many ways, wartime liberalism was vastly different from pre-war liberal governance. McKay argues that these drastic changes were compromises. However, evidence suggests that they were radical changes. Liberalism in wartime Newfoundland was much like the Ship of Theseus: if so many parts of traditional liberalism changed during the war, should it still be considered a "liberal order?" Instead of making comprises, the liberal order metamorphosed into something new: social liberalism in its infancy. A liberalism that realized the community was made of individuals and believed the best way to protect the rights of the individual was to protect the rights of the community.

Notes

INTRODUCTION

1 For more on the liberal order, see Ian McKay, "The Liberal Order Framework: A Prospectus for a Reconnaissance of Canadian History," *Canadian Historical Review* 81, no. 4 (2000): 616–45.

2 McKay, "The Liberal Order Framework," 625, 635.

3 Jean-François Constant and Michel Ducharme, eds., *Liberalism and Hegemony: Debating Canadian Liberal Revolution* (Toronto: University of Toronto Press, 2009), 19.

4 Ibid., 7.

5 John Horne, ed., *State, Society, and Mobilization in Europe during the First World War* (Cambridge: Cambridge University Press, 1997), 4.

6 "Ladies' Patriotic Movement," *Evening Telegram.*

7 1 September 1914; Journal of the Legislative Council, 3 May 1916.

8 For more on the early history of the Newfoundland Regiment, see James Candow, *The Invisibles: A History of the Royal Newfoundland Companies* (St John's: Breakwater Books, 2009).

9 Michael Westcott, *Defending the Dominions: The Naval Defence of Newfoundland during the First World War*, Memorial University, MA thesis, 2013.

10 Tim Cook and Mark Humphries, "The Forgotten Campaign: Newfoundland at Gallipoli," *Canadian Military History* 27, no. 1 (2018): 1–2.

11 For a detailed history of the royal Newfoundland Regiment during the First World War see G.W.L. Nicholson, *The Fighting Newfoundlander: A History of the Royal Newfoundland Regiment* (Montreal and Kingston: McGill-Queen's University Press, 2007).

12 Shannon Ryan, *Fish Out of Water: The Newfoundland Salt Fish Trade, 1814–1914* (St John's, Breakwater, 1986), 236.

13 James Hiller, "The Origins of Pulp and Paper in Newfoundland," *Acadiensis* 11, vol. 2 (1982): 42.

14 For more on the history of the seal hunt in Newfoundland see Shannon Ryan, *The Ice Hunters: A History of Newfoundland Sealing to 1914* (St John's: Breakwater, 1994).

15 Sean Cadigan, *Newfoundland and Labrador: A History* (Toronto: University of Toronto Press, 2009), 7; and John Mannion, "Victualling the Fishery: Newfoundland Diet and the Origins of the Irish Provisions Trade, 1675–1700," *International Journal of Maritime History* 12, no. 1 (June 2000): 8.

16 S.J.R. Noel, *Politics in Newfoundland* (Toronto: University of Toronto Press, 1971); and Melvin Baker and Peter Neary, "Bond, Sir Robert," in *Dictionary of Canadian Biography*, vol. 15, University of Toronto and Université Laval, 2003. For more on Robert Bond see James Hiller, *Robert Bond: A Political Biography* (St John's: ISER Books, 2019).

17 Noel, *Politics in Newfoundland*, 57–8.

18 Cadigan, *Newfoundland and Labrador: A History*, 179.

19 Noel, *Politics in Newfoundland*, 112–14.

20 *Acts of the General Assembly of Newfoundland Passed in the Sixth Year of the Reign of His Majesty, King George V, Special War Session* (St John's: J.W. Withers, 1915), 5–8.

21 Patricia O'Brien, "The Newfoundland Patriotic Association: The Administration of the War Effort, 1914–1918," MA thesis, Memorial University of Newfoundland, 1981, ii. See O'Brien's MA thesis for a detailed account of the NPA's administration of the war effort.

22 "The National Government," *Evening Advocate*, 17 July 1917. For more on formation of a national government see "Is Sir Edward Morris to Say 'You Shall Not Vote,'" *Evening Advocate,* 5 June 1917; "Discreditable Tory Tactics," *Evening Advocate,* 19 June 1917; and "A Demand for an Election," *Evening Advocate*, 1 July 1917.

23 Noel, *Politics In Newfoundland*, 124.

CHAPTER ONE

1 Sheila Roberts Lukins, *Bottoms Up: A History of Alcohol in Newfoundland and Labrador* (St John's: Breakwater Books, 2020), 88.

2 *Proceedings of the House of Assembly*, 17 May 1915.

3 Ibid.

4 *Proceedings of the House of Assembly*, 3 March 1914.
5 Ibid.
6 Ibid.
7 *Proceedings of the House of Assembly*, 21 April 1915.
8 Ibid.
9 *Acts of the General Assembly of Newfoundland Passed in the Sixth Year of the Reign of His Majesty, King George V* (St John's: J.W. Withers, 1915), 62–4.
10 Ibid.
11 "Temperance Meeting at Synod Hall," *Daily News*, 17 November 1914; "Are Temperance Lecturers Fanatics and Cranks?," *Daily News*, 10 December 1914; "The Prohibition Campaign," *Daily News*, 31 July 1915.
12 Greg Marquis, "Alcohol and the Family in Canada," *Journal of Family History* 29, no. 1 (2004): 308–27.
13 "Prohibition Killed," *Mail and Advocate*, 19 May 1915; "Prohibition Resolutions," *Mail and Advocate*, 20 May 1915; and "Thoughts of Theobald," *Evening Telegram*, 22 May 1915.
14 "How Alcohol Effects System, Total Abstinence, Longevity: Even in Small Amounts Alcohol Is Injurious – Low Mortality among Abstainers," *Mail and Advocate*, 16 April 1915.
15 "Dr Geisel's Lectures," *Evening Telegram*, 5 October 1915; and "Prohibition," *Mail and Advocate*, 16 September 1915.
16 "Dr Geisel's Lectures," *Evening Telegram*, 2 October 1915; "Dr Geisel at Bay Roberts," *Evening Telegram*, 7 October 1915; "Dr Geisel at Heart's Content," *Evening Telegram*, 10 October 1915; "Dr Geisel at Catalina," *Evening Telegram*, 15 October 1915; "Dr Geisel at Keels," *Evening Telegram*, 21 October 1915; "Dr Geisel at Kings Cove," *Evening Telegram*, 23 October 1915; and "Dr Geisel at Greenspond," *Evening Telegram*, 25 October 1915.
17 "WCTU," *Evening Telegram*, 29 September 1915.
18 "Vice President Broaders (FPU) Endorses Mr Coaker on Prohibition," *Mail and Advocate*, 6 October 1915.
19 "Composition on Prohibition by a Pupil of a R.C. School in Hr. Main District," *Mail and Advocate*, 12 October 1915.
20 Cheryl Krasnick Warsh, "'John Barleycorn Must Die': An Introduction to the Social History of Alcohol," in *Drink in Canada: Historical Essays*, ed. Cheryl Krasnick Warsh (Montreal and Kingston: McGill-Queen's University Press, 1993), 6–14.
21 Adrian Gregory, *The Last Great War: British Society and the First World War* (Cambridge: Cambridge University Press, 2008), 150.

22 "Prohibition Campaign," *Daily News*, 17 August 1915.
23 "Prohibition Campaign: Big Meeting Last Night," *Daily News*, 11 September 1915.
24 "An Appeal for Prohibition," *Mail and Advocate*, 5 October 1915.
25 "The Prohibition Issue," *Daily News*, 14 September 1915.
26 "Prohibition Resolutions," *Mail and Advocate*, 17 April 1915.
27 "The Question of Prohibition," *Mail and Advocate*, 20 April 1915.
28 "Mr Coaker's Appeal," *Mail and Advocate*, 25 September 1915.
29 "Mr Hickman's Resolutions," *Daily News*, 16 April 1915.
30 Rod Phillips, *Alcohol: A History* (Chapel Hill: University of North Carolina Press, 2014), 240.
31 Ibid.
32 "Prohibition," *Mail and Advocate*, 21 August 1915.
33 "Temperance Rally at College Hall," *Evening Telegram*, 20 April 1915.
34 "Prohibition: Powerful Address Delivered by Rev. W.H. Thomas at Congregational Church," *Mail and Advocate*, 3 May 1915.
35 "The Thoughts of Theobald," *Evening Telegram*, 23 October 1915.
36 "War and Temperance," *Mail and Advocate*, 26 October 1914.
37 "North Star Division, No. 15, Sons of Temperance," *Twillingate Sun*, 17 April 1915.
38 "Closing the Saloons: Urged by Citizen," *Daily News*, 22 September 1915.
39 "Thoughts of Theobald," *Evening Telegram*, 24 July 1915.
40 "Eliminating Waste," *Mail and Advocate*, 16 August 1915.
41 Craig Heron, *Booze: A Distilled History* (Toronto: Between the Lines, 2003), 178.
42 "Last Night's Lecture: A Magnetic Address to a Sympathetic Audience," *Daily News*, 1 October 1915; "Lecture on Health by Dr Carolyn Geisel," *Mail and Advocate*, 8 October 1915; "Dr Geisel's Lectures," *Evening Telegram*, 10 October 1915; and "Dr Geisel at Trinity," *Mail and Advocate*, 14 October 1915.
43 "Are Temperance Lecturers Fanatics and Cranks?," *Daily News*, 10 December 1914. O'Callaghan's claim that France and Russia were winning "battle after battle" while Germany was suffering appalling losses was not true. By December 1914, both sides were firmly entrenched, and there was very little territorial gain for either side.
44 "Reply to Newfoundlander," *Evening Telegram*, 19 October 1915.
45 "A Triumph for Temperance," *Mail and Advocate*, 1 April 1915; "Present War Boosts Cause of Temperance," *Mail and Advocate*, 17 November 1914; "Lesson of the War," *Daily News*, 16 October 1915. "Temperance

Now a World Issue," *Mail and Advocate*, 17 August 1915; and "The World against Alcohol, *Evening Telegram*, 2 November 1915.

46 "Prohibition Carried," *Evening Telegram*, 26 November 1916.

47 Phillips, *Alcohol: A History*, 243–7.

48 Heron, *Booze: A Distilled History*, 180–1.

CHAPTER TWO

1 W.E. Davidson to Arthur Bonar Law, 11 January 1916, Colonial Office Files 194/261; and Mike O'Brien, "Producers versus Profiteers: The Politics of Class in Newfoundland during the First World War," *Acadiensis* 40, no. 1 (2001): 51–2.

2 O'Brien, "Producers versus Profiteers," 52.

3 "Coal Prices," *Daily News*, 19 June 1915.

4 "Thoughts of Theobald," *Evening Telegram*, 19 June 1915.

5 E.P. Morris to A.J. Harvey et al., 4 December 1915, PANL, GN 8.67.

6 J.J. Mullaly to E.P. Morris, 6 December 1915, PANL, GN 8.67.

7 A.J. Harvey to E.P. Morris, 6 December 1915, PANL, GN 8.67.

8 A.H. Murray to E.P. Morris, 6 December 1915, PANL, GN 8.67.

9 "Another Codd," *Mail and Advocate*, 7 December 1915.

10 "Coal Shortage," *Mail and Advocate*, 10 December 1915.

11 "The Thoughts of Theobald," *Evening Telegram*, 11 December 1915.

12 E.P. Morris to Job Brothers & co., 11 December 1915, PANL, GN 8.67; and Robert Job to E.P. Morris, 13 December 1915, PANL, GN 8.67.

13 E.P. Morris to W.E. Davidson, 14 December 1915, PANL, GN 8.67.

14 Ibid.; E.P Morris to D.H. MacDougall, 15 January 1916, PANL, GN 8.67; and "The Coal Situation," *Evening Telegram*, 12 February 1916.

15 "Soft Coal $10.80 a Ton," *Evening Telegram*, 3 January 1916.

16 "The Coal Question," *Daily News*, 4 January 1916. In 1916 J.A. Robinson handed editorial control of the *Daily News* to John Currie.

17 "Opposition Wiling to Aid in Coal Crisis," *Evening Telegram*, 4 January 1916.

18 "The Coal Famine: Barefaced Robbery," *Mail and Advocate*, 4 January 1916.

19 "The Coal Problem," *Daily News*, 5 January 1916.

20 "Interview with Coal Dealers," *Evening Herald*, 4 January 1916.

21 "The Coal Famine: Barefaced Robbery," *Mail and Advocate*, 5 January 1916.

22 "Outline for Adjusting Prices of Coal until April 15th, 1916," 6 January 1916, PANL, GN 8.67.

23 Ibid.
24 J.R. Bennett, colonial secretary, to Morey & Co., 8 January 1916, PANL, GN 8.67; and "Public Notice: Sale of Coal," 11 January 1916, PANL, GN 2.14.22.
25 "Coal Problem," *Evening Telegram*, 10 January 1916; and "The Coal Situation," *Mail and Advocate*, 10 January 1916.
26 A.H. Murray to E.P Morris, 11 January 1916, PANL, GN 8.67.
27 E.P. Morris to D.H. MacDougall, 13 January 1916, PANL, GN 8.67.
28 W.R. Aykroyd, "Beriberi and Other Food-Deficiency Diseases in Newfoundland," *Journal of Hygiene* 30, no. 3 (1930): 359–60; and Sean Cadigan, "The Role of Agriculture in Outport Self-Sufficiency," in *The Resilient Outport*, ed. R.E. Ommer (St John's: Institute for Social and Economic Research, 2002), 241–62.
29 *Acts of the General Assembly of Newfoundland Passed in the Fifth Year of the Reign of His Majesty King George V* (St John's: J.W. Withers, 1914), 9.
30 Ryan, *The Ice Hunters*, 10; and "Flour," *Mail and Advocate*, 12 August 1914.
31 "Destitution," *Mail and Advocate*, 29 January 1915.
32 "The Price of Flour," *Evening Telegram*, 8 February 1915.
33 "Patriots and Patriotism," *Mail and Advocate*, 16 February 1915.
34 "The Times," *Evening Advocate*, 16 March 1917; and "Are We Prepared?," *Evening Advocate*, 2 February 1917.
35 "Food Prices and Control," *Evening Telegram*, 13 April 1917.
36 "The Times," *Evening Advocate*, 16 May 1917.
37 "The Flour Question," *Evening Advocate*, 22 May 1917.
38 "The Commission's Report," *Evening Telegram*, 14 May 1917; and "Food Commission," *Daily News*, 23 April 1917.
39 Journal of the House of Assembly, 30 May 1917.
40 Ibid., 31 May 1917.
41 "Action at Last," *Evening Telegram*, 21 April 1917.
42 "Third Interim Report of Food Commission," *Evening Telegram*, 9 June 1917.
43 Ibid.
44 "The Food Question," *Evening Telegram*, 9 June 1917.
45 "Revelations of the H.C.L. Commission," *Evening Advocate*, 12 June 1917.
46 For more on the NIWA, and their reaction to the cost of living see: Peter McInnis, "All Solid Along the Line: The Reid Newfoundland Strike of 1918," *Labour / Le Travail* 26, no. 1 (1990): 61–84.

47 M.H. Hitchen, secretary NIWA to E.P. Morris, 15 June 1917, PANL, GN 8.89; and M.H. Hitchen, secretary NIWA to E.P. Morris, 22 June 1917, PANL, GN 8.89.
48 *Proceedings of the House of Assembly*, 20 July 1917.
49 *Proceedings of the Legislative Council*, 24 July 1917.
50 Ibid., 26 July 1917.
51 M.H. Hitchens to E.P. Morris, 27 July 1917, PANL, GN 8.89.
52 "Need of Economy," *Evening Telegram*, 29 August 1917.
53 P.T. McGrath to W.E. Davidson, 7 September 1917, PANL, GN 2.14.30.
54 W.E. Davidson to W.F. Lloyd, 10 September 1917, PANL, GN 2.14.62.
55 "Potato Flour," *Evening Telegram*, 27 September 1917; and "Potatoes and Flour," *Evening Advocate*, 27 September 1917.
56 "Potato Flour," *Evening Telegram*, 27 September 1917.
57 "The Flour Situation," *Evening Advocate*, 14 December 1917; and "Must be Faced," *Evening Advocate*, 14 December 1917.
58 "Save Food!," *Evening Telegram*, 27 December 1917.
59 "Victory War Bread Show," *Evening Telegram*, 9 March 1918.
60 "Only A Week Left," *Evening Advocate*, 20 December 1917; "A Few Observations by Observer," *Twillingate Sun*, 13 June 1918; and "The Present Wheat Flour Campaign: Commenced Several Weeks Ago," *Harbour Grace Standard*, 11 October 1918.
61 "Published by Authority," *Evening Telegram*, 10 July 1918.
62 "Blame the Kaiser," *Evening Advocate*, 15 July 1918.
63 "The Present Wheat Flour Campaign: Commenced Several Weeks Ago," *Harbour Grace Standard*, 11 October 1918.
64 Ibid.
65 "Flour and Substitutes," *Evening Telegram*, 25 October 1918.
66 "We Emulate Job," *Daily Star*, 27 December 1918.
67 "An Open Letter to Dr H.M. Mosdell, by a Member of the Board of Food Control," *Evening Advocate*, 3 January 1919.
68 The argument that Newfoundland ought to eliminate waste from the cod fishery predates, but was reinvigorated by, the First World War. For more on this see Sean Cadigan, *Hope and Deception in Conception Bay: Merchant-Settler Relations in Newfoundland, 1785–1855* (Toronto: University of Toronto Press, 1995).
69 "Our Annual Waste: Over 20 Per Cent of Codfishery Thrown Away," *Western Star*, 15 July 1914.
70 "Stop the Waste," *Western Star*, 24 October 1917; and "A Lesson on Industry," *Western Star*, 5 March 1919.

71 "Abundance of Good Food Thrown Away," *Evening Telegram*, 6 March 1915.
72 "The Thoughts of Theobald," *Evening Telegram*, 20 March 1915.
73 "Thoughts upon the Times," *Evening Telegram*, 7 February 1918.
74 "Stop the Waste," *Western Star*, 13 February 1918. The spiny dogfish was a much-hated species in Newfoundland as they were notorious for destroying fishing gear.
75 No title, *Harbour Grace Standard*, 15 February 1918; and "Our National Foods," *Evening Telegram*, 8 March 1918.
76 "Saving Seal Meat," *Evening Advocate*, 9 March 1918.
77 "Statement of Captain Kean," *Evening Advocate*, 9 March 1918.
78 "Sow More Seeds," *Mail and Advocate*, 25 February 1915.
79 "The Country Must Prepare," *Mail and Advocate*, 29 November 1916.
80 "Agriculture," *Evening Telegram*, 5 March 1917.
81 "The Food Shortage," *Evening Telegram*, 5 March 1917.
82 "Newfoundland Agricultural Board," *Evening Telegram*, 11 February 1918.
83 Proceedings of the House of Assembly, 27 June 1917.

CHAPTER THREE

1 For a thorough examination of Canada's tax history see E.A. Heaman, *Tax, Order and Good Government: A New Political History of Canada, 1867–1917* (Montreal and Kingston: McGill-Queen's University Press, 2010).
2 *Proceedings of the House of Assembly*, 31 March 1913.
3 "Premier Announces Further Increases in General Taxation," *Mail and Advocate*, 3 September 1914; and "More Taxes Put On," *Mail and Advocate*, 3 September 1914.
4 "War Is Half the Trouble," *Mail and Advocate*, 16 June 1915.
5 "Fat and Fifty," *Mail and Advocate*, 26 June 1915; and "Two Kinds of Patriotism," *Mail and Advocate*, 30 June 1915.
6 "The Ultimate Stupidity," *Mail and Advocate*, 9 September 1916; *Proceedings of the House of Assembly*, 27 April 1916; and "The Ultimate Stupidity," *Mail and Advocate*, 9 September 1916.
7 "Our Hand to the Plough," *Evening Telegram*, 19 October 1916.
8 "Heavier Taxation at Home," *Evening Telegram*, 22 September 1915.
9 "War Profits," *Mail and Advocate*, 19 October 1915.
10 "Monied Gentry," *Mail and Advocate*, 10 January 1916.
11 "War Taxation," *Evening Telegram*, 25 January 1916; and "Are You Helping to Turn the Key?," *Evening Telegram*, 26 January 1916.

12 "The War Burdens," *Evening Advocate*, 5 January 1917. In 1917, the *Mail and Advocate* changed its name to the *Evening Advocate*.
13 "Conscription of Wealth," *Evening Advocate*, 30 June 1917; and "Men or Money First?," *Evening Advocate*, 31 July 1917.
14 *Proceedings of the House of Assembly*, 26 July 1917; "Excess Profits," *Evening Advocate*, 27 July 1917; and "Taxing Profits," *Daily News*, 27 July 1917.
15 "Legislation Gone Mad," *Evening Telegram*, 27 July 1917.
16 "Mainly in Business Circles," *Evening Advocate*, 28 July 1917.
17 "Advocate Logic," *Evening Telegram*, 30 July 17; and "Sensible Objections to the Act," *Evening Telegram*, 30 July 1917.
18 Manager of the Bank of Montreal, letter to MP Cashin, finance minister, 30 July 1917, PANL, GN 8.4; manager of the Canada Bank of Commerce, letter to MP Cashin, finance minister, 30 July 1917, PANL, GN 8.4; and manager of the Bank of Canada, letter to MP Cashin, finance minister, 30 July 1917, PANL, GN 8.4.
19 "The Profits Tax," *Daily News*, 3 August 1917.
20 *Proceedings of the House of Assembly*, 3 August 1917.
21 Ibid.
22 Ibid.
23 *Proceedings of the Legislative Council*, 3 August 1917; and *Proceedings of the Legislative Council*, 3 August 1917.
24 "Excess Profits," *Evening Advocate*, 27 June 1917.
25 *Proceedings of the Legislative Council*, 3 August 1917; and *Proceedings of the Legislative Council*, 6 August 1917.
26 *Proceedings of the Legislative Council*, 6 August 1917.
27 Ibid.
28 "The Profits Tax," *Evening Advocate*, 7 August 1917; *Proceedings of the Legislative Council*, 6 August 1917.
29 *Proceedings of the Legislative Council*, 6 August 1917; and *Proceedings of the Legislative Council*, 7 August 1917.
30 *Proceedings of the Legislative Council*, 7 August 1917.
31 Ibid.
32 "Miscellaneous by Miranda," *Evening Advocate*, 8 August 1917; and "The Great Refusal," *Evening Advocate*, 8 August 1917.
33 "Business Profits Tax Bill," *Daily News*, 8 August 1917.
34 "A Few Observations by Observer," *Twillingate Sun*, 18 August 1917; and Cadigan, *Death on Two Fronts*, 119.
35 "The Premier and the Profits Tax Bill," *Evening Advocate*, 9 August 1917.

36 E.P. Morris, prime minister, to W.E. Davidson, governor, 8 August 1917, PANL, GN 8.31, Office of the Prime Minister Fonds, Edward Patrick Morris Sous Fonds, legislative council, Increase of Members; and E.P. Morris, prime minister, to W.E. Davidson, governor, 8 August 1917, PANL, GN 8.31
37 "The Sovereign People's Rights Must Be Protected," *Evening Advocate*, August 1917.
38 "Eloquence or Rant?," *Evening Telegram*, 9 August 1917; and "The Constitutional Position," *Evening Telegram*, 10 August 1917.
39 "Are the Fangs of Socialism to Cripple the Legitimate Business of the Colony," *Evening Telegram*, 10 August 1917; and "The Government and the Profits Tax," *Evening Telegram*, 13 August 1917.
40 *Proceedings of the Legislative Council, Special Session*, 16 August 17.
41 Ibid., 20 August 17.
42 Ibid.
43 "The People Now in Control," *Evening Advocate*, 21 August 1917; "A New Age," *Evening Advocate*, 23 August 1917; *Harbour Grace Standard*, 24 August 1917; and "Our Parliament," *Western Star*, 22 August 1917.
44 *Proceedings of the House of Assembly*, 13 May 1918.
45 Shirley Tillotson, *Give and Take: The Citizen Taxpayer and the Rise of Canadian Democracy* (Vancouver: UBC Press, 2017), 21.
46 *Proceedings of the House of Assembly*, 23 April 1918.
47 "Advocates Tax on Incomes," *Evening Telegram*, 1 October 1915.
48 "The Thoughts of Theobald," *Evening Telegram*, 18 November 1916; and "The Thoughts of Theobald," *Evening Telegram*, 10 April 1915.
49 *Proceedings of the House of Assembly*, 23 April 1918.
50 Ibid., 13 May 1918.
51 Ibid.
52 Tillotson, *Give and Take*, 33.
53 "The New Age," *Evening Advocate*, 23 August 1917; and "The Income Tax," *Daily News*, 28 May 1918.
54 *Acts of the General Assembly of Newfoundland Passed in the Eighth Year of the Reign of His Majesty, King George V* (St John's: J.W. Withers, 1917), 211–12.
55 *Acts of the General Assembly*, 115.
56 *Proceedings of the House of Assembly*, 4 May 1918.
57 Ibid.
58 Ibid.

59 *Proceedings of the House of Assembly*, 13 May 1918; *Acts of the General Assembly of Newfoundland Passed in the Eighth and Ninth Years of the Reign of His Majesty, King George V* (St John's: J.W. Withers, 1918), 96.
60 "How A Newfoundland Victory Loan Will Help Win the War," *Evening Telegram*, 19 June 1918.
61 "Your Debt," *Evening Advocate*, 21 June 1918; and "I Will Not Be Responsible," *Evening Telegram*, 27 June 1918.
62 "They Also Serve," *Western Star*, 10 July 1918.
63 "Suppose You Were Going over the Top," *Evening Telegram*, 4 July 1918.
64 "She Has Given Her All," *Evening Telegram*, 13 July 1918.
65 "Support Your Country!," *Evening Telegram*, 14 June 1918.
66 "Your Home Is on Path of the Hun," *Evening Advocate*, 6 July 1918; "Must You Be Begged?," *Evening Advocate*, 18 July 1918.
67 "Two Alternatives," *Evening Advocate*, 20 June 1918.
68 "They Also Serve," *Western Star*, 10 July 1918.
69 "Men and Women Liable for Service," *Western Star*, 24 July 1918.
70 "The Loan Oversubscribed," *Evening Advocate*, 27 June 1918.

CHAPTER FOUR

1 Gerhard Bassler, *Vikings to U-Boats: The German Experience in Newfoundland and Labrador* (Montreal and Kingston: McGill-Queen's University Press, 2006), 116, 139; "Frankfurt Real Spotless Town," *Evening Telegram*, 26 March 1914; and "German Officers Are a Class Apart," *Mail and Advocate*, 24 July 1914.
2 "Tremendous Issue," *Mail and Advocate*, 19 August 1914; and "The Two Germanys," *Mail and Advocate*, 26 August 1914.
3 "Calls It Slander," *Mail and Advocate*, 15 September 1914.
4 "Belgians Tied to Horses Towed along by Germans," *Mail and Advocate*, 20 October 1914; "Germans Cut off Hands of Red Cross Nurses," *Evening Telegram*, 2 October 1914; "First-Hand Story," *Evening Telegram*, 10 October 1915; and "God and Man Will Judge," *Evening Telegram*, 16 October 1916.
5 Horne and Kramer, *German Atrocities*, 2, 292, 420.
6 "A Fallacy," *Mail and Advocate*, 19 October 1914.
7 "German Culture," *Mail and Advocate*, 20 October 1914.
8 No title, *Daily News*, 13 May 1915.
9 "Shoot the Brute," *Daily News*, 2 February 1917.
10 "Kultur and Crime," *Mail and Advocate*, 23 July 1915.

11 "The Leopards Spots," *Evening Telegram*, 3 July 1918; and "Out of the Question," *Evening Telegram*, 18 July 1918.

12 W.E. Davidson, Personal Diary, 19 December 1914, PANL, MG 136.5, Walter Edward Davidson Fonds.

13 "Obituary: R. Von Stein," *Evening Telegram*, 16 July 1914.

14 "Says Von Stein Was in the Pay of the Kaiser," *Mail and Advocate*, 12 September 1914.

15 "Says Report about Von Stein is a False One," *Mail and Advocate*, 15 September 1915.

16 Bassler, *From Vikings to U-Boats*, 141; "We Are Lenient," *Evening Telegram*, 20 October 1914; and "Alien Enemies," *Daily News*, 21 October 1914.

17 "Alien Enemies," *Daily News*, 21 October 1914.

18 A. MacDermott, acting commander H.M.S. Briton, to W.E. Davidson, governor, 6 December 1915, PANL, GN 8.92; and Walter Davidson, governor, letter to Bonar Law, secretary of state for the colonies, 26 July 1915, The National Archives of the United Kingdom, ADM 116/1400/84-86.

19 "A Few Plain Words," *Daily News*, 26 July 1915.

20 "Something to Think About," *Daily News*, 20 July 1915.

21 "We Have Them Here," *Mail and Advocate*, 19 October 1915.

22 P. Turner, deputy head of agriculture and mines to Captain Abraham, intelligence officer, 28 June 1915, PANL, GN 1/10/0 War Files.

23 W.E. Davidson, Personal Diary, 19 December 1914, PANL, MG 136.5; and Bassler, *From Vikings to U-Boats*, 146.

24 W.E. Davidson, Personal Diary, 19 December 1914, PANL, MG 136.5; and W.E. Davidson, Personal Diary, 2 December 1914, PANL, MG 136.5.

25 Statement of Richard Korner to Newfoundland constabulary, 9 November 1940, PANL, GN 13.1.B, box 38, file 90; and W.E. Davidson, Personal Diary, 19 December 1914, PANL, MG 136.5.

26 H.J.B. Woods, postmaster general to J.R. Bennett, colonial secretary, 23 September 1914, PANL, GN 2.14.11.

27 Lewis Harcourt, secretary of state for the colonies to W.E. Davidson, governor, 10 October 1914, PANL, GN 1/10/0; "Prisoner of War," *Mail and Advocate*, 17 October 1914; and "German Prisoners," *Mail and Advocate*, 22 October 1914.

28 W.E. Davidson, governor to Richard Squires, justice minister, 23 October 1914, PANL, GN 1/10/0.

29 W.E. Davidson, Personal Diary, 19 December 1914, PANL, MG 136.5; and War Docket, 1 May – 30 June 1915, PANL, GN 1/10/0.

30 W.E. Davidson, Personal Diary, 23 December 1914, PANL, MG 136.5; Alex Parsons, superintendent HMP to R.A. Squires, justice minister, 9 June 1915, PANL, GN 1/10/0; and W.E. Davidson, Personal Diary, 14 January 1915, PANL, MG 136.5.

31 W.E. Davidson, governor, to J.R. Bennett, colonial secretary, 28 May 1915, PANL, GN 1/10/0; Alex Parsons to R.A. Squires, justice minister, 9 June 1915, PANL, GN 1/10/0; W.E. Davidson to J.R. Bennett, 31 May 1915, PANL, GN 2.14.241; and W.E. Davidson, Personal Diary, 18 January 1915, PANL, MG 136.5.

32 R.J. Korner, prisoner of war, to R.A. Squires, justice minister, 20 April 1916, Memorial University Special Archives and Collections (MUNSAC), COLL 250 Sir Richard Squires Collection, 2.13.004; R.A. Squires to James Benedict, American consul, 22 June 1916, PANL, GN 13.1.B, box 162, file 29.

33 Sheriff's Office, Harbour Grace to R.A. Squires, 11 June 1915, PANL, GN 1/10/10, War Docket May–June 1915; J.M. Bartlett, district inspector for Curling to C.H. Hutchings, deputy minister of justice, PANL, GN 13.1.B, box 162, file 29; James Benedict, American consul to R.A. Squires, justice minister, 24 June 1916, PANL, GN 13.1.B, box 163, file 29; J.M. Bartlett, district inspector for curling to R.A. Squires, justice minister, 15 June 1916, PANL, GN 13.1.B, box 163, file 29; Sheriff's Office, Harbour Grace to R.A. Squires, 11 June 1915, PANL, GN 1/10/10, War Docket May–June 1915; R.A. Squires, justice minister to James Benedict, American consul, 24 June 1916, PANL, GN 13.1.B, box 163, file 29.

34 "Twenty-Four Germans," *Mail and Advocate*, 24 July 1915.

35 J.R. Bennett, colonial secretary to W.E. Davidson, governor, 13 August 1915, GN 1/10/0; W.E. Davidson, governor, to the Duke of Connaught and Strathearn, governor general of Canada, 29 July 1915, PANL, GN 2.14.241.

36 W.E. Davidson, governor to Joseph Outerbridge, chairman of the Reserve Force Committee, 19 October 1915, PANL, GN 2.14.255.

37 W.E. Davidson, Personal Diary, 2 December 1914, PANL, MG 136.5.

38 Bassler, *From Vikings to U-Boats*, 147; and W.W. Halfyard, colonial secretary to F.M. Stirling, private secretary, Government House, 20 February 1919, PANL, GN 1/3/A, Despatch 24.

39 J.R. Bennett, minister of militia to W.W. Halfyard, colonial secretary, 21 October 1918, PANL, GN 2.14.141.

40 Ernst Koch to J. Sullivan, inspector general, 2 September 1915, PANL, GN 13/1/B, box 290, file 17.

41 R.A. Squires, justice minister to W.D. Otter, OIC internment operations, 16 December 1915, MUNSAC, COLL 250, 2.12.012.
42 American Consul, Quebec to P.C. O'Driscoll, justice of the peace, 2 December 1915, MUNSAC, COLL 250, 2.12.012; and R.A. Squires, justice minister to W.D. Otter, OIC internment operations, 18 December 1915, MUNSAC, COLL 250, 2.12.012.
43 R.J. Korner to R.A. Squires, justice minister 27 January 1916, MUNSAC, COLL 250, 2.13.002; and R.A. Squires, justice minister to R.J. Korner, 11 March 1916, MUNSAC, COLL 250, 2.13.003.
44 R.J. Korner to R.A. Squires, justice minister, 20 April 1916, MUNSAC, COLL 250, 2.13.004;
45 R.J. Korner to P.C. O'Driscoll, 20 April 1916, MUNSAC, COLL 250, 2.13.004; and Statement of Richard Korner to Newfoundland constabulary, 9 November 1940, PANL, GN 13.1.B, Department of Justice Files, box 38, file 90.
46 W.E. Davidson, governor to J.R. Bennett, colonial secretary, 11 August 1915, PANL, GN 1/10/0.
47 "German Espionage," *Mail and Advocate*, 31 October 1914.
48 W.E. Davidson, Personal Diary, 19 December 1914, PANL, MG 136.5, Walter Edward Davidson Fonds.
49 "Nardini Held up as German Spy," *Mail and Advocate*, 13 September 1914.
50 "Volunteer Held as Alien Suspect," *Evening Telegram*, 24 February 1915.
51 "Monopolies on Labrador," *Mail and Advocate*, 31 August 1915; and "Arrested at Labrador Suspected of Being Spy," *Mail and Advocate*, 20 August 1915.
52 "Some are Natural Born Fools, Other Grow up with Only Half the Sense They Were Born with," *Mail and Advocate*, 20 September 1915.
53 Rockwell Kent, *After Long Years: Being a Story of Which the Author, for a Change, Is Not the Hero* (New York: Asgaard Press, 1968), 8; and Rockwell Kent to J.S. Benedict, American consul, 4 September 1914, PANL, GN 1/3/A, Despatch 192.
54 Rockwell Kent to J.S. Benedict, American consul, 4 September 1914, PANL, GN 1/3/A, Despatch 192; J.S. Benedict, to E.P. Morris, 5 September 1914, GN 1/3/A, Despatch 192; E.P. Morris, prime minister to J.S. Benedict, American consul, 5 September 1914, GN 1/3/A, Despatch 192; Rockwell Kent to J.S. Benedict, 13 September 1914, PANL, GN 1/3/A, Despatch 192; and J.S. Benedict to Rockwell Kent, 17 September 1914, PANL, GN 1/3/A.
55 Rockwell Kent to J.S. Benedict, American consul, 30 November 1914, PANL, GN 1/3/A, Despatch 192.

56 Kent, *After Long Years*, 9; and J.R. Smallwood, *Newfoundland Miscellany* (St John's: Newfoundland Book Publishers, 1978), 171–2.
57 R.A. Squires to J.R. Bennett, colonial secretary, 11 January 1915, PANL, GN 1.3.A, Despatch 192.
58 Rockwell Kent, "From a British Wilderness," *New Republic*, 22 May 1915.
59 Bassler, *Vikings to U-Boats: The German Experience in Newfoundland and Labrador*, 149; J.R. Smallwood, *Newfoundland Miscellany*, 174.
60 G.H.F. Abraham, to British Ambassador, Washington, 13 June 1917, PANL, GN 8.92.
61 Ibid.; and British Ambassador, Washington to G.H.F Abraham, 14 June 1917, PANL, GN 8.92.
62 W.E. Davidson to E.P. Morris, 14 June 1917, PANL, GN 8.92.
63 G.H.F. Abraham to E.P. Morris, 20 June 1917, PANL, GN 8.92.
64 E.S. Fraser to David Lloyd George, 1 August 1918, PANL, GN 8.82; and H.W. Knox-Niven, personal secretary Government House to V.G.W. Kell, MI5, 4 January 1918, PANL, GN 1/3/A, Despatch 9.
65 V.G.W. Kell to H.W. Knox-Niven, 30 January 1918, PANL, GN 1.3.A, Despatch 9.
66 E.P. Morris to H.W. Knox-Niven, 30 January 1918, PANL, GN 8.92, Despatch 9; C.H. Hutchings, inspector general to W.F. Lloyd, prime minister, 7 May 1918, GN 8.92; Richard Hannevig to P.J. Summers, 10 May 1918, PANL, GN 13/1/B, box 163, file 31; and P.J. Summers to Richard Hannevig, 14 May 1918, PANL, GN 13/1/B, box 162, file 31.
67 A. MacDermott, Commander H.M.S. Briton to C.A. Harris, governor, 21 June 1918, PANL, GN 1/3/A, Despatch 9.
68 N.S. Fraser to David Lloyd George, prime minister, 1 August 1918, PANL, GN 8.82.
69 Bassler, *Vikings to U-Boats*, 159–60.
70 "A Generous Donation," *Evening Telegram*, 19 June 1917; and Bassler, *Vikings to U-Boats*, 331.
71 Lewis Harcourt, secretary of state for the colonies to W.E. Davidson, 5 November 1914, PANL, GN 1/10/0; and Lewis Harcourt to W.E. Davidson, 7 November 1914, PANL, GN 1/10/0.
72 Lewis Harcourt to W.E. Davidson, 31 December 14, PANL, GN 1/1/7.
73 "Mass in the Language of Our Lord," *Evening Telegram*, 27 July 1908; "Mission to Maronites," *Evening Telegram*, 8 September 1910; "Mass in the Language of Our Lord," *Evening Telegram*, 27 July 1908; and "Said Mass," *Evening Telegram*, 4 August 1913.
74 "He That Giveth to the Poor Lendeth to the Lord," *Evening Telegram*, 22 September 1910.

75 "Episcopal Visitation at Bell Island," *Evening Telegram*, 4 July 1912.

76 "Here and There," *Evening Telegram*, 27 April 1912; "Episcopal Visitation at Bell Island," *Evening Telegram*, 4 July 1912; and "Syrian Society's Charitable Work," *Evening Telegram*, 24 April 1913.

77 "Assyrian Patriotic Fund," *Evening Telegram*, 24 December 1914; and Lewis Harcourt to W.E. Davidson, 31 December 14, PANL, GN 1/1/7; and W.E. Davidson, Personal Diary, 19 February 1915.

78 A.B. Sapp, St Joseph's Syrian Benevolent Society to W.E. Davidson, 12 November 1914, PANL, GN 1/10/0.

79 W.E. Davidson, Personal Diary, 19 February 1915, PANL, MG 136.5.

80 *Proceedings of the House of Assembly*, 13 April 1915; and "Proceedings at the House of Assembly," *Mail and Advocate*, 14 April 1915.

81 W.E. Davidson to Lewis Harcourt, 19 February 1915, PANL, GN 1/10/0.

82 W.E. Davidson to Cecil Spring-Rice, 20 January 1915, PANL, 1914 Despatch 190.

83 Donald Avery, *Dangerous Foreigners: European Immigrant Workers and Labour Radicalism in Canada, 1896–1932* (Toronto: McClelland and Stewart, 1979), 37–69. For more on the treatment of enemy aliens on the Canadian home front see Bohdan Kordan, *No Free Man: Canada, The Great War, and the Enemy Alien Experience* (Montreal and Kingston: McGill-Queen's University Press, 2016).

CHAPTER FIVE

1 For more on the impact of war on gender in Britain, see Joanna Bourke, *Dismembering the Male: Men's Bodies, Britain, and the Great War* (Chicago: University of Chicago Press, 1996); Nicoletta Gullace, *The Blood of Our Sons, Men, Women and the Renegotiation of British Citizenship during the Great War* (New York: Palgrave Macmillan, 2002); Jessica Meyer, *Men of War: Masculinity and the First World War in Britain* (Houndsmills: Palgrave Macmillan, 2009); Lois Bibbings, *Telling Tales about Men: Conceptions of Conscientious Objectors to Military Service during the First World War* (Manchester: Manchester University Press, 2011); and Susan Grayzel, *Women's Identities at War: Gender, Motherhood and Politics in Britain and France during the First World War* (Chapel Hill: University of North Carolina Press, 1999). For the Canadian context see Mark Moss, *Manliness and Militarism: Educating Young Boys in Ontario for War* (Toronto: University of Toronto Press, 2014) and Amy Shaw, *Crisis of Conscience: Conscientious Objection in Canada during the First World War* (Vancouver: UBC Press, 2014).

2 Chris Martin, "The Right Course, the Best Course, the Only Course: Voluntary Recruitment in the Newfoundland Regiment, 1914–1918," *Newfoundland and Labrador Studies*, no. 1 (2009): 58.
3 "Patriotism Leads Large Number of Men to Enlist," *Mail and Advocate*, 3 September 1914; and Martin, "The Right Course, The Best Course, The Only Course," 59; and O'Brien, "Out of a Clear Sky," 410.
4 "No Place for Slackers," *Evening Telegram*, 29 November 1916; and "Second Contingent: What Will the Outports Do?," *Western Star*, 9 December 1914.
5 Martin, "The Right Course, the Best Course, the Only Course," 82–3.
6 Jessica Meyer, *Men of War: Masculinity and the First World War in Britain* (Houndsmills: Palgrave Macmillan, 2009), 161–2.
7 "Newfoundland as a German Colony," *Evening Telegram*, 6 January 1915.
8 "Twillingate Shaking Herself," *Twillingate Sun*, 6 February 1915.
9 "German Hunger for Our Colonies," *Evening Telegram*, 17 November 1915.
10 Westcott, *Defending the Dominions*, 46–7; "News Came as Great Shock," *Mail and Advocate*, 9 October 1916.
11 "More Men, and Yet More Men: We Want Them Now," *Western Star*, 8 November 1916.
12 "The Submarine Menace," *Mail and Advocate*, 28 November 1916.
13 "Grand Falls' Response," *Daily News*, 26 February 1916.
14 "The Call of Duty," *Daily News*, 30 November 1914.
15 "What Civilization Means," *Twillingate Sun*, 28 November 1914.
16 "Grand Falls' Response," *Daily News*, 26 February 1916.
17 *Proceedings of the House of Assembly*, 16 March 1916.
18 *Proceedings of the House of Assembly*, 30 May 1917; and "The Late R.J. Devereaux," *Newfoundland Quarterly* (Summer 1920), 20.
19 "An Appeal to the People of Newfoundland," *Evening Advocate*, 12 October 1917; and "A Crisis," *Evening Advocate*, 31 October 1917.
20 *Proceedings of the Legislative Council*, 3 July 1917.
21 "As We See It," *St John's Daily Star*, 26 January 1917.
22 *Proceedings of the Legislative Council*, 3 July 1917; and "Published by Authority," *St John's Daily Star*, 17 October 1917.
23 "Thoughts upon the Times," *Evening Telegram*, 29 December 1917.
24 "Something Must be Done," *Evening Telegram*, 28 February 1918.
25 "Filling the Gaps: The Regimental Recruiting Roster," *Evening Telegram*, 9 April 1918.
26 "Our Duty to the Newfoundland Regiment," *Evening Telegram*, 31 October 1917.

27 "Big Recruiting Campaign Inaugurated," *Evening Advocate*, 4 April 1918; and "An Appeal to the People of the Outports," *Western Star*, 10 April 1917.
28 "State Volunteers," *Daily News*, 21 May 1918.
29 "Shall Newfoundland Fall from Her Honorable Estate?," *Mail and Advocate*, 16 November 1914.
30 "The Slackers," *Daily News*, 4 January 1915.
31 "Has the Right Spirit," *Mail and Advocate*, 16 November 1915.
32 "Conscientious Objectors," *Daily News*, 15 September 1917.
33 "Many Kinds of Slackers," *Western Star*, 3 October 1917.
34 "An Appeal to the People of Newfoundland," *Evening Advocate*, 12 October 1917.
35 "Our Duty to the Regiment," *Evening Telegram*, 31 October 1917.
36 "MEN!," *Evening Advocate*, 10 November 1917.
37 Ibid.
38 "An Appeal," *Evening Advocate*, 15 April 1918.
39 "Men More Men," *Mail and Advocate*, 5 October 1916.
40 "Are Your Folks Ashamed of You for Not Enlisting?," *Evening Telegram*, 2 May 1918.
41 "The Song of the Shirker," *Mail and Advocate*, 13 April 1916.
42 "A Picture of a Slacked in Twenty Years," *Evening Advocate*, 3 May 1918.
43 "A Contrast," *Mail and Advocate*, 7 June 1915.
44 "The Man Who Won't," *Evening Advocate*, 30 November 1917.
45 W.B. Grieve, secretary of recruiting committee to J.R. Bennett, colonial secretary, 16 December 1916, PANL, GN 2.14.275.
46 "No Berths for Slackers," *Daily News*, 17 February 1916.
47 "Now's the Day!" *Evening Telegram*, 23 April 1918
48 "Warning!" *Evening Advocate*, 3 May 1918.
49 J.R. Bennett to Mr Alfred George, 10 May 1916, PANL, 2.14.90.
50 "To the Fishers of Newfoundland," *Evening Telegram*, 30 October 1917.
51 "Last Night's Open-Air Recruiting Meeting a Great Success," *Evening Telegram*, 8 November 1916.
52 *Proceedings of the House of Assembly*, 27 March 1916; and "Manhood!," *Evening Advocate*, 16 November 1917.
53 Glenn Wilkinson, "The Blessings of War: Depictions of Military Force in Edwardian Newspapers," *Journal of Contemporary History* 33, no. 1 (1998): 99.
54 "The Slackers," *Daily News*, 4 January 1915.
55 "Last Night's Recruiting," *Evening Telegram*, 8 November 1916.
56 *Proceedings of the House of Assembly*, 30 May 1917.

57 James Hiller, "Robert Bond and the Pink, White, and Green: Newfoundland Nationalism in Perspective," *Acadiensis* 36, no. 2 (2007): 113–33.
58 Kurt Korneski, "Race, Gender, Class and Colonial Nationalism: Railway Development in Newfoundland, 1881–1898," *Labour / Le Travail* 62 (Fall 2008): 80.
59 "Splendid Patriotic Rally Hears Eloquent Address," *Mail and Advocate*, 27 November 1914.
60 "A Contrast," *Mail and Advocate*, 6 June 1915.
61 "The New Battalion the Call of the Blood," *Evening Telegram*, 8 February 1916.
62 Favours the New Recruitment Movement," *Mail and Advocate*, 18 February 1916.
63 "The Dogged Determination of Our Race Will Win," *Mail and Advocate*, 3 March 1916.
64 Lois Bibbings, *Telling Tales about Men: Conscientious Objectors to Military Service during the First World War* (Manchester: Manchester University Press, 2011), 96–104, 140.
65 "Pres. Coaker Expresses Sympathy for Bereaved," *Mail and Advocate*, 30 January 1915.
66 "Activity of Newfoundlanders," *Evening Telegram*, 17 May 1915.
67 "An Appeal," *Mail and Advocate*, 15 November 1916.
68 "Re-Enforcements," *Evening Advocate*, 22 April 1918.
69 John Fairlie, "British War Cabinets," *Michigan Law Review* 16 (1918): 484.
70 *Proceedings of the House of Assembly*, 30 May 1917.
71 Ibid.
72 "The Times," *Mail and Advocate*, 16 May 1917; and *Proceedings of the House of Assembly*, 30 May 1917.
73 "What Do You Say," *Daily News*, 30 October 1917.
74 "Thoughts for Thought," *Evening Advocate*, 13 November 1917; and "Where Duty Calls," *Evening Advocate*, 6 April 1918.
75 "The Solidarity of the Empire," *Evening Telegram*, 5 January 1915.
76 "Volunteering," *Evening Telegram*, 21 January 1916.
77 "A Stimulus Needed for Recruiting," *Evening Telegram*, 27 January 1916.
78 "Our New Standard Two Battalions," *Evening Telegram*, 5 February 1916.
79 "Are We Rowing Our Weight in the Boat?," *Evening Telegram*, 14 July 1916.
80 "A United Press," *Evening Advocate*, 3 September 1917.
81 "A Last Call," *Daily News*, 11 October 1917.

82 "Play the Man," *Western Star*, 17 April 1918; and "Boys of the Outport We Want Your Help," *Evening Telegram*, 20 April 1918.
83 "The Inevitable Has Happened! Our Eternal Disgrace," *Evening Telegram*, 3 May 1918; and "The Moment of Our Humiliation," *Evening Telegram*, 3 May 1918.
84 "Where Do We Ring In," *Western Star*, 8 May 1918.

CHAPTER SIX

1 *Orders in Council of the Imperial Government Together with Treaties Negotiated between His Majesty the King and Foreign Powers* (Ottawa: Samuel Edward Dawson, 1904), 164; and *Acts of the General Assembly of Newfoundland; Passed in the Fifth Year of the Reign of His Majesty King George V* (St John's: J.W. Withers, 1914), 19–20. For more on conscription across the British Empire see Ilana Bet-El, *Conscripts: Lost Legions of the Great War* (Phoenix Mill: Sutton, 1999); Robin Archer et al., *Conscription Conflict and the Great War* (Victoria: Monash University Press, 2016); and J.L. Granatstein, *Canada at War: Conscription, Diplomacy and Politics* (Toronto: University of Toronto Press, 2020).
2 "Nauseous though Necessary," *Daily News*, 7 January 1916.
3 "Voluntarism or Compulsion," *Western Star*, 22 March 1916.
4 "No Place for Slackers," *Evening Telegram*, 29 November 1916.
5 "A Strong Plea for the Regiment," *Evening Telegram*, 8 September 1917.
6 Paul Crook, "War as a Genetic Disaster? The First World War Debate over the Eugenics of Warfare," *War and Society* 8, no. 1 (1990): 52.
7 Robert Harding, "Glorious Tragedy: Newfoundland's Cultural Memory of the Attack at Beaumont Hamel, 1916–1925," *Newfoundland and Labrador Studies* 21, no. 1 (2006): 24.
8 "The Regiment," *Evening Herald*, 10 November 1917.
9 "The Truth about Conscription," *Evening Telegram*, 12 November 1917.
10 "Recruiting," *Evening Herald*, 15 February 1918.
11 "Stick to the Point," *Evening Telegram*, 18 February 1918; "Last Night's Open-Air Recruiting Meeting a Great Success," *Evening Telegram*, 8 November 1916; and "An Appeal," *Evening Advocate*, 15 April 1918.
12 "Yes, Cowardice!," *Evening Herald*, 18 February 1918.
13 "Cowardice," *Evening Telegram*, 22 February 1918.
14 *Journal of the House of Assembly*, 27 March 1916.
15 Ibid.
16 "The Local Situation," *Evening Herald*, 6 July 1917

17 "Compulsory Service," *Evening Telegram*, 7 July 1917.
18 C.A. Whitemarsh to W.E. Davidson, 12 July 1917, PANL, GN 2.14.105.
19 "Selective Conscription," *Evening Telegram*, 9 April 1918.
20 "Opinions of Orlick," *Evening Telegram*, 11 May 1918.
21 *Proceedings of the House of Assembly*, 23 April 1918.
22 Ibid., 22 April 1918.
23 Ibid., 24 April 1918.
24 Ibid.
25 Ibid., 25 April 1918.
26 Ibid.
27 Ibid.
28 *Proceedings of the House of Assembly*, 26 April 1918.
29 "Press Censor," *Daily News*, 22 February 1917.
30 "Harmonious Harping," *Mail and Advocate*, 20 August 1914.
31 "Now Who Is the Mob Instigator," *Mail and Advocate*, 1 October 1914; and "The War from Our Point of View," *Twillingate Sun*, 22 August 1914.
32 "Now Who Is the Mob Instigator," *Mail and Advocate*, 1 October 1914.
33 "Strong Feeling," *Mail and Advocate*, 17 October 1914; and "Common Sense Writes on Recruiting," *Mail and Advocate*, 18 February 1915.
34 "Patsy's Nightmare," *Mail and Advocate*, 15 January 1916.
35 "Selective Conscription Feasible," *Evening Telegram*, 6 April 1918.
36 "Thoughts for Thought," *Evening Advocate*, 9 April 1918.
37 "Trust the People!," *Plaindealer*, 27 April 1918.
38 *Proceedings of the House of Assembly*, 25 April 1918.
39 *Plaindealer*, 27 April 1918.
40 C.A. Harris to Arthur Long, secretary of state for the colonies, 27 April 1918, PANL, GN 1/3/A, 1918, box 99, Despatch 473.
41 Copy of minutes of executive council, 27 April 1918, PANL, GN 2.14.75; C.A. Harris to Arthur Long, secretary of state for the colonies, 27 April 1918, PANL, GN 1/3/A, 1918, box 99, Despatch 473.
42 *Proceedings of the House of Assembly*, 27 April 1918.
43 P.J. Summers, deputy justice minister, to W.W. Halfyard, colonial secretary, 6 May 1918, PANL, GN 2.14.75; and W.W. Halfyard to P.J. Summers, 7 May 1918, PANL, GN 13.1.B, box 142, file 21.
44 C.A. Harris to Arthur Long, 14 May 1918, PANL, GN 1/3/A, 1918 Despatch 564.
45 "Sedition," *Evening Telegram*, 16 May 1918.
46 W.W. Halfyard to John Currie, Editor Daily News, 18 May 1918, PANL, GN 2.14.75.

47 "Incapacity," *Daily Star*, 23 May 1918; "More of It," *Daily Star*, 23 May 1918; and "Tying Men Up," *Daily Star*, 28 May 1918.

48 Arthur Mews, deputy colonial secretary to R.A. Squires, 30 May 1918, QEII Library, Archives and Special Collections (ASC), COLL-250, 4.01.010.

49 C.A. Harris to W.W. Halfyard, 5 June 1918, PANL, GN 1/3/A, 1918 Despatch 648.

50 R.A. Squires to Reverend Harry Royle, 5 June 1918, ASC, COLL-250, 4.02.005; and R.A. Squires to Gilbert Gosse, Esq., 18 June 1918, ASC, COLL-250, 4.02.005.

51 W.W. Halfyard to C.A. Harris, 5 June 1918, PANL, GN 1/3/A, 1918 Despatch 648;

52 M.P. Cashin to C.A. Harris, 5–6 June 1918, PANL, GN 1/3/A, 1918 Despatch 648.

53 C.A. Harris to M.P. Cashin, 6 June 1918, PANL, GN 1/3/A, 1918 Despatch 648.

54 *Daily Star Publishing Co. v. Grimes, et al.* Supreme Court of Newfoundland, 6 June 1918, Law Society of Newfoundland Law Library; and Conroy & Higgins to W.W. Halfyard, 6 June 1918, PANL, GN 2.14.75.

55 "In His True Colours," *Evening Telegram*, 13 May 1918.

56 *Proceedings of the House of Assembly*, 11 May 1918

57 Shaw, *Crisis of Conscience*, 4.

58 P.J. Summers to C.A. Harris, 1 August 1918, PANL, GN 1/3/A, 1918 Despatch 837; and C.A. Harris to P.J. Summers, 24 August 1918, PANL, GN 1/3/A, 1918 Despatch 837; and C.A. Harris to superintendent of Her Majesty's Penitentiary, 1 September 1918, PANL, GN 1/3/A, 1918 Despatch 837.

59 P.J. Summers to C.A. Harris, 16 November 1918, PANL, GN 1/3/A, 1918 Despatch 1,133; C.A. Harris to superintendent of Her Majesty's Penitentiary, 19 November 1918, PANL, GN 1/3/A, 1918 Despatch 1,133.

60 P.J. Summers to C.A. Harris, 3 September 1918, PANL, GN 1/3/A, 1918 Despatch 1,133; and P.J. Summers to C.A. Harris, 16 November 1918, PANL, GN 1/3/A, 1918 Despatch 1,133.

CHAPTER SEVEN

1 "Women Form Patriotic Association," *Mail and Advocate*, 1 September 1914.

2 Margot Duley, *Where Once Our Mothers Stood We Stand: Women's Suffrage in Newfoundland, 1890–1925* (Charlottetown: Gynergy Books, 1993), 68.
3 "Dastardly Attack on Aged Peer," *Mail and Advocate*, 19 February 1914; "Arson Squad Busy Again," *Mail and Advocate*, 12 March 1914; "Suffragette Battle at Buckingham Palace," *Evening Telegram*, 22 May 1914; and "Militant Has Bomb for Court," *Mail and Advocate*, 25 July 1914.
4 "To Vote or Not to Vote," *Twillingate Sun*, 4 April 1914.
5 "Just Like a Woman," *Mail and Advocate*, 8 May 1914.
6 "Helpful," *Mail and Advocate*, 8 May 1914.
7 "Suffragists," *Evening Telegram*, 22 June 1914.
8 Duley, *Where Once Our Mothers Stood*, 40–1.
9 Ibid., 50–1.
10 Margot Duley, "Armine Nutting Gosling: A Full and Useful Life," in *Creating this Place: Women, Family, and Class in St John's, 1900–1950*, ed by Linda Cullum and Marilyn Porter (Montreal and Kingston: McGill Queen's University Press, 2014), 126–9.
11 Ibid., 129.
12 "Women's Patriotic Association," *Daily News*, 15 September 1914.
13 Mabel LeMessurier, "A Visit to the Headquarters of the W.P.A.," *Distaff*, 1917, CNS.
14 Women's Patriotic Association Minute Book of General Committee, 17 October 1914, PANL, MG 635.1.
15 Adelaide Browning, "The Red Cross," *Distaff*, 1916, CNS; and Women's Patriotic Association Minute Book of General Committee, 14 May 1917, PANL, MG 635.1.
16 *Journal of the Legislative Council*, 3 May 1916.
17 Ibid.
18 "Xmas Gifts for Ours," *Mail and Advocate*, 4 December 1915.
19 Women's Patriotic Association Minute Book of General Committee, 1 September 1914, PANL, MG 635.1.
20 "Women's Work in Relation to War," *Daily News*, 27 November 1914.
21 Ibid.
22 "A Widow's Patriotism," *Daily News*, 7 December 1914.
23 "Inspiring Work of the Women of Newfoundland," *Evening Telegram*, 17 December 1914; Arthur Dale, *First Aid: The Independent Journal for the Ambulance and Nursing Services*, August 1913, https://issuu.com/museumoftheorderofstjohn/docs/first_aid_1912-1914; and "Inspiring Work of the Women of Newfoundland," *Evening Telegram*, 17 December 1914.

24 "The Work of the WPA," *Daily News*, 20 January 1915.
25 "Socks," *Daily News*, 3 February 1915.
26 "What Happens to Socks," *Twillingate Sun*, 23 January 1915.
27 "Our Soldiers Abroad," *Mail and Advocate*, 9 January 1915.
28 "The W.P.A.," *Mail and Advocate*, 30 November 1915.
29 Ibid.
30 "The W.P.A.," *Mail and Advocate*, 1 December 1915.
31 "Backs up Our Demands for a Public Meeting," *Mail and Advocate*, 2 December 1915.
32 "Letter from Mrs Browning," *Mail and Advocate*, 2 December 1915.
33 Ibid.
34 "A Reply to Mrs Browning," *Mail and Advocate*, 3 December 1915.
35 "Doesn't Agree with Letter from Mrs Browning," *Mail and Advocate*, 14 December 1915.
36 "Winter Comforts for our Soldiers in the Trenches," *Western Star*, 1 December 1915.
37 "The Work of the WPA," *Daily News*, 8 December 1915.
38 W.E. Davidson, governor, to A. Steel-Maitland, chairman Newfoundland War Contingent Association, 2 December 1915, PANL, GN 1/10/0.
39 "Clothing for 'Our' Regiment," *Mail and Advocate*, 11 December 1915.
40 "Comforts for Our Soldiers," *Mail and Advocate*, 22 November 1916.
41 "The Selfish Women," *Mail and Advocate*, 8 September 1916.
42 "A Noble Mother," *Daily News*, 4 February 1915.
43 "Mothers of Men," *Daily News*, 4 February 1915.
44 Suzanne Evans, *Mothers of Heroes, Mothers of Martyrs: World War I and the Politics of Grief* (Montreal and Kingston: McGill Queen's University Press, 2007), 8, 159.
45 "Volunteers of New Bonaventure," *Mail and Advocate*, 14 April 1915.
46 W.E. Davidson, Personal Diary, 1 December 1914
47 "Appeal for Men," *Evening Telegram*, 7 April 1917.
48 "More Particularly to the Newfoundland Rejected Volunteers," *Evening Advocate*, 16 April 1918.
49 "The White Feather," *Evening Telegram*, 29 November 1916.
50 "Why Worry about Them?," *Evening Telegram*, 6 August 1917.
51 *Proceedings of the House of Assembly*, 22 March 1916.
52 *Proceedings of the House of Assembly*, 7 April 1916.
53 Ibid.
54 "The Regimental Badge," *Evening Telegram*, 3 October 1916; and "1st Newfoundland Regiment," *Mail and Advocate*, 7 October 1916.
55 "Resents Insult Offered Navy," *Mail and Advocate*, 12 October 1916.

56 Joseph Outerbridge to J.R. Bennett, 11 September 1916, PANL, GN 2.14.276.

57 R.A. Squires to J.R. Bennett, 29 September 1916, PANL, GN 2.14.276.

58 Miriam Wright, "Women in the Newfoundland Fishery," in *Framing Our Past: Constructing Canadian Women's History in the Twentieth Century*, ed by Lorna R. McLean, Kate O'Rourke, Sharon Anne Cook (Montreal: McGill Queen's University Press, 2001), 343; Marilyn Porter, "'She Was Skipper of the Shore Crew': Notes on the Sexual Division of Labour in Newfoundland," *Labour / Le Travail* 15 (1985): 111–16. For more on the role of women in the creation of state and society in Newfoundland see Linda Kealy, ed., *Pursuing Equality: Historical Perspectives on Women in Newfoundland* (St John's: ISER, 1993); and Marilyn Porter and Linda Cullum, eds., *Creating This Place: Women, Family, and Class in St John's, 1900–1950* (Montreal and Kingston: McGill-Queens University Press, 2014).

59 "Women of the Empire," *Daily News*, 26 March 1915.

60 "The Thoughts of Theobald," *Evening Telegram*, 27 May 1916.

61 "Woman Suffrage," *Mail and Advocate*, 20 December 1916.

62 A New Franchise," *Daily News*, 15 September 1917.

63 "Woman Suffrage," *Evening Advocate*, 16 November 1917.

64 "Woman's Triumph," *Evening Telegram*, 29 March 1917.

65 Susan Kent, *Making Peace: The Reconstruction of Gender in Interwar Britain* (Princeton: Princeton University Press, 1993), 141.

66 Nicoletta Gullace, *The Blood of Our Sons, Men, Women and the Renegotiation of British Citizenship during the Great War* (New York: Palgrave Macmillan, 2002), 3–4, 119.

67 "Conscientious Objectors," *Daily News*, 15 September 1917.

68 Margot Duley, "The Unquiet Knitters of Newfoundland: From Mothers of the Regiment to Mothers of the Nation," in *A Sisterhood of Suffering and Service: Women and Girls of Canada and Newfoundland during the First World War*, ed. Sarah Glassford (Vancouver: UBC Press, 2012), 51, 67–9.

69 Ibid. For information on Newfoundland nurses and Voluntary Aid Detachment workers (VADS) see Terry Bishop-Stirling, "'Such Sights One Will Never Forget:' Newfoundland Nursing in the First World War in Glassford," *A Sisterhood of Suffering and Service: Women and Girls of Canada and Newfoundland during the First World War* (Vancouver: UBC Press, 2012).

70 *Proceedings of the House of Assembly*, 9 March 1925.

Index